D1718967

# Ecclesiological Investigations

*Series Editor*

Gerard Mannion

# Volume 13

Dumitru Staniloae: An Ecumenical
Ecclesiology

Other titles in the series:

# Dumitru Staniloae: An Ecumenical Ecclesiology

Radu Bordeianu

t&t clark

Published by T&T Clark International
*A Continuum Imprint*
The Tower Building, 11 York Road, London SE1 7NX
80 Maiden Lane, Suite 704, New York, NY 10038

www.continuumbooks.com

**British Library Cataloguing-in-Publication Data**
A catalogue record for this book is available from the British Library

ISBN: 978-0-567-33481-7 (hardback)

Typeset by Newgen Imaging Systems Pvt Ltd, Chennai, India
Printed and bound in Great Britain

*To my family*

# CONTENTS

# ACKNOWLEDGMENTS

While the cover credits only one person as the author of this book, it is the fruit of many meaningful encounters. My mentor at Duke University, Geoffrey Wainwright, inspired me to study ecumenical ecclesiologies. My dissertation director at Marquette University, Michael Fahey, S.J., uncharacteristically insisted that I write my dissertation on the theology of Dumitru Staniloae. Characteristically, I refused … but not for long. I am deeply indebted to my *Doktorväter* for guiding me as I discovered the riches of Staniloae's theology.

The manuscript went through a long journey of improvements under the careful eyes of the editors who helped me publish some of these passages as journal articles or book chapters, which are used here with permission. My doctoral students and teaching assistants reflected on various parts of this text, especially Ann Vinski who engaged with it assiduously, as a veritable editor. Various grants from Duquesne University, such as the Presidential Scholarship Award, NEH Endowment Fund, and the Wimmer Family Foundation research grant helped me in the research phase. My Department Chair, George Worgul has been a mentor and tireless supporter. The Ecclesiological Investigations Research Network, especially Gerard Mannion (to whom I am forever indebted), facilitated the publication with T&T Clark/Continuum, where I encountered a wonderful editorial team. The faithful and the clergy of the Holy Trinity Greek Orthodox Churches in Raleigh, NC and Pittsburgh, PA showed me that Church is, indeed, communion.

Last, but not least, I would like to thank my family for keeping me grounded, for their support and sacrifice while this book was birthed.

# INTRODUCTION

The Church is a communion in the image of the Trinity. Being adopted children of the Father, the members of the Church are gathered together as the Body of Christ in the Holy Spirit, who is the Spirit of communion both in the Trinity and in the Church. Because there is a continuum of grace between the Trinity and the Church, the same relationships that exist among trinitarian persons are manifested in creation in general, and the Church in particular. In this way, the Trinity fills the world and the Church, determining their mode of existence. Intratrinitarian relationships are manifested in the relationships between humankind and nonhuman creation, the Church and the world, local and universal aspects of the Church, clergy and the people, and among various charisms. The Romanian Orthodox theologian Dumitru Staniloae (1903–1993) contributed significantly to an ecumenical understanding of these themes.

The theological principle underlying these remarks is that there is a continuum of grace, a communication between the Trinity and the Church. Oftentimes, contemporary ecclesiology gives the impression that the Trinity and the Church are two parallel realities, mirroring each other. According to this type of theology, what is regarded as a distorted Triadology (e.g., the Filioque) can have disastrous ecclesiological consequences, such as the primacy of the institution over charisms or the subordination of the synod of bishops to the Pope. Other times the Trinity and the Church appear separate from each other, where God stands so much above the Church that God always comes upon the Church from the outside; the Church is not always united with God. And yet, is there no true relationship between the Trinity and the Church? In the second chapter I argue that the Church is not merely a reflection of the Trinity, but that the Trinity descends to our plane and the Church is lifted up in the Trinity. As Origen wrote, "The Church is filled with the Trinity."

Another trend in contemporary ecclesiology is to analyze the role of the Son and the Spirit in the Church, while leaving the relationship between the Father and the Church underdeveloped. Ecclesiology struggles to be trinitarian. There has been a salutary shift away from monistic, or, more precisely, christomonistic ecclesiology, by focusing on the role of the Spirit in the Church. But the journey is not yet complete. Oftentimes, the result is a binitarian tendency in ecclesiology, which is disinterested in the relationship between the Father and the Church. Staniloae, however, offered a fully trinitarian ecclesiology, address-ing the role of all three persons of the Trinity in the Church. I present these rela-tionships in the second part of the book where, for reasons of systematization, I address the presence of each trinitarian person in the Church in a distinct chapter, but never in isolation from the other two persons.

If the Trinity is indeed present in the world and the Church, how is the com-munion among the divine persons manifested in nonhuman creation, among the ordained and nonordained charisms of the Church, or among various local churches as they constitute the *Una Sancta*? In the third part of the book I attempt to present Staniloae's understanding of the Church as communion among these various aspects of ecclesiology, as a contribution toward the cause of Christian unity. In order to emphasize this contribution, throughout the book I engage Staniloae in dialogue with various Vatican II documents, as well as several prominent Catholic and Orthodox theologians. Among these, Yves Congar, Walter Kasper, Vladimir Lossky, Paul Evdokimov, Nikolas Afanassieff, Nikos Nissiotis, Georges Florovsky, John Zizioulas, and Kallistos Ware stand out. Additionally, I humbly propose my own solutions to the challenges that ecumenical ecclesiologies face today.

### Raising Awareness of Staniloae's Ecumenical Relevance

This book is also meant to promote the thought of the greatest Romanian theologian of all times and probably the most important Orthodox theolo-gian of the twentieth century. There is currently a significant interest in his work, but, unfortunately, most of Staniloae's writings are not translated into languages of international circulation. Isolated from the rest of the world by a repressive Communist regime, Staniloae did not have a chance to present his contribution to the West. More than 20 years after the fall of the Iron Curtain, his publications are still largely unknown and need proper attention for at least six reasons.

*First*, the multitude of Staniloae's works makes a thorough study of his theology, if not impossible, then certainly intimidating. He was a very pro-lific theologian; his academic work consists of 1149 titles, not to mention his earlier cultural and sociopolitical publications.[1] He was able to make this significant theological contribution despite opposition from a commun-ist regime that censured his publications and incarcerated him for 5 years.

---

1   See Virginia Popa, *Parintele Dumitru Staniloae: Bio-bibliografie* [*Father Dumitru Staniloae: Bio-Bibliography*] (Iasi: Trinitas, 2004), 17–102.

Consequently, several universities awarded him honorific titles such as Doctor Honoris Causa: Thessalonica, Tübingen, St. Serge, Belgrade, Athens, and Bucharest. In 1991, he became a member of the Romanian Academy, being the first theologian admitted to this most prestigious academic institution. Throughout his academic career, he remained a dedicated husband, father, and priest.

Undoubtedly, his figure dominates Romanian Orthodox theology and his authority is gradually extending outside the borders of Romania and Orthodoxy, for which reason many important contemporary theologians have written appreciative words about him. For example, Andrew Louth considers that, among Orthodox theologians, Staniloae "is not marginal, he is not even simply a bridge between East and West, or between Russian and Greek Orthodoxy: he is at the center of what many would regard as the liveliest and most original movement in modern Orthodox thought [i.e., neo-patristic synthesis]."[2] Jürgen Moltmann, a good friend of Staniloae, refers to him as "the most influential and creative contemporary Orthodox theologian."[3] Olivier Clément considers that "Father Dumitru Staniloae is certainly the greatest Orthodox theologian of the present day. When it will be translated in the Western languages, his work will prove to be one of the major creations of the Christian thought of the second half of our century."[4] Lucian Turcescu and Kallistos Ware consider that Staniloae occupies "a position in present-day Orthodoxy comparable to that of Karl Barth in Protestantism and Karl Rahner in Roman Catholicism."[5] Danut Manastireanu, an Evangelical Romanian theologian, writes that Staniloae "is

---

2  Andrew Louth, "The Orthodox Dogmatic Theology of Dumitru Staniloae," in *Dumitru Staniloae: Tradition and Modernity in Theology*, ed. Lucian Turcescu (Iasi, Romania; Palm Beach, FL: Center for Romanian Studies, 2002), 57.

3  "Introduction" to Dumitru Staniloae, *Orthodoxe Dogmatik*, trans. Hermann Pitters, 3 vols., *Ökumenische Theologie 12, 15, 16* (Zürich, Gütersloh: Benziger Verlag, Gütersloher Verlagshaus Gerd Mohn, 1984–1995), 10. Quoted in Ronald G. Roberson, "Dumitru Staniloae on Christian Unity," in *Dumitru Staniloae: Tradition and Modernity in Theology*, ed. Lucian Turcescu (Iasi, Romania; Palm Beach, FL: Center for Romanian Studies, 2002), 104.

4  Olivier Clément, "Le Père Dumitru Staniloae et le génie de l'Orthodoxie Roumaine," in *Persoana si Comuniune. Prinos de Cinstire Parintelui Profesor Academician Dumitru Staniloae la implinirea varstei de 90 de ani* [*Person and Communion: Offering to Honor Professor Academician Dumitru Staniloae on His Ninetieth Birthday*], ed. Mircea Pacurariu and Ioan I. Ica jr. (Sibiu: Ed. Arhiepiscopiei Ortodoxe Sibiu, 1993), 82.

5  Lucian Turcescu, "Introduction," in *Dumitru Staniloae: Tradition and Modernity in Theology*, ed. Lucian Turcescu (Iasi, Romania; Palm Beach, FL: Center for Romanian Studies, 2002), 8. See also Kallistos Ware, "Foreword," in *The Experience of God: Revelation and Knowledge of the Triune God*, ed. Dumitru Staniloae (Brookline, MA: Holy Cross Orthodox Press, 1998), xxiv.

undoubtedly the most important Romanian theologian of any Christian tradition to date."[6]

Despite the importance of Staniloae's theology, its study is barely in its
infancy. It is impossible here to look at Western perceptions of the East, but a
quick glance at five major journals offers a significant insight about what constitutes Orthodox theology in the West. Until recently, Staniloae was mentioned
episodically together with Zizioulas and Lossky, and sometimes Florovsky and
Schmemann appeared as other representatives of Orthodoxy. Around 2005,
Staniloae began to be regarded as an alternative to Zizioulas and Lossky,
but mention of him remains drastically minimal. Overall, Staniloae is quoted
3.5 times less than Zizioulas and almost four times less than Lossky. The ratio is
even more unfavorable to Staniloae when counting only Catholic and Protestant
journals, which rarely mention him.[7] The East needs to make its theologians
better known to the West, offering other Orthodox voices besides Zizioulas and
Lossky. Staniloae's ecclesiology is a much-needed alternative.

2)  *Second*, only an infinitesimal percentage of Staniloae's works have been translated into languages of international circulation. As a result, Staniloae is both
misunderstood and insufficiently known. Especially in chapters one and seven,
I attempt to clear up some misconceptions that are the result of a fragmentary
reading of Staniloae's work by providing a panoramic picture of his theology
on the subjects of the relationship between theology, spirituality, and Liturgy, as
well as universal priesthood. In this endeavor, I am forced to offer more numerous and lengthier quotes than usual.[8] Staniloae had to do the same when writing
his patristic theology, given the insufficiency of Romanian translations from the
Fathers at that time. He later contributed significantly with numerous patristic
translations.

3)  *Third*, in Romania Staniloae is treated as a myth, being less quoted in context than misquoted or simply misrepresented. Ideas that seem to the speaker

---

6  Danut Manastireanu, "Dumitru Staniloae's Theology of Ministry," in *Dumitru
   Staniloae: Tradition and Modernity in Theology*, ed. Lucian Turcescu (Iasi, Romania;
   Palm Beach, FL: Center for Romanian Studies, 2002), 126. See also *Parintele
   Dumitru Staniloae in constiinta contemporanilor: marturii, evocari, amintiri* [*Father
   Dumitru Staniloae in Contemporary Conscience: Witnesses, Accounts, Memories*]
   (Iasi: Trinitas, 2003). This entire volume contains appreciative comments by some of
   the most important theologians who studied or have been influenced by Staniloae's
   theology.

7  Based on *Theological Studies, Pro Ecclesia, Journal of Ecumenical Studies, St
   Vladimir's Theological Quarterly*, and *Sobornost*, between 1992 and 2009.

8  Unless otherwise specified, all translations from Romanian and French are mine. My
   translations use inclusive language, but throughout the book I also quote existing
   translations that are not inclusive.

to sound Orthodox are attributed to Staniloae without any references, and the affirmation is impossible to trace given the magnitude of the Staniloaean corpus. Based on marginal aspects of his thought and certainly not as a result of a balanced reading of his work, he is sometimes portrayed as antiecumenical, which leads to the *fourth* reason for studying Staniloae's theology.

*4)*

As I attempt to show throughout the book, Staniloae was far from being antiecumenical, despite the occasional highly polemical tone that he adopted. In response to the scholastic influence experienced by Orthodox theology during its "Western captivity," Staniloae wrote a "neo-patristic synthesis," which restores the importance of patristic writings and engages with contemporary scholarship. He also used Western terminology, consistent with his understanding of "open sobornicity," which is defined as the acceptance of valid theological insights in Western theologies without altering the essence of Orthodox teaching. His work provides a model for creative engagement with the West. Even when not written with an ecumenical purpose in mind, his theology is relevant to the cause of Christian unity, so it is only unfair that Staniloae would be hijacked by antiecumenical groups who take Staniloae's remarks out of context and use them to support their rhetoric.

I am deeply concerned about the growing antiecumenical attitude in Christianity in general, and in Orthodoxy in particular. Although relatively small in number, the voices that deem ecumenism as pan-heresy[9] tend to dominate the

---

9   In their *Patriarchal and Synodal Encyclical on the Sunday of Orthodoxy* (February 21, 2010), the Ecumenical Patriarch Bartholomew and the Synod express their concern with attitudes of "fanaticism or bigotry," "intolerance and extremism" within Orthodoxy. In very courageous and unequivocal terms, they write: "The Orthodox Church does not fear dialogue because truth is not afraid of dialogue. On the contrary, if Orthodoxy is enclosed within itself … it will become an introverted and self-contained group, a 'ghetto' on the margins of history. This is why the great Fathers of the Church never feared dialogue with the spiritual culture of their age—indeed even with the pagan idolaters and philosophers of their world—thereby influencing and transforming the civilization of their time and offering us a truly ecumenical Church.… With the mutual agreement and participation of all local Orthodox Churches, the Ecumenical Patriarchate has for many decades conducted official Panorthodox theological dialogues with the larger Christian Churches and Confessions.… These dialogues, together with every effort for peaceful and fraternal relations of the Orthodox Church with other Christians, are unfortunately challenged today in an unacceptably fanatical way—at least by the standards of a genuinely Orthodox ethos—by certain circles that exclusively claim for themselves the title of zealot and defender of Orthodoxy. As if all the Patriarchs and Sacred Synods of the Orthodox Churches throughout the world, who unanimously decided on and continue to support these dialogues, were not Orthodox. Yet, these opponents of every effort for the restoration of unity among Christians raise themselves above Episcopal Synods of the Church

public discussion of Orthodox involvement in ecumenism. They employ tactics of intimidation and deception, rarely engage in theological analysis of the issues at stake, and are never able to produce evidence of ecumenical documents in which Orthodox representatives would have corrupted the essence of the faith.

This antiecumenical phenomenon is not limited to Orthodoxy. If in the past, divisions within the Church coincided with clearly marked denominational lines, today I sense more of a trans-denominational schism, which tends to focus on moral issues and openness to the other. Ultra-conservatives in one church feel more at home with ultra-conservatives in another church than with the ultra-liberals in their own denomination. The case is the same with ultra-liberals. I label both of these polarizing positions as "ultra" because I notice a gradual disappearance of moderate attitudes, open to dialogue, and their replacement with a refusal to listen to the other and unfounded judgmental, caricaturist opinion. The threat of "ultra"-ism is so stringent that we arrived at this ironic situation, where denominations are actually beneficial for ecumenism, providing structures that initiate, support, and implement the results of dialogue. These denominational structures should be transcended only as a result of an open dialogue that aims to visibly manifest the unity of the Church and renounce the sinfulness of our divisions, and not as a means of further dividing the Church.

Assuming the necessity of dialogue, many of us, Orthodox theologians, justify our presence in ecumenical discussions as an opportunity to affirm the fullness of our faith and to bear testimony to the apostolic tradition that we have so faithfully preserved throughout two millennia of constant martyrdom and theological struggles. But are we also there to learn from other Christians? Few among us would admit it. Even fewer would apply it. And yet, Staniloae's concept of open sobornicity commends it. Orthodox Christians can and must learn from the other instances of God's manifestation outside the Orthodox space. The tension between the affirmation that Orthodoxy represents the fullness of

---

to the dangerous point of creating schisms within the Church. In their polemical argumentation, these critics of the restoration of unity among Christians do not even hesitate to distort reality in order to deceive and arouse the faithful.... They condemn those who conduct these dialogues as allegedly 'heretics' and 'traitors' of Orthodoxy, purely and simply because they converse with non-Orthodox, with whom they share the treasure and truth of our Orthodox faith. They speak condescendingly of every effort for reconciliation among divided Christians and restoration of their unity as purportedly being 'the pan-heresy of ecumenism' without providing the slightest evidence that, in its contacts with non-Orthodox, the Orthodox Church has abandoned or denied the doctrines of the Ecumenical Councils and of the Church Fathers." http://www.patriarchate.org/documents/sunday-orthodoxy-2010. The Patriarch's remarks resemble quite closely those of John Zizioulas in "The Orthodox Church and the Third Millennium." *Sourozh* 81 (August 2000): 31.

the faith and the possibility, or even necessity, to learn from others is inevitable. But the two sides of the equation do not contradict each other, just as Staniloae affirmed both the fullness of Revelation in Christ and the possibility, or even necessity, to progress in the development of revealed truth. Dialogue for him was a duty commended by Christ so that the entire Church would grow in the truth; Orthodoxy has a significant contribution in this sense, and it cannot deprive other churches of its treasure, nor can it be oblivious to the gifts of other Christians.

*Fifth*, Orthodoxy is oftentimes perceived as distanced from society and its needs, indifferent to the world and missions, and overly mystical. But Staniloae had a different attitude. His beginnings as a publicist were actually primarily dedicated to social issues, and less to theology. Between 1929 and 1946, he was an editor at "Telegraful Roman [The Romanian Telegraph]," which advocated an Orthodox viewpoint on issues of national life and culture, and he participated at some meetings of "Rugul Aprins [The Burning Bush]," a cultural organization that I discuss in Chapter 4. Moreover, his theology is applicable to many social issues, showing the role of the Church to manifest the Kingdom of God as already here, in society, in creation, in the human being, as the first fruits of eternity. Throughout the book I discuss the relationship between the Church and the Kingdom, as well as several practical issues, such as depersonalization, missions based on the relationship between Christ and the Spirit, and the Liturgy after Liturgy. Among all the social issues to which the latter expression refers, I focus on eco-activism, or the eucharistic and ascetical attitude toward creation, as a manifestation of our natural priesthood.

The reader will notice that Staniloae was only episodically explicit on these issues and will probably ask: Is it fair to apply Staniloae's theology to contemporary social issues? Was Staniloac's view of personhood too narrowly connected with his understanding of the role of the person in the Church (especially in a liturgical context), thus rendering its application to society artificial? The answer is twofold. First, theologically, Staniloae considered that the Church is fully manifested in the Liturgy, where the person is best affirmed in union with the rest of the community; hence his insistence on the Church as a model of communion in society, after the image of the Trinity. Second, Staniloae was politically limited by communist censure. The dictatorial regime confined the Orthodox Church within its liturgical borders, denying its mission toward society, forbidding religious education and charitable works. In his suffering under communist rule that included 5 years of imprisonment, Staniloae was representative of a Romanian Orthodoxy that was considered outcast, even though almost 90 percent of the Romanian population was Orthodox. His political voice was obviously muted in those years, which covered most of his theological career.

And yet, Staniloae managed to criticize communist ideology by addressing areas of theology that were most relevant during that oppressive regime. For example, if Communism advocated a community devoid of personal character-istics, Staniloae proposed inter-personal trinitarian relationships as the model and driving force for communion as unity in diversity. If communist authori-ties treated people as objects, Staniloae affirmed the value and dignity of each human being. Even when he discussed divine *taxis*—the order within immanent Trinity—Staniloae affirmed that order is not devoid of freedom, which is very significant in the context of an oppressive regime. Thus, his theology can, and urgently needs to, be applied to contemporary social issues.

*Sixth*, critics might say that Staniloae is inconsistent. Sympathizers, such as myself, would argue that Staniloae's theology responded to an ever-changing context. He wrote in a long period of great change. His corpus consists of approximately 1200 titles, spanning over approximately 70 years, years in which Romania went from a period of economic prosperity and optimistic reconstruc-tion between the two world wars, to the Second World War, to Communist dictatorship (including Staniloae's 5 years of incarceration), to another period of optimism and newfound freedom, after the 1989 Revolution.

The ecumenical world went through seismic changes as well. Early in his career, Staniloae encountered a bitter, controversial attitude between Orthodox, Catholics, and Protestants. In his native Transylvania, contacts between Orthodox and Catholic theologians inevitably centered on the issue of Uniatism (as Byzantine Catholic churches were named in his context), a controversial subject given the political, economic, and physical pressure under which various Orthodox communities were forced to embrace the union with Rome. During Communism, however, these Byzantine Catholic churches were dissolved force-fully by the political regime, and coerced into becoming Orthodox or simply going underground. Staniloae saw this instance as a restoration of justice—undoubtedly a blemish on his magnificent work. Moreover, early in his career, when studying in the West, he encountered a neoscholastic Catholic theology and a strong Protestant reaction to it, again, at a time when ecumenism was barely beginning.

That situation was soon to change: the World Council of Churches (WCC) was formed in 1948, which raised many questions about the nature of the unity it sought. The Toronto Assembly (1950) alleviated some of these suspicions, and all Orthodox churches became members of the WCC. The 1960s were marked by an opening of the Catholic Church towards other Christians, in the aftermath of the Second Vatican Council, when Catholic theology was freed from neoscho-lasticism. The WCC went through its own evolution, from an inclusivist agenda to a much more pluralist approach to doctrinal union. Many Orthodox did not welcome this change, but started doubting the WCC's interest in unity in faith, which led to the suspicion that ecumenism means compromising one's faith or, at the lest, that bilateral dialogues are preferable to WCC-sponsored ecumenical activities. Orthodoxy, too, shifted from a neoscholastic captivity back towards its patristic roots, from a theoretical discourse, to a lived experience. Given all these changes in and around Romania, in and around Orthodoxy, naturally, Staniloae reacted differently throughout his career. There is unquestionably a significant delay in his reaction, mainly because of Communist isolation. But there is also a heightened sensitivity to the world around him and to the changes within him, the years of prison having marked him considerably. The reader will discover a complex theologian, one who inspires awe.

With these considerations in mind, I explore Staniloae's ecclesiology as ecumenical and trinitarian, attempting to support the thesis that the Church is a communion that shares in the intratrinitarian communion.

# PART I

# ECUMENICAL ECCLESIOLOGY

# Chapter 1

## OPEN SOBORNICITY: STANILOAE'S
## INTERACTION WITH THE WEST

Orthodox theology suffered an unhealthy influence during its "Western captivity." Its neoscholastic theology was overly intellectualistic, an academic exercise divorced from spirituality. In line with several notable predecessors, Eastern and Western alike, Georges Florovsky has called for a departure from the previous manual tradition. He proposed a "neo-patristic synthesis" that would incorporate the methodology and theology of patristic writings while engaging ecumenically with contemporary scholarship. As a historian, however, Florovsky did not write such a theology systematically.

In the present chapter, I contend that Staniloae wrote a "neo-patristic synthesis." His work represents a creative development of the Orthodox patristic, spiritual, and liturgical tradition in dialogue with modern thought, thus being relevant for contemporary Church and social issues. To support this thesis, after a brief analysis of Orthodox theology in the fifteenth to twentieth centuries, I present theological and biographical elements that attest to Staniloae's departure from manual theology, contrasting neo-patristic with neoscholastic theology. I then analyze his adoption of the three offices of Christ and the designation of seven sacraments as instances of open sobornicity. I thus hope to provide a methodology of constructive engagement with the West and correct the misconception according to which Staniloae was antiecumenical, an opinion that is based on mere marginal aspects of his works.

### From Old to New (or Actually Older):
### Orthodox Theology after the Fall of Constantinople (1453)

Prior to 1453, Orthodox theology was done either by the Fathers and ecclesiastical writers of the patristic era, or in the spirit of the Fathers in postpatristic times. This latter period marks a decline in the quality of Orthodox theology, with notable exceptions such as Symeon the New Theologian, Nicholas Cabasilas, and Gregory Palamas. Setting aside the polemics of this period, the interaction between East and West was minimal at best. Augustine's *De Trinitate* was translated only in the thirteenth century.[1] Greek theologians began to engage constructively (even appreciatively) with the West, especially with Thomas Aquinas,[2] during the fourteenth century.

The situation changed under Ottoman rule. Given the practical difficulties to theologize freely, the East turned rather uncritically to the West: when responding to Catholic missionary activities, it used the already-made Protestant answers;[3] when enamored with Western models of education, Orthodoxy adopted Catholic theology uncritically or sent its youth to study at Protestant schools without prior initiation in Orthodox theology. At that time, German, Italian, French, and English schools provided the only opportunity to obtain a higher education.[4] As a counterreaction to this Western influence, at times the East adopted an ultraconservative, highly polemical attitude that resulted in the simple repetition of patristic formulas. Thus, the encounter between East and West resulted in the impoverishment of Orthodox theology either because of foreign influences suffered without much discernment, or because of stifling creativity for fear of the West.

### *Western Captivity*

To what extent was Orthodox theology influenced by the West in this period? Alexander Schmemann writes about the "Western captivity of the East."[5] (*Nouvelle théologie* or *ressourcement* Catholic theologians would probably also speak of the Western captivity of the West, given the predominance of neoscholasticism at that time). Georges Florovsky was probably the Orthodox theologian who condemned this period most vehemently, calling it—under Luther's inspiration, of course—"the Babylonian captivity" of Orthodox theology. He noted that Peter Moghila's *Confession* was organized according to

---

1  George E. Demacopoulos and Aristotle Papanikolaou, "Augustine and the Orthodox: 'The West' in the East," in *Orthodox Readings of Augustine*, ed. George E. Demacopoulos and Aristotle Papanikolaou (Crestwood, NY: St Vladimir's Seminary Press, 2008), 15.

2  John Meyendorff, *Byzantine Theology: Historical Trends and Doctrinal Themes* (New York: Fordham University Press, 1983), 104–09.

3  The *Confessio Fidei* of Patriarch Cyril Lukaris was censured for its Calvinist doctrine by several Orthodox synods.

4  George A. Maloney, *A History of Orthodox Theology since 1453* (Belmont, MA: Norland Pub. Co., 1976), 305–06.

5  Alexander Schmemann, *Great Lent: Journey to Pascha* (Crestwood, NY: St Vladimir's Seminary Press, 1974), 131.

anti-Protestant catechisms that appeared during the Counter Reformation era, being more closely linked to Catholic literature than to Orthodox spiritual life. Although key Catholic doctrines such as the primacy of the pope were repudiated, the initial version argued in favor of the doctrine of the purgatory and a specific moment in the Liturgy when the bread and wine become the Body and Blood of Christ.[6] Even though the *Confession* was not so much doctrinally in error, the choice of language and the uncritical use of Catholic argumentations against Protestantism made Florovsky write about

> Moghila's Latin "pseudomorphosis" or "crypto-Romanism." . . . The impression is created that Orthodoxy is no more than a purified or refined version of Roman Catholicism. This view can be stated quite succinctly: "Let us omit or remove certain controversial issues, and the rest of the Roman theological system will be Orthodox." Admittedly, in some ways this is true. But the theological corpus that is thereby obtained lacks or severely reduces the native genius and the ethos of the Eastern theological tradition.[7]

Florovsky's criticism of Moghila extended to the establishment of the Kiev Academy, in which Catholic methodology and doctrine (including the Immaculate Conception) were being taught following Latin textbooks. Why was Moghila so important in Florovsky's view?

> This was the first outright encounter with the West. One might even have called it a free encounter had it not ended in captivity, or more precisely, surrender. But for this reason, there could be no creative use made of the encounter.[8] . . . There emerged an imitative and provincial

---

6  Florovsky considered that the *Confession* remained heavily influenced by Catholicism even after its discussion at the Synod in Iasi (1642) and the amendments and translation into Greek by Meletios Syrigos, himself educated at Padua, where he became an adherent of Bellarmine.

7  Georges Florovsky, *Ways of Russian Theology: Part One*, ed. Richard S. Haugh, trans. Robert L. Nichols, vol. 5, *Collected Works of Georges Florovsky, Emeritus Professor of Eastern Church History, Harvard University* (Belmont, MA: Nordland Pub. Co., 1979), 77.

8  Florovsky reinforced this idea when writing: "Russian theology imitatively experienced every major phase of modern Western religious thought—Tridentine theology, the baroque period, Protestant orthodoxy and scholasticism, pietism and freemasonry, German idealism and romanticism, the Christian-social ferment following the French Revolution, the expansion of the Hegelian school, modern critical historiography, the Tübingen school and Rischtlism, modern romanticism, and

scholasticism, in its literal sense a *theologia scholastica* or "school theology."[9]

The Jesuit theologian George Maloney has a milder opinion about Orthodoxy's encounter with the West. Orthodoxy's scholasticism, he contends, was unique in that it never developed into a speculative science and remained in continuation with the writings of the Fathers.[10] Kallistos Ware is even more optimistic, considering that the Western influence affected primarily the form that Eastern theology took, never its substance.[11] Staniloae concurred:

> Sometimes, under similar influences, a theological diversity appears in the bosom of one and the same national Orthodox Church. Russian theology of the Ukraine, which came under Polish domination, was greatly influenced by Roman Catholic theology during the 16th and 17th centuries, whereas after Peter the Great brought Russia into close cultural interrelationship with Prussia, Russian theology underwent a Lutheran influence. But by the second half of the 18th and 19th centuries and especially in the 20th century, simultaneously with the orientation of Russia towards the Balkans, its theology became profoundly patristic and mystical. Greek theology began, by the end of the Byzantine Empire, to come under the influence of Roman Catholic scholasticism, and after the Reformation

---

symbolism. In one way or another all of these influences successively entered into Russia's cultural experience. However, only dependence and imitation resulted—no true encounter with the West has yet taken place. That could only happen in the freedom and equality of love." Georges Florovsky, *Ways of Russian Theology: Part Two*, ed. Richard S. Haugh, trans. Robert L. Nichols, vol. 6, *Collected Works of Georges Florovsky, Emeritus Professor of Eastern Church History, Harvard University* (Belmont, MA: Nordland Pub. Co., 1987), 300–01.

9   Florovsky, *Ways of Russian Theology: Part One*, 85.

10  Maloney, *A History of Orthodox Theology since 1453*, 302–03. Maloney adds that Orthodoxy did not form several schools of theology, as happened in the West with the disciples of Thomas Aquinas, Duns Scotus, or Bonaventure, among others.

11  Timothy (Kallistos) Ware, *The Orthodox Church*, New ed. (London, New York: Penguin Books, 1997), 93. Although Florovsky argued that the substance of Orthodox theology was Westernized, thereby disagreeing with Ware, Florovsky also believed that Orthodox spirituality remained unaffected, resulting in the divorce between theology and Church life: "Theological thought gradually digressed from hearing the rhythm of the Church's heart and thereby lost the 'way' to this heart.... [T]heological problematics lost their proximity to life and ... the Truth of God became a school exercise limited to specialists and professionals." Georges Florovsky, "Western Influences in Russian Theology," in *Aspects of Church History, Collected Works 4* (Belmont, MA: Nordland, 1975), 178–79.

up to the 20th century, some theologians came under Protestant influence, while others remained under that of the Roman Catholic. It is true that these two *Western influences were of a formal rather than spiritual nature* and did not succeed in making either the Greeks or the Russians leave the essential bounds of Apostolic Tradition, so jealously guarded in Orthodoxy.... Romanian theology, which like the Greek and Russian also came under the formal influence of Western theology up to the 19th century, *in the last 40 years* has discovered the new Russian theology and has begun *creatively to develop the works of the Holy Fathers*. We can say that ... we witness ... the return of all Orthodox theology to a spirit *specifically Eastern and patristic*. [emphases mine] [12]

Eastern and Western theology of this period of crisis is labeled scholastic because it includes scholasticism-proper, but most of the time it refers to neoscholastic theology, with the surprising addition of Protestant theology. What constitutes scholastic or manual theology?

- Intellectualist approach to faith and the world, as opposed to intellectual description of faith (and its logical consequences) for catechesis[13]
- Philosophy as the criterion for theological truth as opposed to development within the limits set by the Fathers
- Theology as speculative science[14]

---

12  Dumitru Staniloae, "Unity and Diversity in Orthodox Tradition," *Greek Orthodox Theological Review* 17, no. 1 (1972): 33–34.

13  A. N. Williams's contrast between Origen and the Enlightenment is illuminating in this sense: "[Origen's] purpose is nonetheless quite different from that of the Enlightenment thinkers who made natural arguments for the existence of God, for he declares that the faith is not something that needs to be proved by human reason, and that his purpose in pursuing particular points is only to follow the inquiry where it logically leads. The line between the two is very fine, of course, and Origen does not trouble to explain where he would draw it. It seems to run between the differing sorts of intention, the desire, which he implicitly repudiates, to look intellectually strong in the eyes of the world, and the rightful wish to inform inquirers about the faith in a way that is readily graspable, this latter purpose being one also of catechesis, and hence not one a Christian teacher could plausibly reject." Anna N. Williams, *The Divine Sense: The Intellect in Patristic Theology* (New York: Cambridge University Press, 2007), 66–67.

14  Since Russia has been at the center of the stage in terms of the Westernization of Orthodox theology, it is proper to quote Fyodor Dostoyevsky here. Father Paisy tells young novice Alyosha: "secular learning, having united itself into a great power, has studied all the celestial things that were bequeathed to us in the Holy Books, and after the cruel analysis of scholars of this world there remains of all the

- Concentration upon unnecessary rational speculations[15]
- Overemphasis on cataphatism, to the detriment of apophatism
- Lack of concern with a personal encounter with God (theology being divorced from spirituality and the life of the Church)
- Separation from the liturgical life of the Church (theology not inspired by Liturgy, theology not incorporated into Liturgy)
- Ecclesiology understood through canons, organization, order (juridical), as opposed to Eucharist and sacraments (communal)
- Diminishment of a theocentric anthropology

There are several notable reactions to manual theology. First, the philokalic movement began in the eighteenth century with a textual compilation by Nikodemus and Makarios, and then its translation into Slavonic, Romanian and other languages.[16] This hesychast literature represents a spiritual approach to theology, in contrast with the rationalism of neoscholasticism. Second, the departure from Western theology continued more intensely in the nineteenth century, when most Orthodox countries in Eastern Europe obtained political independence and ecclesiastical autocephaly. Third, the Slavophil movement intended to move away from the West (Catholic and Protestant alike) and toward Russia's messianic dream. The genius of Slavic Orthodoxy became concentrated around the

---

earlier holiness absolutely nothing at all. But their study was conducted piecemeal, and they missed the whole; indeed, such blindness is positively worthy of marvel. Whereas the whole stands right before their eyes immovably as ever, and the gates of hell shall not prevail against it." Fyodor M. Dostoyevsky, *The Brothers Karamazov: A Novel in Four Parts and and Epilogue,* trans. David McDuff, Second ed. (London: Penguin Books, 2003), 225–26.

15  See Aquinas' unnecessary speculations in *Summa Theologiae* IIIa, q. 3, art. 5–7 on "whether each of the divine Persons could have assumed human nature," "whether several divine Persons can assume one and the same individual nature," or even "two human natures," when in fact Revelation affirms that only the Son took on one human nature, while the Father and the Spirit did not become incarnate.

16  The earliest attempts to collect spiritual writings are attributed to Basil the Great and Gregory of Nazianzen, while in the twentieth to fourteenth centuries such collections circulated at Athos. In 1782, Nikodimos Hagioritos and Makarios of Corinth published in Venice the Greek version of the *Philokalia*. In 1793, Paisii Velichkovskii published the Slavonic version, having translated it in Romania. In 1857, Bishop Ignatii Brianchaninov and later Theophan the Recluse published another Slavonic translation. Although there was an older fragmentary Romanian translation, Staniloae is credited with the Romanian translation, adding many writings and abundant notes to the Greek version. Other contemporary translations include abbreviated or incomplete versions in English, French, German, and Italian.

notion of sobornicity and the contrast between law/institution and love/charism.[17] Fourth, early twentieth-century Orthodox theologians became more and more disenchanted with neoscholastic theology and explicitly set out to depart from it. Nicholas Afanassieff returned to the eucharistic and charismatic character of the early Church. One of his students, Alexander Schmemann, continued his work in liturgical theology and participation of the people in the public worship of the Church. Another one of Afanassieff's students, John Meyendorff, put the Fathers back into the spotlight, being instrumental in the rediscovery of Gregory Palamas. Vladimir Lossky, too, returned to the Fathers, emphasizing apophatic theology in contrast with the overly cataphatic theology of the West.[18] Most notably, Florovsky called for a neo-patristic synthesis; going beyond the repetition of earlier thought, this theology *ad mentem Patrum* can be preached, has spiritual consequences, and represents the key to Christian unity.[19] In a creative interaction

17  See Aidan Nichols, *Theology in the Russian Diaspora: Church, Fathers, Eucharist in Nikolai Afanas'ev* (Cambridge: Cambridge University Press, 1989), 1–24. Boris Jakim and Robert Bird, *On Spiritual Unity: A Slavophile Reader, Library of Russian Philosophy* (Great Barrington, MA: Lindisfarne Books, 1988).
   Ware considers that Alexei Khomiakov (1804–1860) was the first Russian theologian to break away from excessive dependence upon Western theology. Khomiakov argued that all Western Christianity, whether Catholic or Protestant, shares the same assumptions and upholds the same fundamental point of view, while Orthodoxy is something entirely distinct and should return to its own authentic sources. However, during his lifetime, Khomiakov exercised little or no influence on the theology that was taught in Orthodox academia. Ware, The Orthodox Church, 124–25.

18  For an overview of patristic studies in early twentieth century and an advocacy for neo-patristic synthesis, see Bishop Hilarion Alfeyev, "The Faith of the Fathers: The Patristic Background of the Orthodox Faith and the Study of the Fathers on the Threshold of the 21st Century," *St Vladimir's Theological Quarterly* 51, no. 4 (2007): 379–88.

19  Georges Florovsky, "Patristic Theology and the Ethos of the Orthodox Church," in *Aspects of Church History, Collected Works 4* (Belmont, MA: Nordland, 1975), 17–18, 22, 29. Concerning neo-patristic synthesis, Florovsky wrote: "It should be more than just a collection of Patristic sayings or statements. It must be a *synthesis*, a creative reassessment of those insights which were granted to the Holy Men of old. It must be *Patristic*, faithful to the spirit and vision of the Fathers, *ad mentem Patrum*. Yet, it must also be *Neo-Patristic*, since it is to be addressed to the new age, with its own problems and queries." Florovsky's "Address at 80 Years of Age" in Andrew Blane, "A Sketch of the Life of Georges Florovsky," in *Georges Florovsky: Russian Intellectual and Orthodox Churchman*, ed. Andrew Blane (Crestwood, NY: St Vladimir's Seminary Press, 1993), 154. For an overview of Florovsky's application of neo-patristic synthesis to various theological themes, see George H. Williams, "The Neo-Patristic Synthesis of Georges Florovsky," in *Georges Florovsky: Russian Intellectual and Orthodox Churchman*, ed. Andrew Blane (Crestwood, NY: St Vladimir's Seminary Press, 1993), 287–329, esp. 292.

with the West,[20] Florovsky called for writing in the same patristic spirit, or in "the mind of the Fathers"[21] and the rediscovery of the "catholic mind," which is the language of the Scriptures, the worshipping Church, and the Fathers.[22]

All these instances of Orthodox theology mark a gradual departure from the previous manual tradition, unhealthily influenced by the West. How does Staniloae fit into this picture?[23]

### Staniloae's Engagement with the West

At times, Staniloae's engagement with the West is markedly polemical for three reasons. First, he was not current with the developments in the theologies that he criticized because of his isolation behind the Iron Curtain. He engaged mostly with Catholic and Protestant theologies of the late nineteenth and early twentieth centuries and with the classical Latin tradition, which he encountered early in life as a student in the West. These theologies are frequently criticized by modern Catholic

---

20   Florovsky wrote: "Returning to the fathers, however, does not mean abandoning the present age, escaping from history, or quitting the field of battle. Patristic experience must not only be preserved, but it must be discovered and brought into life. Independence from the non-Orthodox West need not become estrangement from it. A break with the West would provide no real liberation.... And genuine historical synthesis lies not in interpreting the past, but in creatively fulfilling the future." Georges Florovsky, *Ways of Russian Theology: Part Two*. Translated by Robert L. Nichols. Edited by Richard S. Haugh. Vol. 6, *Collected Works* (Belmont, MA: Nordland Pub. Co., 1987), 301, 308.

21   Georges Florovsky, "St. Gregory Palamas and the Tradition of the Fathers," in *Bible, Church, Tradition, Collected Works 1* (Belmont, MA: Nordland Publishing, 1972), 107–08. In the same article, Florovsky recommended going beyond "archaic formulas," and simple "appeal to antiquity," providing Gregory Palamas as an example of "creative extension of ancient tradition" "in complete conformity with the mind of the Church," as opposed to a "theology of repetition." (pp. 105–06, 114, 120)

22   Georges Florovsky, "The Church: Her Nature and Task," in *Bible, Church, Tradition, Collected Works 1* (Belmont, MA: Nordland Pub. Co., 1972), 58. Florovsky, "Patristic Theology," 181–82.

23   Early in the twentieth-century Romania, translations were very popular, especially from dogmatic treatises by Russian theologians of the late nineteenth century (e.g., Peter Ternovskoi, Antonii Amfiteatrov, Makarii Bulgakov, Filaret Gumilevskii, Silvestr Malevanskii, Filaret Drozdov and Alexei Khomiakov) or Greek theologians such as Chrestos Andrutsos, whose *Dogmatiké* and *Symboliké* formed the basis for original Romanian compendia. Several dogmatic treatises written in the form of standard Greek and Russian manuals of the nineteenth century preceded Staniloae. Maloney, *A History of Orthodox Theology since 1453*, 291.

theologians, too.[24] Second, Staniloae reacted against neoscholastic theology as it was being done by Orthodox and Catholic theologians at that time, as I show in the next section. And third, if Staniloae's criticism of Catholicism is oftentimes very sharp, it is because of his personal experience with Byzantine Catholic proselytism in his native region of Transylvania, which even took violent forms such as bombing monasteries or villages that opposed the union with Rome.[25]

Consequently, especially in the first part of his academic career, Staniloae used caricatures, unfair generalizations,[26] and his sources are sometimes hard to trace.[27] Louth goes as far as to describe Staniloae's attitude toward the West as nonreceptive, negative, and even uncomprehending, despite occasional engagements with Barth, Rahner, Balthasar, Schlier, and Althaus, to mention only a few.[28] But Louth is not entirely right.

After he retired, Staniloae became more receptive to the changes in Catholic theology, especially concerning its more sacramental, spiritual ecclesiology. He was certain that schism could not endure.[29] Roberson considers that this change was determined by Staniloae's direct involvement with ecumenism:

> Staniloae's experience as a participant at the second plenary session of the international Catholic-Orthodox dialogue at Munich in 1982 seems to have caused him to greatly moderate his views on the Catholic Church. In an interview published in 1988, he stated that Orthodoxy and Catholicism "are not divided by essential differences." He was pleasantly surprised at Munich to see

---

24  Ronald G. Roberson, "Contemporary Romanian Orthodox Ecclesiology: The Contribution of Dumitru Staniloae and Younger Colleagues" (Doctoral dissertation, The Pontifical Oriental Institute in Rome, 1988) 163–64.

25  Despite these considerations, Ion Bria remarked that "he has a profound sense of the unity of all Christians and he never adopts an attitude of anti-ecumenism." Ion Bria, "The Creative Vision of Dumitru Staniloae: An Introduction to His Theological Thought," *Ecumenical Review* 33, no. 1 (1981): 57. See also Stefan L. Toma, *Traditie si actualitate la pr. Dumitru Staniloae* [*Tradition and Actuality in Fr. Dumitru Staniloae*] (Sibiu: Agnos, 2008), 237–45.

26  For example, he considered that "Catholicism is *rationalist* and *immanentist* [i.e., empirical], while Orthodoxy is *mystical* and *transcendentalist*. The rationalism of Catholicism has its source in Roman positivism." Dumitru Staniloae, *Natiune si Crestinism* [*Nation and Christianity*], ed. Constantin Schifirnet (Bucuresti: Elion, 2003), 19.

27  Roberson, "Contemporary Romanian Orthodox Ecclesiology" 49.

28  Andrew Louth, "The Orthodox Dogmatic Theology of Dumitru Staniloae," *Modern Theology* 13, no. 2 (1997): 260–61. This review article is reprinted in Louth, "Staniloae's Dogmatics (Reprint 2002)," 53–70.

29  Roberson, "Dumitru Staniloae on Christian Unity," 117. Roberson refers here to Dumitru Staniloae, "In problema intercomuniunii [On the Issue of Intercommunion]," *Ortodoxia* 23, no. 4 (1971): 583–84.

that there was a broad agreement on issues that had been significant causes of division in the past. He emerged hopeful that a solution may even be found to the problem of the papacy which would integrate the bishop of Rome into the communion of the Church in a way acceptable to the Orthodox.[30]

Staniloac dedicated much energy to the study of ecclesiology and ecumenism. As a thematic bibliography shows,[31] he contributed to the cause of Christian unity with 65 articles and many references in his other writings. He praised the ecumenical movement and its purpose to reestablish the unity of the Church, recommending that it must seek the most intimate presence of Christ among the faithful, as it is experienced in the Orthodox Church.[32] This is why Staniloae wrote about our obligation to maintain ecclesial unity: "Salvation is communion in Christ (koinonia) and therefore the obligation of Christians to strive to maintain and develop their ecclesial unity through love is plain: 'For the love of Christ gathers us together' (2 Cor. 5.14)."[33] He also encouraged Orthodox theologians to study the teachings of other churches in an irenic spirit.[34] Indeed, there is a need to present the relevance of Staniloae's theology to ecumenism, based on the current developments of Western theologies.

*Staniloae's Departure from Neoscholasticism: A Theological Biography*

Staniloae's attitude toward the West changed over time, probably because his theology moved from a rejection of neoscholasticism to the positive affirmation of neo-patristic synthesis. This journey is reflected in his theological biography.

In 1922, Staniloae began the study of theology at the University of Cernauti. Disappointed by the rationalistic manual theology that he was taught there,

---

30   Roberson, "Dumitru Staniloae on Christian Unity," 113. Roberson refers here to Ioanichie Balan, ed., *Convorbiri Duhovnicesti* [*Spiritual Conversations*], vol. 2 (Roman: Editura Episcopiei Romanului si Husilor, 1988), 92–93.

31   Gheorghe F. Anghelescu and Ioan I. Ica jr., "Parintele Prof. Acad. Dumitru Staniloae: Bibliografie Sistematica [Father Professor Academician Dumitru Staniloae: Systematic Bibliography]," in *Persoana si Comuniune: Prinos de Cinstire Parintelui Profesor Academician Dumitru Staniloae la implinirea varstei de 90 de ani*, ed. Ioan I. Ica jr. and Mircea Pacurariu (Sibiu: Editura Arhiepiscopiei Ortodoxe Sibiu, 1993). See also *Bibliografia Parintelui Academician Profesor Dr. Dumitru Staniloae* [*The Bibliography of Father Academician Professor Dr. Dumitru Staniloae*], (Bucuresti: EIBMBOR, 1993).

32   Dumitru Staniloae, *Teologia Dogmatica Ortodoxa* [*Orthodox Dogmatic Theology*], Second ed., vol. 2 (Bucharest: EIBMBOR, 1997), 176.

33   Dumitru Staniloae, *Theology and the Church*, trans. Robert Barringer (Crestwood, NY: St Vladimir's Seminary Press, 1980), 204.

34   Ibid., 121.

he left after only a year to study Literature at the University of Bucharest.[35] He then returned to the study of theology, learned Russian in order to read Sergey Bulgakov, and familiarized himself with thinkers such as Kant, Hegel, and Schopenhauer. Staniloae next went to learn Greek and study the Fathers in Athens where, unfortunately, the patristic tradition was largely ignored, just as in Romania. Between 1928 and 1929, he studied Byzantine history in Munich. There he read the second edition of Karl Barth's *Commentary on Romans* (1922), from which Staniloae later acknowledged to have gained "the affirmation of a living God, the affirmation of the transcendence of God before man."[36] Staniloae balanced this affirmation with the theology of Gregory Palamas (whom he studied in Berlin, Paris, and Constantinople from 1929 to 1930), who distinguished between God's essence and energies, allowing for God's real involvement with humankind and the world without compromising his essential unknowability and transcendence.[37] Between 1929 and 1946, Staniloae taught Dogmatic Theology at the Theological Institute in Sibiu.

---

35 Charles Miller writes: "His early theological training, therefore, followed a rationalistic German model based upon the principles of scholastic metaphysics. 'One never had to think about God,' Staniloae recalled, 'everything had been said.' And so, except for the acquisition of a methodical research technique, he gained little from his initial theological studies, and even abandoned his interest in dogmatics. When he turned to the study of church history he was equally frustrated. Although in the course of study he discovered the Hesychast tradition of spirituality and theology, his scholastic manuals described Hesychasm as 'strange.' [Dumitru Staniloae and M. A. Costa de Beauregard, *Ose comprendre que je t'aime* (Paris: Cerf, 1983), 18–19.]" Charles Miller, *The Gift of the World: An Introduction to the Theology of Dumitru Staniloae* (Edinburgh: T&T Clark, 2000), 13.

36 Staniloae and Costa de Beauregard, *Ose comprendre que je t'aime*, 22. Miller's translation.

37 The distinction-in-unity between God's essence and his uncreated energies, generally ascribed to Gregory Palamas, although certainly present in early patristic writings, was not always fully represented during Orthodoxy's "Western captivity," but Staniloae rediscovered its importance. As Dan Ciobotea (a disciple of Staniloae and now Patriarch of Romania) puts it, "the Palamite teaching is ignored in the *Dogmatics* of Adrutsos, and allowed no more than a passing mention in that of Trembelas. There is no reference to it in the main text of Fr. Michael Pomazansky's *Orthodox Dogmatic Theology*, although a few lines are devoted to St. Gregory Palamas in an appendix. Fr. Dumitru's is thus the first dogmatics in which the distinction is seen as fundamental to the Orthodox understanding of God. (Dan I. Ciobotea, "Une dogmatique pour l'homme d'aujourd'hui [Review of Teologia Dogmatica Ortodoxa]," *Irénikon* 54, no. 4 (1981): 473. Quoted and translated in Ware, "Foreword," xxi.) Moreover, as Stefan Toma points out, Staniloae worked directly with manuscripts, translated, commented, and was instrumental in the rediscovery of Palamas. Toma, *Tradition and Actuality*, 49.

In 1930, Staniloae translated Chrestos Andrutsos's *Handbook of Dogmatics*. As he translated this work, Staniloae became more and more dissatisfied with it, adopting a wholly different theological method and vision by writing in the spirit of the Church Fathers. In 1938 he published a pioneering study of the theology of Gregory Palamas, and, in 1943, *Jesus Christ, or the Restoration of Humankind*. In the latter volume, Staniloae relied heavily on Maximus the Confessor and other Fathers, as he would in all his future works.

In 1946, under pressure from the newly established communist regime, Staniloae had to resign from the Theological Institute in Sibiu and was later transferred to Bucharest. Shortly thereafter, he was the victim of an unjust communist trial, which resulted in his condemnation to five years of imprisonment. Staniloae preferred not to talk about these terrible five years, in which he was mentally and physically abused through violent interrogations, isolation, hunger, and beatings.[38] However, Staniloae confessed later that he learned the Jesus Prayer in prison.[39] He also admitted that the years of incarceration taught him that theology was not sufficiently "in touch" with the people. Here was yet another reason to depart from neoscholasticism by tying together dogma and spirituality.[40] Consequently, Staniloae's theology was transformed. He was not content with Lossky's understanding of apophatism simply as negative theology and his lack of appreciation for cataphatism. Staniloae presented the spiritual aspect of both our affirmations and negations about God, culminating with an experiential, beyond-rational aspect of apophatism.[41]

---

38   His daughter, Lidia, writes: "the extreme suffering he underwent was an experience that brought him even closer to God.... He passed through that hell with a luminous smile on his lips, and with confidence that God gives us hardships to purify us so that we might obtain the future life, a reality that presupposes effort and a powerful will." Lidia Staniloae, "Remembering My Father," in *Dumitru Staniloae: Tradition and Modernity in Theology*, ed. Lucian Turcescu (Iasi, Oxford, Palm Beach, Portland: The Center for Romanian Studies, 2002), 21. For more details on Staniloae's life, see Lidia Staniloae, *Lumina faptei din lumina cuvantului: impreuna cu tatal meu, Dumitru Staniloae* [*The Light of the Deed from the Light of the Word: Together with My Father, Dumitru Staniloae*] (Bucuresti: Humanitas, 2000).

39   'Préface' to Dumitru Staniloae, *Prière de Jesus et expérience de Saint Esprit*, *Théophanie* (Paris: Desclée De Brouwer, 1981), 11.

40   Staniloae and Costa de Beauregard, *Ose comprendre que je t'aime*, 28.

41   See Radu Bordeianu, "Orthodox Spirituality: A Practical Guide for the Faithful and a Definitive Manual for the Scholar. By Dumitru Staniloae. Translated from the Romanian by Archimandrite Jerome (Newville) and Otilia Kloos. South Canaan, Pennsylvania: St. Tikhon's Seminary Press, 2002. ISBN 1-878997-66-1. Pp. 397 [Book Review]," *Archaeus* 12–13 (2007–2008): 414.

Therefore, Staniloae regarded theology as a personal experience rather than an abstract philosophical system, and emphasized the complementarity between cataphatism and apophatism, characteristic of his departure from scholastic theology toward a neo-patristic synthesis.[42] He achieved this kind of theology by drawing from three sources: Revelation (Scripture and Tradition), Liturgy, and contemporary thought.

The first source of his theology is Revelation. One aspect of Revelation is the Bible, and Staniloae might give the impression that his theology is not biblical enough. True, at times he slips into the realm of logical speculation and does not quote the Bible consistently. At the same time, his theology is profoundly biblical, going well beyond the temptation of systematic theology to use the Bible simply for decorative purposes, to support arguments that otherwise could stem from logical deductions, rather than being rooted in Revelation. Many of Staniloae's statements are implicitly biblical concepts or derived from exegetical analysis. Other times, he quoted the Bible abundantly and dedicated entire books to biblical theology, such as *The Evangelical Image of Jesus Christ*.[43] Throughout this book and primarily in the second part, I hope to show the profoundly biblical character of Staniloae's theology.

The other aspect of Revelation is the patristic tradition of the Church. Staniloae studied the Church Fathers thoroughly, reading the Greek authors in their original language and translating many of their works, such as the Romanian *Philokalia* in 12 volumes.[44] He showered the translations abundantly with his commentaries, many informed by Western scholarship. However, Staniloae considered that the works of the Fathers needed to be taken a step further, due to their limited cultural and even theological character.[45] This is why he wrote in

---

42  Louth, "Staniloae's Dogmatics," 254, 58.

43  Dumitru Staniloae, *Chipul evanghelic al lui Iisus Hristos* (Sibiu: Editura Centrului Mitropolitan Sibiu, 1991).

44  Dumitru Staniloae, *Filocalia sau Culegere din scrierile Sfintilor Parinti care arata cum se poate omul curati, lumina si desavirsi* [*The Philokalia or Collection from the Writings of the Holy Fathers that Shows How One Can Be Purified, Illumined and Perfected*], Fourth ed., 12 vols. (Bucuresti: Harisma-Humanitas, 1993–).

45  For example, as I show in the next chapter, Staniloae considered that the iconodoules of the eighth century could have explained better the relationship between Christ and the icon, and how the veneration passes on to the prototype, had they had the benefits of a fully explicit theology and terminology of the uncreated energies. Dumitru Staniloae, *Spiritualitate si comuniune in Liturghia Ortodoxa* [*Spirituality and Communion in the Orthodox Liturgy*] (Craiova: Editura Mitropoliei Olteniei, 1986), 65. See also Dumitru Staniloae, *The Experience of God: Revelation and Knowledge of the Triune God*, trans. Ioan Ionita and Robert Barringer, Second ed., vol. 1 (Brookline, MA: Holy Cross Orthodox Press, 1998), 252.

the "Foreword" to his *Dogmatics*: "We tried to understand the teaching of the Church in the spirit of the Fathers, but, at the same time, to understand it as we think that they would have understood it today. I believe that they wouldn't ignore our times, as they didn't ignore theirs."[46]

The second source of Staniloae's theology is the Liturgy.[47] In his book *Spirituality and Communion in the Orthodox Liturgy*, for example, he builds a communion ecclesiology on the foundation of the Liturgy and, vice versa, explains the theological, communal aspects of the Liturgy. The worshipping Church is both the source and the interpretative lens of Staniloae's theology.

A third source is contemporary thought. Louth writes about Staniloae's engagement with contemporary philosophy such as Buber, or with Nikolai Berdiaev and other Russian émigrés:

> Fr. Dumitru is both clearly open to modern ideas and at the same time finds here concepts that crystallize in a striking way intuitions of the Fathers. He does not try to reduce the notion of the personal to something patristic (as some Orthodox writers sometimes seem to do); rather he recognizes in this aspect of modern thought the deepening of a patristic insight.[48]

Due to communist isolation, however, Staniloae was not heavily influenced by his contemporaries. Born and raised in Communist Romania, I have bitter memories of this oppressive regime. When I began to study Staniloae, my natural inclination was to emphasize the negative consequences of living and writing under communist isolation. But in 2002 I have interviewed Roman Braga,

---

46  Dumitru Staniloae, *Teologia Dogmatica Ortodoxa* [*Orthodox Dogmatic Theology*], Second ed., vol. 1 (Bucharest: EIBMBOR, 1996), 7. This passage was not included in the English translation. There is no doubt among scholars who have studied Staniloae's theology that Maximus the Confessor was the Church Father who inspired him the most. [Louth, "Staniloae's Dogmatics," 257.] Staniloae also relied heavily on Pseudo-Dionysius the Areopagite [Gheorge Dragulin, "Pseudo-Dionysios the Areopagite in Dumitru Staniloae's Theology," in *Dumitru Staniloae: Tradition and Modernity in Theology*, ed. Lucian Turcescu (Iasi, Romania; Palm Beach, FL: Center for Romanian Studies, 2002).], Athanasius of Alexandria, John Chrysostom, Gregory of Nyssa, Gregory of Nazianzen, Basil the Great, John Chrysostom, John of Damascus, and Gregory Palamas, to name a few.

47  Louth writes about Staniloae's thought: "one of the sources of Orthodox theology comes into its own: that is the liturgical ceremonies of the Orthodox Church, not just the texts, but also what takes place, what is expressed through what is done." Louth, "Staniloae's Dogmatics," 264.

48  Ibid., 261–62.

a Romanian intellectual and hieromonk who knew Staniloae closely; they were convicted at the same trial. Braga was the first to point me to the positive consequences of writing under communist persecution. By being isolated from the West and even from the rest of the Orthodox world—says Braga—Staniloae developed a positive affirmation of the Orthodox faith as opposed to a theology in opposition to other theologians. His theology could thus grow naturally, without being framed by polemics originating outside his tradition. I agree. But this does not mean that isolation is good in and of itself. One can only wonder how Staniloae's theology would have been enriched by more meaningful dialogues with other theologians.

For the reasons mentioned above I consider that Staniloae was the first Orthodox theologian to successfully break away from the manual tradition.[49] This affirmation does not diminish the importance of other theologians who embarked on the same quest, paved the way, and pointed the direction, but were more concerned with historical and nonsystematic theology than Staniloae. I am not accusing Russian theologians such as Bulgakov, Florovsky, or Lossky of neoscholasticism. But Staniloae began his departure towards a neo-patristic theology as early as 1930, independent of other theologians, or even earlier, if one recalls his discontent with manual theology as taught in Orthodox schools. His departure from neoscholasticism is particularly evident in his biography and in the importance that he placed on the complementarily between cataphatism and apophatism, as well as on the personal encounter with God, which results in a theology with spiritual consequences. Furthermore, as an excellent patristic scholar and translator, Staniloae relied heavily on the Fathers, while also rooting his theology in the Liturgy and contemporary thought, thus writing a neo-patristic synthesis. His theology remains more affirmative and concerned with proclamation than responsive and dialogical. And yet, his limited (though intense) encounter with the West is most helpful for contemporary ecumenism, especially concerning open sobornicity.

## Open Sobornicity

In 1971, Staniloae wrote an article entitled "Open Sobornicity," a term aptly summarized by Turcescu as the acceptance of every valid theological

---

49  Others would concur. See Turcescu, "Introduction," 7. For a description of Staniloae as "neo-Orthodox" theologian writing a "neo-patristic" synthesis, see also Maciej Bielawski, *Parintele Dumitru Staniloae, o viziune filocalica despre lume* [*Father Dumitru Staniloae: A Philokalic Vision of the World*], trans. Ioan I. Ica jr., *Dogmatica* (Sibiu: Deisis, 1998), 74–77.

insight in other theological traditions without running the risk of doctrinal relativism.[50]

Staniloae wrote this article as a positive reaction to the "Scripture and Tradition" document of the Faith and Order meeting in Aarhus (1964). The document notes the unity of the Gospel as reflected in diverse, complementary, or even contradictory biblical testimonies.[51] These testimonies reflect the diversity of God's actions in different historical circumstances and the diversity of human answers to God's actions. So—in what Staniloae calls a justified and wise declaration—the document recommends that biblical interpreters should not attach themselves to just one biblical passage, as central as it may seem, because this would lead to a misunderstanding of the richness and variety of the Bible. Staniloae then applied this recommendation to ecclesiology; most schisms are due to the unilateral attachment to a scriptural passage, without regard to the diversity of the Bible. Church unity became understood not as a balanced unity of apparently contradictory points, but as a uniformity that suppressed the complexity of ecclesial life. Staniloae added:

> The restoration of unity is for Western Christianity a matter of abandoning the plane of exclusivist alternatives. It must rediscover the spirit of Orthodoxy which does not oppose one alternative or the other, but embraces in its teaching and equilibrium the points affirmed by both forms of Western Christianity.... Of course, we must not pride ourselves with a satisfactory actualization of Orthodoxy on the plane of spirituality and with efficacy in the lives of the faithful.[52] Besides this, Orthodox sobornicity nowadays must be enriched with the spiritual values actualized by Western Christians.[53]

---

50  Lucian Turcescu, "Eucharistic Ecclesiology or Open Sobornicity?," in *Dumitru Staniloae: Tradition and Modernity in Theology*, ed. Lucian Turcescu (Iasi, Romania; Palm Beach, FL: Center for Romanian Studies, 2002). In the same volume, Roberson analyzes "open sobornicity" and its value for promoting Christian unity. Roberson, "Dumitru Staniloae on Christian Unity," 120–22.

51  On the contributions of Ernst Käsemann and Raymond Brown in this sense, as well as another description of the same development within the WCC, including the Fourth World Conference of Faith and Order, Montreal (1963), see Michael Kinnamon, *The Vision of the Ecumenical Movement and How It Has Been Impoverished by Its Friends* (St. Louis: Chalice Press, 2003), 55ff.

52  To give just one example, Staniloae admitted that, at times, Orthodoxy has fallen into the temptation to emphasize either ordained or universal priesthood over the other. This is why, for the Orthodox, unity in diversity, or "sobornicity must be more than a theory; it must be a practice."

53  Dumitru Staniloae, "Sobornicitate deschisa [Open Sobornicity]," *Ortodoxia* 23, no. 2 (1971): 171.

Staniloae's concern here is to call both sides to action and counteract triumphal attitudes that de-entice Orthodoxy from being open to Western values. All churches need to learn from each other not only to maintain diversity, but also to come to a symphonic unity, without uniformity,[54] just as the Scripture is unitary and diverse at the same time. Being confined within one's own limits means to regard a certain experience of God's actions as ultimate and exclusive; this results in a limited experience of God. However, God's actions in different historical contexts, although valuable, have a relative value in the sense that only if we search for the other manifestations of God's revelation and bring them together in unity, do we find God fully. Concretely, Orthodoxy could benefit from Catholicism by strengthening its unity, while it could learn from Protestantism to give more value to all instances of God's revelation. Staniloae concluded:

> Sobornicity is more than embracing in common all the modes of reve- lation and expression of God into the world or in life.... Sobornicity is also an increasingly comprehensive and embracing openness towards God who is above these [revelations]; it is a continuous advancement in God's infinitely spiritual richness. This sobornicity that is *open*, transparent, and continuously surpassed, also implies a certain *theological pluralism*. [emphases mine][55]

These considerations are not intended in a relativistic sense, as if there were no unique truth of Revelation. Nor do they negate the understanding of the Orthodox Church as the one that possesses the fullness of truth. Instead, they are meant to say that Orthodoxy needs to be enriched (even corrected) by other historical instances of God's revelation. At the same time, Staniloae added, Orthodoxy can bring an important contribution to the ecumenical movement by looking for the living spiritual core in doctrinal formulations. Rather than regarding its doctrinal formulae as rigid expressions opposed to equally rigid expressions used by the other churches, Orthodoxy should seek to uncover the living meanings of other confessions of faith. The spiritual effects of these doc- trines might be identical,[56] despite differences in semantics and terminology, as it is often (though not always) the case. Unsurprisingly, Staniloae added: "Western theology often leads toward the same spiritual and mystical core of Revelation,

---

54 See the same idea in Dumitru Staniloae, "Coordonatele ecumenismului din punct de vedere Ortodox [The Coordinates of Ecumenism from the Orthodox Perspective]," *Ortodoxia* 19, no. 4 (1967): 517–18.

55 Staniloae, "Open Sobornicity," 178.

56 Staniloae, *Theology and the Church*, 221–22.

and so by this path comes to merge with Orthodox theology."[57] Thus, Staniloae proposed a "spiritual interpretation" of dogmas as a means toward unity.

How is open sobornicity implemented concretely, here and now, when the East does not have eucharistic communion with the West? Through "spiritual intercommunion," as a form of intercommunion that consists in common study, prayer, and action among Christians.[58] This intercommunion leads to open sobornicity because, through its exercise, "the Holy Spirit multiplies the 'connections' among Churches, [connections] through which their life in Christ may be transmitted from one Church to another, thus becoming more and more alike."[59]

In his own special way, despite his occasional polemical tone, Staniloae was considerably open to the West. He applied open sobornicity both knowingly and unknowingly. He relied on Western philosophers and theologians, biblical and patristic scholarship. He also adopted the positive influences that Western theology had upon Orthodoxy, such as the three offices of Christ or the designation of seven sacraments, sometimes unaware of their Western origin.

## The Three Offices of Christ

Louth criticizes Staniloae for adopting Orthodox manual theology that was in turn influenced by Western theology:

> Christ's work of redemption is presented in terms of Christ's threefold office as Prophet, Priest, and King. Fr. Dumitru declares that it is patristic (without any references), but it was only with Calvin's *Institutes* that the notion of Christ's threefold office assumed the structural significance with which he invests it. There is nothing wrong with an Orthodox borrowing from Calvin, though it would be gracious to admit it: Fr. Dumitru, however, was probably borrowing from Orthodox Dogmatics. But it is this dependence on the structure of earlier Orthodox Dogmatics (which

---

57   Ibid., 217.

58   These exercises form a true communion, albeit less than eucharistic communion. Staniloae did not explain the historic origin for his terminological choice of "spiritual intercommunion." It is probably related to Origen's use of "spiritual communion" as a designation of the benefits of attending the Divine Liturgy and partaking of God's words, even when not receiving the Eucharist (*In Num.* 16:9, *In Mt.* 11.14). See a repudiation of Origen's concept in Nicolas Afanassieff, *The Church of the Holy Spirit*, trans. Vitaly Permiakov (South Bend, IN: Notre Dame University Press, 2007), 57, 287.

59   Dumitru Staniloae, "Teologia Euharistiei [The Theology of the Eucharist]," *Ortodoxia* 21, no. 3 (1969): 361.

borrowed their structure from Catholic and Protestant models) that may conceal dangers.[60]

First, there is no doubt that Christ's threefold office as Prophet, Priest,[61] and King is a theological construct consecrated by Calvin.[62] Louth, however, dismissed too easily the affirmation that this notion is of patristic origin, for Staniloae's lack of references. Even though systematized by Calvin, the notion of Christ's threefold office is certainly present in the Bible and patristic tradition.[63]

---

60 Louth, "Staniloae's Dogmatics," 259.

61 Staniloae used the Romanian word, "arhiereu," which means bishop or literally, high priest. However, in accordance with common English usage, I translate it with "Priest."

62 John Calvin, *Institutes of the Christian Religion*, ed. John T. McNeill, trans. Ford Lewis Battles, vol. 1 (Louisville, KY: Westminster John Knox Press, 2006), 494. Chapter 15 in book 2 of the first volume is entitled, "To Know the Purpose For Which Christ Was Sent By the Father, And What He Conferred Upon Us, We Must Look Above All at Three Things in Him: the Prophetic Office, Kingship, and Priesthood."

63 Without any exegesis or mentioning the texts that do not explicitly state that Jesus is King, Prophet, Priest, here are some of the most relevant examples from the Gospels and the Letter to the Hebrews:

   Jesus is King: Mt. 21.5; Lk. 19.38; Jn 12.13, 15. Parables that make reference to Jesus as king: Mt. 22.2–14; 25.31–46, etc. Jesus is "King of Israel": Jn 1.49. "King of the Jews": Mt. 2.2; 27.11, 29, 37, 42; Mk 15.2, 9, 12, 18, 26, 32; Lk.23.3, 37, 38; Jn 18.33, 37 twice, 39; 19.3, 19, 21 twice.

   Jesus is Prophet: Mt. 21.11, 46; Lk. 4.24, 44; 7.16; 24.19; Jn 4.19; 6.14; 7.40; 9.17.

   Jesus is Priest or "high priest": Heb. 2.17; 3.1; 4.14, 15; 5.1, 5, 6, 10; 6.20; 7.11, 15, 16, 17, 21 twice, 26; 8.1, 3; 9.11; 10.21. Jesus "holds his priesthood permanently": Heb. 7.24.

   There are also patristic examples in this sense. Macarius affirmed: "Spiritual men, who are anointed with the heavenly unction, become Christs according to grace, so that they too are kings, priests, and prophets of heavenly mysteries." (Homily 27:4, PG 34:696BC, Homily 17:1, PG 34:624BC, quoted in Paul Evdokimov, *The Sacrament of Love: The Nuptial Mystery in the Light of the Orthodox Tradition*, trans. Anthony P. Gythiel and Victoria Steadman (Crestwood, NY: St Vladimir's Seminary Press, 1985), 88.) Maximus the Confessor stressed that Joachim (Virgin Mary's father) and Joseph were descendants of David, whose tribe was intermingled with that of Judah, so the kingly and priestly tribes have been intermingled; hence Christ is both Priest and King because he is both God and human. (Saint Maximus the Confessor, *Viata Fecioarei Maria* [*The Life of Virgin Mary*], trans. Ioan Ica Jr. (Sibiu: Deisis, 1999), 7.) Moreover, in Calvin's above-mentioned chapter, the third footnote makes reference to Thomas Aquinas' *Summa Theologiae* IIIa q. 22, art. 1, rp 3, which reads: "Wherefore, as to others, one is a lawgiver [i.e., prophet], another is a priest, another is king; but all these concur in Christ as the fount of all grace."

   These examples are not meant to challenge the fact that Calvin was the first to stress Christ's threefold office as clearly and emphatically as he did.

More importantly, this notion became part of Orthodox ecclesiastical tradition, which represents the continuous adaptation of the unchanging Holy Tradition, so as to make it relevant to present times. Staniloae accepted this possibility, of Orthodoxy borrowing valid concepts from other theologies as long as there are sufficient biblical and patristic grounds to do so. Louth is equally open to this possibility in his affirmation that "there is nothing wrong with an Orthodox borrowing from Calvin." So one can conclude that Staniloae was influenced by the West in this instance, and I consider it a case of open sobornicity, despite Staniloae's unawareness of the Calvinist development of the three offices of Christ.

Louth's second criticism is that Staniloae's use of the traditional dogmatic structure may conceal dangers. Louth did not provide a more specific description of these dangers. Nor did he offer an alternative manner of presenting Christ's offices. Staniloae did both: he exposed some dangers of scholastic descriptions of the three offices and departed from them. He reacted against Bulgakov's sharp separation of the three offices, as if before his Passion Christ was only Prophet, during his Passion only Priest, and then at the end of his ministry only King.[64] Moreover, Staniloae criticized the separation of the prophetic aspect of pastoral life from the priestly and kingly offices (to which Staniloae sometimes refers as the works of illumination, sanctification, and perfection, respectively). This is symptomatic of the scholastic separation between theology, spirituality, and pastoral life, rooted in the separation between reason, feelings, and will, thus not looking at the human being as a whole. On the contrary, Staniloae argued, biblical and patristic writings point to the interdependence between these human capacities; hence, the three offices are sometimes

---

64   According to Staniloae, Christ was Prophet, Priest, and King in all the stages of his mission on earth: "Jesus's three offices ... always co-exist together even though, in each stage [of Jesus's life], one of them is more prominent. When he was teaching as prophet, Jesus was also performing miracles as king, and through teaching, he was exercising a certain kingly power on the souls. He also taught through his Passion. And from his death to his second coming, even though his kingly office is more prominent, shining in his heavenly glory and exercising a greater dominion over the souls, he also continues to teach through the Holy Spirit and to sacrifice himself in the Eucharist or to intervene to the Father as priest forever." Dumitru Staniloae, *Iisus Hristos sau restaurarea omului* [*Jesus Christ or the Restoration of Humankind*], Second ed. (Craiova: Editura Omniscop, 1993), 347–48. Staniloae did not mean to discard completely Bulgakov's assertion that certain events in Jesus' life correspond to one of the offices, since Staniloae organized the second part of his book, *Jesus Christ or the Restoration of Humankind*, according to the three offices.

designated as one ministry, that of sanctification.[65] Implicit here is both the preservation of the mystery of Christ's work against excessive systematization and our participation in Christ's three offices. While I discuss the latter in the eighth chapter, suffice it to say here that our priestly, prophetic, and kingly manifestations are possible only because we share in, and as a result of, Christ's three offices. Being united with Christ and sharing in his manifestations, the Church becomes "a tightly knit community that advances in the bosom of the Trinity,"[66] being raised with Christ in the Trinity. Staniloae's discussion of the three offices of Christ goes well beyond a cold oversystematization of Christology, and is ultimately a chapter of trinitarian theology with spiritual consequences. This is certainly a departure from scholastic theology.

In summary, the notion of the threefold office of Christ originated with Calvin, and, if taken to extreme, it conceals the dangers of rationalization of theology, separation between theology and spirituality and, I might add in light of Staniloae's critique of Bulgakov, the clear separation of the three offices, contrary to the Scriptures. Departing from such theology, Staniloae presented a neo-patristic synthesis that leads to an encounter with God through participation in Christ's three offices in the Church through the Spirit, without claiming to exhaust the mystery of God's saving presence in our lives.

### The Designation of Seven Sacraments[67]

Louth also criticizes Staniloae for adopting the Latin designation of the seven sacraments:

> The idea of seven sacraments, distinct and set apart from other sacramental acts, is a Western idea that only emerges in the twelfth century. It was

---

65 Dumitru Staniloae, "Temeiurile teologice ale ierarhiei si ale sinodalitatii [The Theological Foundations of Hierarchy and Synodality]," *Studii Teologice* 22, no. 3–4 (1970): 167–68.

66 Staniloae, *Spirituality and Communion*, 140–41.

67 The Greek term for sacrament is *misterion* and, beginning with Tertullian, it has been translated into Latin as *sacramentum*; hence the common usage of the word sacrament in the Western world, both Protestant and Catholic. Some English-speaking Orthodox theologians prefer *mysteries*, while others are comfortable with *sacrament*. I translate Staniloae's Romanian term, *taina* with *sacrament*. However, when I occasionally use translations other than mine, I respect their use of *mystery*. Staniloae would most likely be neutral in the debate on whether to use a term of Greek origin, or one with a Latin root, since the Romanian *taina* comes from the Slavonic *taina*, which means mystery.

only accepted by the Orthodox under pressure from the West, explicitly, by the Emperor Michael VIII Paleologos after the Council of Lyon (1274), and in reaction against Protestant influence by such as Dositheos and Peter Mogila. In the West it was bound up with the notion of Dominical institution and the mystique of the number seven. It is made easier in the West by the clear separation of baptism and confirmation. Fr. Dumitru has to keep to this separation, although it corresponds to no reality in Orthodox practice, and finds himself defending Dominical institution in a very forced way. It also leads him to misunderstand some of the ingenuity devoted to this topic by Catholic theologians such as Karl Rahner. It also means that he draws a veil over the variety of ways in which sacraments are treated by the Fathers, very nearly sealing himself off from some of the sources of his theology (e.g. Nicholas Kabasilas, whom he quotes a good deal, both of whose major works, his *Commentary on the Divine Liturgy* and his *Life in Christ*, presuppose a rather different, more Dionysian approach to the sacraments). Here, it seems to me, the structure has become a strait-jacket, though what is pressed into the strait-jacket is often arresting and profoundly moving (it also means that some of his sacramental teaching appears elsewhere in his teaching on creation as a gift bearing the mark of the cross, for instance).[68]

Did Staniloae indeed defend the Dominical institution of all the sacraments in a forced way? A careful reading of the *Dogmatics* (the basis of Louth's critique) shows that the Dominical institution is at best marginal in the 133 pages that Staniloae dedicates to the sacraments, and in the case of marriage it is simply nonexistent.[69] True, Staniloae considered that the Anointing of the Sick originates, "through the Apostles, from Christ himself,"[70] thus confirming Louth's criticism. But elsewhere Staniloae acknowledged that Christ did not explicitly institute all the sacraments. Instead, the Apostles have applied different events in Jesus' life or his sayings to their pastoral necessities, resulting in the sacraments.[71]

Furthermore, Louth considers that the demarcation of the seven sacraments from other sacramental acts is a Western idea that emerged only in the twelfth

---

68  Louth, "Staniloae's Dogmatics," 259–60.
69  Staniloae, *Dogmatics 3*, 118–35.
70  Ibid., 135.
71  Dumitru Staniloae, "Numarul Tainelor, raporturile intre ele si problema Tainelor din afara Bisericii [The Number of the Sacraments, Their Relationships, and the Problem of the Sacraments Outside the Church]," *Ortodoxia* 8, no. 2 (1956): 192.

century.[72] He assumes that Staniloae was unaware of the lateness of this development. And yet, Staniloae agreed with Louth's chronology and was even more detailed, naming pope Alexander III and Peter Lombard for the West, and adding to Paleologos's name that of the monk Job of Iasi.[73] Thus, unlike Staniloae's involuntary acceptance of Christ's three offices discussed above, he was aware that the number seven designating the sacraments originated in the West, and yet he adopted it. This was certainly an instance of open sobornicity!

Ware, too, would probably disagree with Louth's criticism. He believes that the formalization of the seven sacraments is of Western origin, but he also states that the setting apart of the seven sacraments from other sacramental acts is actually found in early Eastern Fathers well before the twelfth century. There was no consensus on the number of the sacraments (ranging from two to ten) in the patristic period, and those who spoke of seven actually included some liturgical acts other than what we consider today to be the seven sacraments.[74] Thus, it is not surprising that the East, too, would want to settle this issue, and I regard Staniloae's advocacy for the Western solution as another instance of open sobornicity.

Karl Felmy mentions two more interesting facts about the seven sacraments. First, he attributes this delimitation to the discussions surrounding Cyril Lukaris's *Confessio Fidei* which, with its Calvinist influence, brought this issue to the fore. Felmy also mentions that the delineation between the seven sacraments and the other services of the Church is not reflected in liturgical books. There is no book dedicated solely to the sacraments. The *Euchologion* (*Trebnik*), the book most commonly used in pastoral life, does not include all the sacraments, especially those performed by the bishop, such as Ordination.[75] Moreover, the Eucharist generally stands as a book by itself, the *Liturgikon*. Hence, Louth's observations

---

72  Lambert Leijssen places this development even earlier: "This process of acknowledgment culminated in the theology of Peter Lombard (1095–1160) and, further, in the official doctrine of the church as established in the councils of Florence (1439) and Trent (1547). Scholastic theology had a clear definition of the sacrament as 'a visible sign of an invisible grace.'" Lambert J. Leijssen, *With the Silent Glimmer of God's Spirit: A Postmodern Look at the Sacraments*, trans. Marie Baird (New York/ Mahwah, NJ: Paulist Press, 2006), 19. However, the date that is generally accepted for the official establishment of the number seven for the sacraments is 1547, with the first canon of the Council of Trent, as a reaction against Luther who challenged Catholic sacramental theology.

73  Staniloae, "Number of the Sacraments," 191.

74  Ware, *The Orthodox Church*, 275.

75  Karl C. Felmy, *Dogmatica experientei ecclesiale: Innoirea teologiei ortodoxe contemporane* [*The Dogmatics of Ecclesial Experience: The Renewal of Contemporary Orthodox Theology*] (Sibiu: Deisis, 1999), 234–35.

concerning the demarcation between sacraments and sacramentals are not completely unwarranted.[76]

Louth's final criticism refers to Staniloae's less than Dionysian approach to
sacraments, as a result of their limitation to seven. Since Louth did not provide any further clarifications, one is left suspecting that his criticism refers to
Dionysius' treatment of Baptism and Chrismation together.[77] Louth contended
that the separation between Baptism and Chrismation corresponds to no reality
in Orthodox practice. But a careful reading of Dionysius shows that the anointing with Myron does not refer exclusively to the completion of Baptism, but
also to the consecration of new church buildings, so it is a sacrament that can
stand on its own. Moreover, Louth overlooked the fact that a person who has
been baptized validly elsewhere is received in the Orthodox Church through
Chrismation, unaccompanied by Baptism. This is also the case of persons who,
although initially Orthodox, subsequently embraced other religions but eventually came back to Orthodoxy. Chrismation can thus be administered separate
from Baptism and Staniloae was correct to count them as distinct sacraments.
Having said that, Staniloae did not separate Baptism and Chrismation totally,
especially given their unity together with the Eucharist in the early rites of
initiation.[78]

Several other elements show that Staniloae was able to avoid the dangers
concealed in borrowing from scholastic theology. Besides form, two themes that
concern scholastic sacramental theology are the matter used and the officiant
of the sacrament. I will analyze these points in detail in the last two chapters, in
the discussions of the sacramentality of creation and the communion between

---

76  I translate the Romanian *ierurgii* with "sacramentals" (or as Aquinas used it in
    Latin, *sacramentalia*—Summa I–II, Q. cviii, a. 2 ad 2um; III, Q. lxv, a. 1 ad 8um),
    which refers to Church services other than the seven sacraments. Ware is one of the
    English-speaking Orthodox theologians who uses this term in Ware, *The Orthodox
    Church*, 276.

77  See for example *The Ecclesiastical Hierarchy* II, IV in Pseudo Dionysius the
    Areopagite, *Pseudo-Dionysius: The Complete Works*, trans. Colm Luibheid and
    Paul Rorem, *The Classics of Western Spirituality* (New York: Paulist Press, 1987),
    208, 32. Staniloae was no stranger to Dionysius, whose works he translated and
    commented upon extensively, adopting his theological ethos. Gheorghe Dragulin
    actually praised Staniloae precisely for his Dionysian approach to sacraments.
    Pseudo Dionysius the Areopagite, *Sfantul Dionisie Areopagitul: Opere complete si
    Scoliile Sfantului Maxim Marturisitorul* [*Saint Dionysius the Areopagite: Complete
    Works and the Scholias of Saint Maximus the Confessor*], trans. Dumitru Staniloae
    (Bucuresti: Paideia, 1996), 130. See Dragulin, "Pseudo-Dionysios the Areopagite in
    Dumitru Staniloae's Theology," 80.

78  For a historical and theological analysis, see Staniloae, "Number of the Sacraments,"
    202–03.

the clergy and the people as they concelebrate the Eucharist. Here it is enough to quote Staniloae's remark about the combination of elements that constitute the sacrament: "Neither the material, nor the words spoken, nor the gestures performed, taken by themselves, constitute the [sacrament. Rather, the sacrament] is accomplished in the coming together of two human subjects who through faith are open to the Holy Spirit in the context of the Church."[79] This personalist approach marks a significant point of departure from neoscholasticism.

Staniloae also reacted against the Catholic influence upon Orthodox manual theology[80] that adopted the scholastic understanding of the indelible character conferred by some of the sacraments. (Character is a scholastic term designating an indelible stain imprinted on the soul.) Staniloae preferred to write about the relationship that is eternally established between God and the recipient of the sacrament, emphasizing the encounter between God and humans taking place in the sacraments. Moreover, he rejected the scholastic understanding of character as biblically and patristically unfounded.[81]

Finally, Staniloae stressed repeatedly that the East emphasizes the spiritual experience, the encounter with God, which sacraments produce. The Church in its totality becomes a sacrament because Christ (the sacrament of God who is the origin of all sacramentality) unites himself with the Church and sustains the Church's continuous growth as a sacrament.[82] Such descriptions of the sacraments in no way conceal the dangers mentioned by Louth and reveal clearly Staniloae's departure from scholasticism, while adopting Western concepts in the process of open sobornicity.

The preceding paragraphs are not intended to portray Louth as an unsympathetic critic of Staniloae. He is actually very appreciative of Staniloae's contribution and notes that he wrote the *Dogmatics* under considerable restraints. In 1976 the Romanian Orthodox Church had been granted grudging permission by the Communist Party to publish a handbook of dogmatics for theological

---

79   Staniloae, *Dogmatics 3*, 8. Miller's translation.

80   Silvester Malevansky, Maltzev, V.I. Ekzemplarski, Al.D. Kuzetov, N.G. Popov.

81   Staniloae, "Number of the Sacraments," 206–07.

82   Dumitru Staniloae, "Din aspectul Sacramental al Bisericii [Of the Sacramental Aspect of the Church]," *Studii Teologice* 18, no. 9–10 (1966): 531–32. See also Dumitru Staniloae, "Transparenta Bisericii in viata Sacramentala [The Transparence of the Church in Sacramental Life]," *Ortodoxia* 22, no. 4 (1970): 501–16. Moreover, Staniloae affirmed that "The divine life, the divine energies of the Trinity, present in the humanity of the Son and descended to us through the Holy Spirit, overflow into human beings through the sacraments. Their purpose is to transform gradually the existence of the faithful according to the image of the Human-Christ." Staniloae, "Number of the Sacraments," 195.

institutes. Staniloae had to produce a book that would look to the censors like a dogmatic handbook, after the neoscholastic model of Russian manuals. Thus, the only kind of theology that Staniloae was allowed to write was influenced by scholasticism in form,[83] though, as I have argued, decisively departing from scholasticism in content. While I agree with Louth concerning Staniloae's theology written during Communism, the notion of Christ's threefold office predates Communism, appearing, for example, in *Jesus Christ or the Restoration of Humankind*, first published in 1943. The same is true in the case of the seven sacraments.

I submit that it was Staniloae's choice to affirm Christ's threefold office and the seven sacraments, consistent with his understanding of open sobornicity. Staniloae presented an intrinsically Orthodox theology, which was enriched by Western categories.

### Can the West Influence the East?

Can Orthodox theologians introduce new categories that are not found in the Fathers? Can they adopt categories that originate in other Christian theologies and adapt them to Orthodox theology? Despite criticizing Staniloae for doing precisely that, elsewhere Louth responds in the affirmative.[84] Before him, Florovsky did not call for the simple repetition of old patristic formulae, but for theologizing according to "the mind of the Fathers" in dialogue with others. For his part, Staniloae rejected the claim of manual theologies to supply comprehensive formulae repeated mechanically, because they inhibit the progress of theological thought. In contrast, "today we think that the terms of every dogmatic formulation indicate—as though they were signposts—the entrance where we are admitted to the depths of the abyss, but we do not think that they assign limits to these depths."[85]

Staniloae constructively used Western insights to reach new depths of Orthodox theology. As previously stated, even concepts that are not of Orthodox origin can be incorporated into Orthodox ecclesial tradition, as long as they are consonant with Scripture and Tradition, concerned with a personal encounter with God, and balance cataphatism with apophatism. Rather than being perceived as the foe, the West becomes the friend that helps the East develop

---

83   Louth, "Staniloae's Dogmatics (Reprint 2002)," 60.
84   Andrew Louth, "What is Theology? What is Orthodox Theology?," *St Vladimir's Theological Quarterly* 51, no. 4 (2007): 435–44.
85   Staniloae, *Theology and the Church*, 214–15.

its own legacy. East and West acknowledge the revealing work of God in each other, revelation that extends beyond the patristic era.

One could propose two brief examples where Eastern theology, in its encounter with the West, might progress. First, we should reopen the discussion about the number of sacraments. In the context of a divided Christendom, the distinction between sacraments and sacramentals is necessary; the Orthodox allow different forms of prayer with other denominations, but, as a general rule, prohibit sharing in the sacraments. There are, however, some notable exceptions: (1) any baptized Christian can be received in the Orthodox Church through Chrismation without needing a second baptism; (2) weddings are allowed even if only one of the spouses is Orthodox so as not to deprive them of the sacrament, and the U.S. Joint Committee of Orthodox and Catholic Bishops decided to even allow concelebrated weddings,[86] a decision that, to my knowledge, has not been implemented yet; and (3) the Orthodox Church recognizes some of the ordinations of other denominations. Remarkably, as early as 1956, Staniloae approved of the practice to receive Anglican priests in the Orthodox Church without reordination.[87] One should not draw too many conclusions from exceptions, but, at the same time, these exceptions point to the need to reevaluate either the rule that the Orthodox do not share in sacramental communion with other churches, or the number of the sacraments that are not shared in a divided Christendom. That number might be reduced to one—the Eucharist. In its encounter with the West, Orthodoxy is enticed to address these issues.

Second, in dialogue with the West, the East might rediscover apophatism. I refer here neither to Chrestos Yannaras's "apophaticism of the person" (understood as the infinite possibilities of encountering the human or divine person),[88] nor Staniloae's experiential apophatism (described above). I consider that Orthodox theology excels in these regards. Instead, I refer here to negative theology, where terms do not fully express the divine mystery. This is the

---

86 The "Pastoral Statement on Orthodox-Roman Catholic Marriages" (1990) recommends "that when an Orthodox and Catholic marry there be only one liturgical ceremony in which either one or both priests are present, with the rite being that of the officiating priest ... [and] that such marriages be recorded in the registries of both churches." John Borelli and John H. Erickson, eds., *The Quest for Unity: Orthodox and Catholics in Dialogue* (Crestwood, NY: St Vladimir's Seminary Press, 1996) 239–43.

87 Staniloae, "Number of the Sacraments," 215.

88 Andrew Louth, "[Book Review of] Aristotle Papanikolaou, *Being with God: Trinity, Apophaticism, and Divine-Human Communion*," *St Vladimir's Theological Quarterly* 51, no. 4 (2007): 447.

aspect of apophatism that Lossky has consecrated, precisely in his most vehement criticism of the West for its lack of apophatism. And yet, it seems that contemporary Western, not Eastern theologians are most determined to find new ways to express trinitarian theology and alternatives to the person-nature terminology.[89] Perhaps discouraged by these Western attempts, Eastern theologians did not follow the same path. And yet, the Cappadocians were adamant that God is above our linguistic categories, and Orthodox theologians need to produce a neo-patristic synthesis that would bring to light the divine mystery, revealing more and more the super-abundant, luminous darkness of the Trinity. In recent times, the West seems to lead the path in the direction traced by the Cappadocians.

## *Conclusion*

Staniloae made an important contribution to the departure of Orthodox theology from the manual tradition, while also engaging constructively with the West. His achievement is significant for ecumenism, providing in the concept of open sobornicity a valuable methodology. In adopting the Western categories of the three offices of Christ and the seven sacraments, Staniloae presented a neo-patristic theology characterized by a balance between cataphatism and apophatism, personal encounter with God, rootedness in the biblical, patristic, and liturgical Tradition of the Church, and engagement with contemporary thought.

---

89   To give just one example, in his trinitarian theology, Barth prefers "modes of being" to "persons." Karl Barth, *Church Dogmatics: The Doctrine of the Word of God*, trans. G.W. Bromiley, Second ed., vol. 1 (Edinburgh: T&T Clark, 1999), 299.

Chapter 2

## FILLED WITH THE TRINITY: THE RELATIONSHIP
## BETWEEN THE TRINITY AND THE CHURCH

Twentieth-century theologians tend to take the relationship between Triadology and ecclesiology for granted.[1] Sometimes, because a true relationship between the Trinity and the Church has not been carefully established, the Church is seen as a parallel reality, somehow unrelated to the Trinity; it is not always clear how the two intersect.[2] Moreover, while seeing the Church as a reflection of the Trinity, some theologians accuse what they perceive to be a distorted Triadology of having catastrophic consequences in the life of the Church. Such is the case of Vladimir Lossky, who considered that the Filioque automatically leads to institutionalism, juridicism, clericalism, individualism, and subjecting the college of bishops to the primacy of the Pope. Hence, in order to advance the Orthodox-Catholic dialogue on the ecclesiological consequences of the Filioque, I analyze Staniloae's contention that there is a continuum between the Trinity and the Church such that these two are not simply parallel realities where the Church mirrors our diverse or even conflicting understandings of the Trinity.

Based on Staniloae's theology, while also taking it (sometimes considerably) further, I propose (1) four models for the relationship between the Trinity and the Church: reflection, icon, sacrament, and the ecclesiological consequences of

---

1  Notable exceptions are the discussions of the relationship between God *in se* and God *pro nos*, or between *theologia* and *oikonomia* in Catherine Mowry LaCugna, *God for Us: The Trinity and Christian Life* (San Francisco: Harper Collins, 1992). John Meyendorff and Michael A. Fahey, *Trinitarian Theology East and West: St. Thomas Aquinas—St. Gregory Palamas* (Brookline, MA: Holy Cross Orthodox Press, 1977), 40–41. Gary D. Badcock, *Light of Truth & Fire of Love: A Theology of the Holy Spirit* (Grand Rapids: William B. Eerdmans Publishing Company, 1997), 252–55.

2  John Behr, "The Trinitarian Being of the Church," *St Vladimir's Theological Quarterly* 48, no. 1 (2003): 68.

*theosis.*[3] These four models result in the assertion that (2) the same relations that exist within the Trinity are manifested in the life of the Church, an affirmation that is relevant for the discussion of the (3) ecclesiological consequences of the Filioque. Thus, I hope to show not only that Staniloae's theology is trinitarian (a thesis that I develop further in the second part of the book) but also ecumenical, in light of the previous chapter.


### Four Models for the Relationship between the Trinity and the Church

#### The Church as a Reflection of the Trinity

According to the reflection model, trinitarian theology is automatically and analogically reflected in the life of the Church. I will attempt to show both the strengths and limitations of this approach.

While Staniloae did not explicitly define this reflective model, he repeatedly applied it. For instance, he affirmed in Dionysian language that the three triads of the celestial hierarchy and the threefold hierarchy of the Church (bishop, priest, and deacon) reflect the Trinity.[4] Moreover, he wrote that "the light of the Church represents the unity that the Son of God came to restore between humankind and him, after the *model and power* of the Holy Trinity"[5] [emphasis mine].

These examples represent constructive applications of the reflective model, where ecclesiology mirrors Triadology and the Church is truly a reflection of the Trinity. The reflection model is confined to the theoretical realm, in which our discourse of the Trinity shapes our discourse of the Church, but does not transfer

---

3  Staniloae summarized these elements (Church as icon, sacrament, *theosis*—united with Christ in the Spirit) when he affirmed that, through grace, the faithful are "images, visible signs of the invisible sacramental and pneumatic presence of Christ." Staniloae, *Theology and the Church*, 107.

4  Dumitru Staniloae, "Introducere [Introduction]," in *Sfântul Dionisie Areopagitul* [*Saint Dionysius the Areopagite*] 13.

5  Dumitru Staniloae, *Iisus Hristos, lumina lumii si indumnezeitorul omului* [*Jesus Christ, the Light of the World and the One Who Deifies Humankind*], Colectia Dogmatica (Bucuresti: Editura Anastasia, 1993), 214. Staniloae also added that "the *foundation and model* of creation and salvation would thus be God's mode of being in the Holy Trinity," that is, in communion among the three persons, so the Trinity is the model of the entire creation, and especially of the Church. Staniloae, *Jesus Christ or the Restoration of Humankind*, 76. Along the same lines, Ware affirms: "What Fr. Dumitru terms the 'divine intersubjectivity' of the Trinity constitutes the model and paradigm of all human relationships, and more specifically the model and paradigm of the Church." Ware, "Foreword," xx.

to the concrete, practical reality of the Church. In other words, if our Triadology is distorted, so will become our ecclesiology, but a faulty Triadology does not automatically impoverish the life of the Church. Our limited knowledge of the mystery of the Trinity and the Church cannot inevitably influence God's relationship with the Church. Hence, the weakness of the reflective model is that it allows for the application of what one perceives as erroneous Triadology to the practical life of the Church, which is presented as automatically impoverished. As I argue later in this chapter, this is Lossky's case when describing the ecclesiological consequences of the Filioque in the Catholic Church.

In summary, while the reflection model supports a theoretical relationship between Triadology and ecclesiology, it does not establish a direct relationship between the Trinity and the actual life of the Church. Implied here is that both Triadology and ecclesiology can fail to correspond to the actual life of the Trinity and the Church. When dealing with authentic theologies of the Trinity and the Church, however, the reflection model becomes illustrative of the direct relationship between the Trinity and the Church. In the next three sections, I present other models that establish such a direct relationship, a communication, or a continuum between the Trinity and ecclesial life, and where theology describes this direct relationship, as opposed to conditioning it.

### The Church as Icon of the Trinity

Staniloae wrote about love among human beings: "This unperfected love between us presupposes, however, the perfect love between divine persons with a common being. Our love finds its explanation in the fact that we are created in the image of the Holy Trinity, the origin of our love."[6] Several elements stand out in this passage. First, our unperfected love points to the perfect love among the persons of the Trinity in such a way that our love finds its explanation and origin in the Trinity. Second, for our love to originate in the Trinity, there must be a communication of grace from the Trinity toward us, and so there is a continuum of grace between divinity and humanity.[7] Third, this communication is based on our creation in the image (in Greek, *eikon*) of the triune God.

---

6  Staniloae, *The Experience of God* 1, 245.

7  Stressing that the Trinity communicates its "power" or energy to the community that bears its image, Staniloae affirmed: "if we are to grasp this supreme unity of a number of distinct persons, we have need of power from that very unity itself, and must make use of the imperfect unity among human persons as an obscure image of the Holy Trinity." Ibid., 251.

This terminology of pointing to a higher reality (the type-archetype relationship), the type finding its explanation and origin in the archetype, the type being a presence of grace and an image of the archetype, is language associated with the theology of the icon. I interpret Staniloae's words to mean that the love among human persons is an icon of the intratrinitarian love and that, as the visible type that points to its invisible archetype, the Church is an icon of the Trinity.[8] Thus, the Church as communion of love reveals the Trinity as loving communion.

Of course, much of Staniloae's theology of the icon is based on Theodore the Studite, especially his affirmation that icons receive a relative veneration.[9] Significantly, Staniloae added that those who defended the veneration of icons in the eighth century did not benefit yet from a fully explicit theology of the uncreated energies.

> This would have given them the possibility to explain the connection between Christ and his icon, a connection that they affirm, yet without sufficient explanation. Because they have not explained sufficiently the sense of the term, "relative veneration," "veneration that passes on to the prototype," they did not explain that "the passing on" from icon to prototype does not mean a separation between Christ and icon, or a distance between [Christ] and [the icon]. This is why they affirm both (that is, both the passing on and the interior connection between them), but they do not present a unitary explanation, a synthesis.[10]

This passage is very important because it creates a bridge between the type and the archetype, namely divine grace or uncreated energies, through which there is a continuum between the icon and the one represented on it. Yet Staniloae went beyond traditional theology of the icon by affirming that the Theotokos and the saints are icons of Christ, since Christ shines in them and his image was imprinted on them, as "the pneumaticized dwelling places of Christ, whose humanity is fully pneumaticized through the Holy Spirit."[11]

---

8  One can refer to the Church as the icon of the Trinity only metaphorically, not in the proper sense of the word, because one cannot paint an icon of the Trinity, since the Father and the Spirit did not become incarnate, but only the Son did.

9  Staniloae affirmed that the icon is a presence of the divine that penetrates the material through grace. Consequently, the affirmation of "the seventh Ecumenical Council that the veneration given to the icon 'passes on,' 'ascends' to the person that is represented, or to the archetype, to its living model . . . [also implies] the work of Christ unto the one who looks at the icon." Staniloae, *Spirituality and Communion*, 61–62.

10  Ibid., 65.

11  Ibid., 55.

If I were to take Staniloae's affirmation a step further, given that the Theotokos and the saints make up the Church together with the rest of the faithful,[12] living or departed, I would say that the entire Church is an icon of the Trinity, who is present in the Church through God's uncreated energies. The people gathered in the Church become, in a certain sense, Trinity by grace, especially in regard to their communion of love. This affirmation will be discussed further in the section on divinization.

Staniloae also stated explicitly that the Church is an icon of the Trinity based on Maximus the Confessor's *Mystagogia*[13] (a work that Staniloae translated and commented on extensively) and on a longstanding Eastern tradition.[14] In the first part of the *Mystagogia*, Maximus affirmed that the Church is an "icon and figure of God,"[15] adding that the Church "has towards us the same energy as God does, as icon of the same energy as its archetype."[16] The Church is an icon of God because it does what God does, conforming itself to its archetype, and because the same energies or operations that effect union in God are at work in the Church.[17] As icon, the Church is an instrument through which God

---

12   Staniloae has repeatedly affirmed the iconic presence of Christ in the faithful, especially when gathered for the Eucharist, but also in the context of charity and missionary endeavors. For example, see Staniloae, *Dogmatics 2*, 153–54.

13   Saint Maximus the Confessor, "Mistagoghia: Cosmosul si sufletul, chipuri ale Bisericii [*The Mystagogy: The Cosmos and the Soul, Images of the Church*]," translated by Dumitru Staniloae. *Revista Teologica* 34, no. 4–5; 6–8 (1944). Reprint in Saint Maximus the Confessor, *Sfantul Maxim Marturisitorul: Mystagogia: Cosmosul si Sufletul, Chipuri ale Bisericii [Saint Maximus the Confessor: The Mystagogy: The Cosmos and the Soul, Images of the Church]*, trans. Dumitru Staniloae (Bucuresti: EIBMBOR, 2000).

14   See, for example, Alexander Golitzin, "Hierarchy Versus Anarchy? Dionysius Areopagita, Symeon the New Theologian, Nicetas Stethatos, and Their Common Roots in Ascetical Tradition," *St Vladimir's Theological Quarterly* 38, no. 2 (1994): 168. Alexander Golitzin, *Et Introibo Ad Altare Dei: The Mystagogy of Dionysius Areopagita, with Special Reference to Its Predecessors in the Eastern Christian Tradition* (Thessaloniki: Patriarhikon Idryma Paterikon Meleton, 1994), 403–04.

15   Most Romanian and French translations use the term icon to render the Greek *eikon*. (For example, Maximus refers to the Church as "*túpon kaì eikóna Theoũ*" PG 91, 663D.) The most popular English translations by Dom Julian Stead, O.S.B. and George C. Berthold, however, use the term, image. I will use the term icon.

16   Translated in Alain Riou, *Le Monde et l'Église selon Maxime le Confesseur, Théologie Historique 22* (Paris: Beauchesne, 1973), 140–41. I prefer to use Alain Riou's translation here, since it expresses more clearly the relationship between the Trinity (as archetype) and the Church (as icon) than the existing English translations.

17   Saint Maximus the Confessor, *The Church, the Liturgy and the Soul of Man: The Mystagogia of St. Maximus the Confessor*, trans. Dom Julian Stead O.S.B. (Still River, Massachusetts: St. Bede's Publications, 1982), 68. Chapter 1.

works in the world. Moreover, the Church does what God does in figure, in the sense that the services performed in the Church, even though they appear to have only a limited scope, have in fact a larger effect, being addressed to the entire universe, bringing it to unity. As Staniloae commented in his translation of the *Mystagogia*, God starts from a small group, the Church, in order to bring the whole creation to himself:

> The Church is cosmos partly united with God, on the one hand, and cosmos drawing closer to the full union with Christ and under his leadership, on the other.... Christ begins from a small circle of humans with the intention to extend his perfecting work to the entire creation. [At this point Staniloae quoted the *Mystagogia* and added that implied here is] the will of the faithful to participate in the Liturgy of the Church and, as they go outside the Church, to bring the spirit of union with God and of union of creation in God.[18]

In a general sense, the entire world is united with God. In a special sense, the Church is in full union with Christ, so Staniloae affirmed the cooperation between Christ and the faithful to fully incorporate creation into the Church. Christ works through the Church to gather the world in himself. This contention is very important because it qualifies the understanding of the Church as icon of the Trinity in synergic terms.

In conclusion, Staniloae affirmed an iconic relationship between the Trinity and the Church. On the one hand, the Church reveals the Trinity, which would otherwise be beyond our reach; one contemplates God by observing the work of the Trinity in the Church. On the other hand, the Trinity informs the Church, since the Church does what the Trinity does, as the type that is filled with, and communicates the grace of, the archetype. Better than the reflection model, the understanding of the Church as icon establishes the direct presence of the Trinity in the Church.

## The Church as Sacrament of the Trinity

As I show in more detail in Chapter 7, Staniloae referred to the Church as the third sacrament. The first sacrament is the world, created to make God transparent in it, or to make God manifest so that the world has a sacramental-liturgical

---

18   Dumitru Staniloae, "Locasul Bisericesc Propriu-Zis, Cerul pe Pamant sau Centrul Liturgic al Creatiei [The Church Temple: Heaven on Earth or the Liturgical Centre of Creation]," in *Sfantul Maxim Marturisitorul: Mystagogia: Cosmosul si Sufletul, Chipuri ale Bisericii* (Bucuresti: EIBMBOR, 2000), 74–75.

and a revelatory function.[19] The second sacrament is Christ, who is fully God's presence; the Trinity is revealed and acts through Christ.[20] As a consequence of the second sacrament or as an "extension of the mystery of Christ" arises the third sacrament, namely the Church,

> in which God the Word re-establishes and raises to a more accentuated degree his unity with the world, [a unity] established through the act of creation and weakened by the sin of humankind.... Christ is the real Head, or the fundamental hypostasis of the Church, which he constitutes and sustains, continuously imprinting his life in [the Church], or in its members, kept in unity among them and with him.[21]

Christ acts as a sacrament of the Trinity and, by extension, the Body of Christ (the Church) also becomes the sacrament of the Trinity, through which the tri-une God acts and reveals himself. Similar to the iconic considerations of the previous section, the designation of the Church as sacrament establishes a con-tinuum between the Trinity and the Church and affirms the direct relation-ship between the two, going beyond the parallelism of the reflection model. Staniloae's remarks bring a significant contribution to Orthodox theology in which references to the Church as sacrament are rather scarce.[22]

## The Ecclesiological Consequences of Theosis

To a Western audience, Staniloae's understanding of *theosis*, divinization, or deification seems foreign, but Staniloae is in continuation with a longstanding Eastern Tradition that affirms the possibility of utmost union by grace (not by

---

19  Staniloae, *Jesus Christ, the Light of the World*, 31. See also Dumitru Staniloae, *The Experience of God: The World—Creation and Deification*, trans. Ioan Ionita and Robert Barringer, vol. 2 (Brookline, MA: Holy Cross Orthodox Press, 2000), 45. Dumitru Staniloae, "Creatia ca dar si Tainele Bisericii [Creation as Gift and the Sacraments of the Church]," *Ortodoxia* 28, no. 1 (1976): 28.

20  Staniloae, *Dogmatics 3*, 13. Staniloae, *The Experience of God 1*, 67.

21  Staniloae, *Dogmatics 3*, 10–11.

22  Though only in passing, Nikos Nissiotis wrote that the Church "has to be accepted as a great sacrament, the *mysterion par excellence*." Nikos Nissiotis, "Pneumatological Christology as a Presupposition of Ecclesiology," *Oecumenica* (1967): 251. Similarly, *Lumen Gentium* 1 defines the Church as "a sacrament—a sign and instrument, that is, of communion with God and of unity among all men." Council II Vatican, *Vatican Council II: The Conciliar and Postconciliar Documents*, ed. Austin Flannery O.P., New Revised ed., vol. 1 (Northport, NY: Costello Publishing Company, 1998), 350.

nature, as in the person of Jesus Christ) between God and human persons. Based on the distinction-in-unity between God's essence and his uncreated energies, he defined *theosis* as "God's perfect and full penetration of the human being."[23] Moreover, "just as the one who is loved, if they respond to love, becomes as the one whom they love, more so the human person, enlightened by Christ, is made as Christ, although through grace, not nature. Being full of Christ, the human person lives his divinity."[24]

According to Staniloae, divinization is not only an eschatological gift, but it is also something to be achieved during this life, and then continually fulfilled in eternity. Actually, Staniloae considered that the Church is already holy as a whole, despite the presence of sinful individuals in it,[25] so divinization is something already attained by the community of the Church, even though some (or most) members of the Church have not reached it yet.

Because the Church is the locus of deification, *theosis* has a profound communitarian-ecclesiological dimension.[26] In his commentary on Symeon the New Theologian, Staniloae drew from the Pauline language of 1 Cor. 12, affirming that Christ is "present in the members of his Body; he makes himself present . . . in each believer and the believers are and feel like members of Christ. [As Symeon put it in his 15th hymn,]

> And I, the unworthy, am the hand and the foot of Christ.
> I move the hand and Christ fully is my hand.
> I move the foot and, behold, it shines like Him. [. . .]
> And we will all become together gods [small g] through God [capital G]."[27]

Both Symeon and Staniloae used the image of the faithful as members of the Body of Christ because *theosis* takes place only in the community

---

23  Dumitru Staniloae, *Orthodox Spirituality: A Practical Guide for the Faithful and a Definitive Manual for the Scholar*, trans. Archimandrite Jerome (Newville) and Otilia Kloos (South Canaan, PA: St. Tikhon's Seminary Press, 2002), 362.

24  Staniloae, *Jesus Christ or the Restoration of Humankind*, 227.

25  Staniloae, *Dogmatics 2*, 177–86.

26  Personal *theosis* results in utmost communion with God, other people, and the rest of creation. Staniloae, *Jesus Christ, the Light of the World*, 186–87. This is why Bartos affirms that "Staniloae's ecclesiology reveals, above all else, his understanding of deification as being communal in character.... We are saved in communion, in the Church, and in creation." Emil Bartos, "The Dynamics of Deification in the Theology of Dumitru Staniloae," in *Dumitru Staniloae: Tradition and Modernity in Theology*, ed. Lucian Turcescu (Iasi, Romania; Palm Beach, FL: Center for Romanian Studies, 2002), 234–35.

27  Quoted in Staniloae, *Jesus Christ or the Restoration of Humankind*, 227–28.

of the Church or, as Staniloae stated it, "spiritual ascent begins and ends in the Church."[28] One's divinization is not individualistic, but is based on the entire Church community and for the benefit of the Church. Thus, *theosis* extends from the person to the entire Church community and vice versa, from the Church united by grace with the Trinity to the person. These affirmations, even though they bear slightly eschatological overtones, are relevant in a discussion of the relationship between the Trinity and the Church in this present age. Together with the previous considerations of the Church as reflection, icon, and sacrament of the Trinity, these remarks establish not only an analogous relationship, but also a continuum of grace originating in the Trinity and manifested in the Church. Consequently, Staniloae arrived at the conclusion that the same relations that exist within the Trinity are at work in the Church.

### Same Relations within the Trinity and the Church

For Staniloae, "the trinitarian relations are seen as the basis for the relation of the Trinity to creation,"[29] with direct application in the life of the Church. Triadology has ecclesiological consequences, since the Father, Son, and Holy Spirit have the same kind of relationships within the Trinity and in the Church: "As a work of raising up believers to intimate communion with God, salvation and deification are nothing other than the extension to conscious creatures of the relations that [exist] between the divine persons."[30]

As I show in the next chapter, the extension of intratrinitarian relations into the world was made possible by the Christ event. Given the theandric, or better, theanthropic (i.e., divine-human) character of Christ, the same person whom the Father loves eternally as Son encompasses the entire humankind after the incarnation. Hence, the eternal Father-Son relationship extends to humanity and, more specifically, to the Church, the community of God's adoptive children. In other words, the Son places all his human brothers and sisters in a filial relationship with the Father. In turn, the Father loves the Church as the Body of Christ because of his paternal relationship with the Son, and this Father-Son

---

28  Staniloae, *Orthodox Spirituality*, 353.
29  Dumitru Staniloae, "The Procession of the Holy Spirit from the Father and His Relation to the Son, as the Basis of our Deification and Adoption," in *Spirit of God, Spirit of Christ: Ecumenical Reflections on the Filioque Controversy. Faith and Order Paper No. 103*, ed. Lukas Vischer, *Faith and Order Paper No. 103* (Geneva: World Council of Churches, 1981), 178.
30  Staniloae, *The Experience of God 1*, 248.

relationship represents the basis for human relationships of paternity and sonship.[31]

Similarly, the Spirit dwells in the Church, which is the Body of Christ, because the Spirit rests from eternity in the Son.[32] The Holy Spirit also represents the possibility of extending the love between the Father and the Son to human beings because the Spirit is the third person who fulfills the loving relationship between the Father and the Son. In our relationship with God, creation, and among ourselves, "he is the Spirit of communion, because the Spirit is communion in the Holy Trinity, too."[33] Thus, the Holy Spirit (and the uncreated energies with which the work of the Spirit is generally associated) represents the outpouring of trinitarian love into the Church.[34] Of course, human beings are not in communion with the trinitarian persons to the same degree that the Father, Son, and Holy Spirit are in communion among themselves. The faithful are penetrated by the activity of the Spirit, so they can have only a relation "through grace," where the uncreated energies represent the bridge between the Trinity and the Church, allowing intratrinitarian relationships to be manifested in both the Trinity and the Church.[35] More on the trinitarian being of the Church will be said in the second part of the book.

The Trinity renders the Church not only into a union sharing in the love between the Father, Son, and Holy Spirit, but also into a communion of unity in diversity in which its members remain distinct in union with other persons. Because Christ is both human and divine, he "imprints his unity according to his divinity with the Father and the Holy Spirit, in the unity according to his humanity with the other people gathered in him."[36] Human unity thus becomes a manifestation of intratrinitarian unity, going beyond a simply analogous relationship between the two, where the Trinity is simply a model of unity in diversity for humankind. Rather, because the incarnation brought intratrinitarian relationships down to the human level, the incorporation of the members of the

---

31  Ibid., 246.
32  Staniloae, "The Procession of the Holy Spirit," 179.
33  Staniloae, *Orthodox Spirituality*, 318–21.
34  Staniloae, *The Experience of God 1*, 268. Staniloae's affirmation that "Only through the Holy Spirit, therefore, does the divine love radiate to the outside" is very similar to the first antiphon in the fourth tone in the Orthodox service of Matins: "By the Holy Spirit shall every soul be given life and be elevated through purification, and be made radiant through the mystery of the Triune Unity." *Orthros: The Resurrectional Hymns for Sunday*, trans. Spencer T. Kezios (Northridge, CA: Narthex Press, 1996), 75.
35  Staniloae, *Theology and the Church*, 28.
36  Staniloae, *Spirituality and Communion*, 376–77.

Church into Christ safeguards the personal character of our union with each other and with God. According to Staniloae,

> The eternal communion after which we yearn has its origin and fulfillment in the one eternal co-essentiality of the divine persons of the Trinity. And if unity without confusion between the divine persons is assured by their sharing in a common nature, then certainly the communion between God and those who believe is assured by their participation, through grace, in the divine nature or in the energies irradiating from the common nature of the three divine persons, which is to say, from their loving community. But human nature, subsisting in a multiplicity of persons, must have some resemblance to the divine nature as this subsists in the three persons, if, in a divine person [i.e., the Son], it is to be able to be united with the divine nature.[37]

Consequently, the same relationships of unity and diversity within the imma-nent Trinity are manifested in the economy of salvation and represent the basis for unity in the world and in the Church defined as communion, or *koinonia*.

Based on the affirmation that the same intratrinitarian relationships are man-ifested within the Trinity and the Church, Staniloae submitted his famous thesis that, because humanity is raised up to an "eternal communion with the Holy Trinity," the Trinity represents "the structure of perfect communion."[38] Indeed, as Origen wrote, the Church is "filled with the Trinity,"[39] an affirmation that will be explored further in the second part of the book.

Up to this point, I have attempted to analyze the "mechanisms" of the con-tinuum between the Trinity and the Church. The same relationships that exist within the Trinity are manifested in the Church not only theoretically as a reflection, but also directly through grace. God is manifested directly through

---

37  Staniloae, *The Experience of God 1*, 70–71. Similar to Staniloae, Forte comments on *Lumen Gentium* 3: "The Church is the icon of the Holy Trinity, i.e., her commu-nion is structured in the image and likeness of the Trinitarian communion.... So by analogy the Church can be likened to the divine communion: one in the diversity of Persons, in a fruitful exchange of relations." Bruno Forte, *The Church: Icon of the Trinity. A Brief Study*, trans. Robert Paolucci (Boston: St. Paul Books & Media, 1991), 28.

38  Staniloae, *The Experience of God 1*, 67. Staniloae originally published the article, "Sfanta Treime, structura supremei iubiri [The Holy Trinity: Structure of Supreme Love]," *Studii Teologice* 22 (1970). He gave the same title to the chapter on the Trinity in his *Dogmatics*. Staniloae, *Theology and the Church*, 73–108.

39  Origen. *Selecta in Psalmos* 23, 1 PG 12,1265B. Quoted it in Staniloae, *Theology and the Church*, 39.

uncreated energies in the Church, rendering the Church into an icon, sacrament, and union with God in *theosis*. How are these models relevant to a discussion of the ecclesiological consequences of the Filioque?[40]

### The Filioque and Its Ecclesiological Implications?

Throughout most of its history, the Filioque caused theological and pastoral tensions. These conflicts, however, did not reverberate into ecclesiology until very recently. The Filioque is at the heart of neither Orthodox nor Catholic theology,[41] so it need not be the focus of our dialogue. Staniloae did not ignore this issue, but neither did he write his Pneumatology around it. He was more concerned with, and effective in, proclaiming the Orthodox teaching on the procession of the Holy Spirit, than refuting the Catholic teaching on the procession of the Spirit from the Father and the Son. I try to do the same: after few remarks on the Filioque (issues and points of convergence), I will discuss its relationship to ecclesiology.

### The Filioque

Briefly stated, the West added the phrase, "and the Son" (*Filioque* in Latin) to the original Greek version of the Nicaeo-Constantinopolitan Creed describing the procession of the Spirit from the Father. The West intended it as a clarification, but the East perceived it as an error or sometimes even as a heresy. Some have

---

40  Another possible application of the theoretical principles outlined in the first part of this chapter is that of depersonalization, understood as the diminishing of human freedom, equality, and dignity as a manifestation of the loss of the importance of the person. Depersonalization occurs first when the person is subjected to suffering, such as communist oppression, poverty in an aggressive market economy, or war. Second and paradoxically, depersonalization is also the result of individualism, where the individual rises above the community to the detriment of the members of the community, and without respecting their dignity, equality, and freedom. See Radu Bordeianu, "Filled with the Trinity: The Contribution of Dumitru Staniloae's Ecclesiology to Ecumenism and Society," *Journal of Eastern Christian Studies* 62, no. 1–2 (2010): 79-84.

41  In this sense, Congar affirmed that a careful reading of both Eastern and Western traditions would reveal the fact that they profess the same trinitarian faith. Yves Congar, *I Believe in the Holy Spirit: The River of the Water of Life Flows in the East and in the West*, trans. David Smith, vol. 3 (New York: Seabury Press, 1983), 199–203.

even seen it as the main cause of the disunity between East and West, resulting in each side caricaturizing the other position.[42]

The dialogue has also been obstructed by the fact that East and West did not speak the same language. Greek theology almost always restricts the theological use of *ekporeuesthai* ("proceed," "issue forth") and its related noun, *ekporeusis* ("procession") to the coming-forth of the Spirit from the Father, as ultimate origin. In contrast, other Greek words, such as *proienai*, "go forward," refer to the sending of the Spirit in the world from the Father and the Son, the second person being an intermediary origin, since the Spirit proceeds from the Father and rests in the Son. The Latin word *procedere* suggests simply "movement forwards," and is used to translate both of these Greek theological terms. Maximus the Confessor, in his *Letter to Marinus* (PG 91.133-136), was the first to explain this terminological confusion surrounding the Filioque.[43] In the same letter, Maximus proposed an Orthodox understanding of the Filioque. The Spirit proceeds from the Father as from his source, and he is bestowed by the Father and the Son, because he is interior to both of them, by virtue of their perichoresis. He proceeds also from the Son not as from the original source, but because he rests in the Son, being received by the Son from the Father. This is why he is also called the Spirit of the Son.

These considerations are not meant to trivialize the controversy. At a deeper level, it is based on theological differences:

> By the Middle Ages, as a result of the influence of Anselm and Thomas Aquinas, Western theology almost[44] universally conceives of the identity

---

42   The North American Orthodox-Catholic Theological Consultation states, "It is not true, for instance, that mainstream Orthodox theology conceives of the procession of the Spirit, within God's eternal being, as simply unaffected by the relationship of the Son to the Father, or thinks of the Spirit as not "belonging" properly to the Son when the Spirit is sent forth in history. It is also not true that mainstream Latin theology has traditionally begun its trinitarian reflections from an abstract, unscriptural consideration of the divine substance, or affirms two causes of the Spirit's hypostatic existence, or means to assign the Holy Spirit a role subordinate to the Son, either within the Mystery of God or in God's saving action in history." North American Orthodox-Catholic Theological Consultation, "The Filioque: A Church-Dividing Issue? An Agreed Statement of the North American Orthodox-Catholic Theological Consultation. Saint Paul's College, Washington, DC. October 25, 2003," *www.usccb.org/seia/dialogues.htm* (2003): III.

43   Ibid., III.1.

44   Congar might be able to explain the "almost" used by the Consultation. He pointed to the diverse understandings within scholastic theology of person and relationship. Duns Scotus was very open to the Greek way of expressing the trinitarian mystery. Following Bonaventure and several other theologians, he affirmed, "the Person in

of each divine person as defined by its "relations of opposition"—in other words, its mutually defining relations of origin—to the other two, and concludes that the Holy Spirit would not be hypostatically distinguishable from the Son if the Spirit "proceeded" from the Father alone…. Eastern theology, drawing on the language of John 15:26 and the Creed of 381, continues to understand the language of "procession" (*ekporeusis*) as denoting a unique, exclusive, and distinctive causal relationship between the Spirit and the Father, and generally confines the Son's role to the "manifestation" and "mission" of the Spirit in the divine activities of creation and redemption.[45]

Staniloae's main criticism of the Filioque was that, when Catholic theology affirms that the Father and the Son cause the Holy Spirit to proceed as from a single principle, the distinction between the Father and the Son is blurred. For him, the Orthodox affirmation of trinitarian intersubjectivity presupposes that

just as the divine Father experiences the subjectivity of the Son in his own subjectivity as parent, without mingling the two but rather intensifying them, so too does the Son experience the paternal subjectivity of the Father in his own filial subjectivity, that is, as Son. *In the Holy Trinity all is common and perichoretic, and yet in this common movement of the subjectivity of the one in the other there is no confusion of the distinct modes in which this subjectivity is experienced together.* [emphases mine][46]

A further implication of these considerations is that, for Staniloae, the Filioque affects the unity of the Trinity in the sense that the Holy Spirit "is seen somewhat outside of the unity between the Father and the Son."[47] Staniloae addressed many other facets of this issue from a historical, terminological, and ecclesiological perspective. His analysis is very well informed. As I show momentarily, however, some of the logical implications that Staniloae deduced from Catholic statements go too far.

---

God is constituted, not by relationships, but by something absolute, namely the (first) substance or supposit that is distinguished by a certain property. That property is identical with the relationship in question." Anselm and Aquinas did not accept this judgment, but Grosseteste and others did. Congar, *I Believe in the Holy Spirit 3*, 180.

45  Consultation, "The Filioque: A Church-Dividing Issue?" III.2.a.
46  Staniloae, *The Experience of God 1*, 263.
47  Staniloae, *Spirituality and Communion*, 393.

The positive result of the discussion surrounding the Filioque is that Staniloae emphasized some important points of Orthodox theology. I discuss them at length in the fifth chapter, but they could be summarized as follows:

- The Holy Spirit represents the love of the Father for the Son.
- The Son responds to the love of the Father through/in the Spirit.
- The Spirit returning to the Father from the Son bears the personal character of the Son, or the Son imprints some aspects of his personality to the Spirit. The Spirit is enriched in the sense of now being also the Spirit of the Son.
- Consequently, the Spirit is not only the Spirit of the Father, but is also eternally and unceasingly the Spirit of the Son.
- Since the Spirit of the Father and the Spirit of the Son are one and the same, there is no fourth hypostasis within the Trinity.
- The begetting of the Son cannot be thought of without the Spirit, since the Spirit is the beginning and the end of the Son's birth.
- Conversely, the procession of the Spirit cannot be thought of without the Son, since the Son is the beginning and the end of the Spirit's procession.
- Begetting and procession are inseparable and simultaneous.[48]

Most, if not all of these points that Staniloae made in regard to the procession of the Spirit are elements that both Catholic and Orthodox traditions have in common. Bilateral national and international Orthodox-Catholic documents[49] present many other instances in which the two traditions might find a common

---

48  All these points represent a summary of Staniloae, *Orthodox Spirituality*, 53–54 and Staniloae, *Theology and the Church*, 102ff. Many nuances need to accompany these statements. For example, in regard to the role of the Father as origin, it is important to add Staniloae's quite lengthy explanation as to why the Spirit does not proceed from the Father alone in Dumitru Staniloae, "Le Saint Esprit dans la théologie Byzantine et dans la réflexion Orthodoxe contemporaine," in *Credo in Spiritum Sanctum—Pisteuo eis to Pneuma to Agion: Atti del Congresso Teologico Internazionale di Pneumatologia in occasione del 1600o anniversario del I Concilio di Constantinopoli e del 1550o anniversario del Concilio di Efeso, Roma 22-26 marzo 1982* (Vatican: Libreria Editrice Vaticana, 1983), 661–69. Moreover, under the influence of Sergey Bulgakov who affirmed that there is no causality in God, Paul Evdokimov considered that we should go past the anthropomorphic language of causality. However, Evdokimov was not always consistent and wrote about the Father as cause. He stated that the Spirit proceeds eternally from the Father by *procession of origin* and from the Son by *procession of manifestation*. Paul Evdokimov, *L'Orthodoxie* (Paris: Desclée de Brouwer, 1979), 139.

49  See for example the first statement of the Joint International Commission for Theological Dialogue between the Orthodox and Catholic Church (1982), entitled "The Mystery of the Church and of the Eucharist in Light of the Mystery of the Trinity."

ground in regard to the procession of the Spirit, but this is not the place to analyze them all. One thing is certain: the attitude toward the Filioque is changing
on both sides. Among the Orthodox, as I show shortly, an increasing number
of theologians consider the Filioque not to be a Church-dividing issue. Among
Catholics, several recent events point to Rome's willingness to recognize the normative character of the original creed of Constantinople. For example, in the presence of Ecumenical Patriarchs Dimitrios I (December 1987) and Bartholomew I
(June 1995), and Romanian Patriarch Teoctist (October 2002), Pope John Paul
II proclaimed the Creed in Greek, without the Filioque. Moreover, the document
*Dominus Iesus: On the Unicity and Salvific Universality of Jesus Christ and
the Church,* issued by the Congregation for the Doctrine of the Faith in August
2000, mentions the text of the Creed of 381 without the Filioque. Earlier on,
in September 1995, the Vatican published the document "The Greek and Latin
Traditions Regarding the Procession of the Holy Spirit," which affirms that

> The Catholic Church acknowledges the conciliar, ecumenical, normative
> and irrevocable value, as the expression of one common faith of the Church
> and of all Christians, of the Symbol professed in Greek at Constantinople
> in 381 by the Second Ecumenical Council. No confession of faith peculiar
> to a particular liturgical tradition can contradict this expression of faith
> taught and professed by the undivided Church. [The Filioque, obviously,
> does not contradict the Creed of 381.][50]

Based on these terminological, theological, and historical elements, the North
American Orthodox-Catholic Theological Consultation issued the following
statement, of historic importance: "our traditions' different ways of understanding the procession of the Holy Spirit need no longer divide us."[51] This means
that, if the Filioque were the only cause of Orthodox-Catholic disunity, these
two churches should now be reunited.

On the one hand, a lot of progress has been made in regard to the Filioque, and
some even propose that it should no longer divide Catholics and the Orthodox.

---

50   Quoted in Consultation, "The Filioque: A Church-Dividing Issue?" II.
51   Ibid.: IV. Long before the Consultation, Congar mentioned that the Latin position
     did not hinder the Church's being one for almost seven centuries and made refer-
     ences to several Orthodox theologians, such as Damaskinos of Tranoupolis, who
     affirmed that the schism between the West and the East had other causes than the
     Filioque. Congar also quoted Basile Krivocheine who considered that "this question
     is concerned more with theology than directly with faith itself.... Disagreements of
     this kind, as St. Basil the Great wrote, can be easily overcome later, after reunion, in
     the course of life together over a long period and study together without polemics."
     Congar, *I Believe in the Holy Spirit* 3, 190, 202–03.

On the other hand, the disagreement shifted toward ecclesiology. There is a rather recent history of debates on whether the Filioque has any major ecclesiological consequences or not. After outlining the major positions in this debate, I will point to a third option not as a clear-cut solution, but as a helpful focus for future discussions in order to ensure ecumenical progress.

## Ecclesiological Implications of the Filioque: Status Quaestionis

Relevant to the present debate, Ware identifies two positions within Orthodoxy. On the one hand, the strict position, or the "hawks," represented especially by Lossky, consider that the Filioque implies the subordination of the Spirit to the Son if not in theory, then surely in practice. As a result, insufficient attention is given to the Spirit in the Church, in the world, and in spirituality. Since the Filioque also overemphasizes the oneness of God to the detriment of God's three-ness and gives priority to essence over persons,[52] Lossky thought, the Catholic Church faces numerous ecclesiological problems, including papal totalitarianism, clericalism, institutionalism, and the litany of "isms" could continue.[53] Also

---

52  See, for example, Vladimir Lossky, "Concerning the Third Mark of the Church: Catholicity," *One Church [Edinaia Tserkov]* 19 (1965). Lossky wrote in a markedly polemical context, rejecting the Catholic teaching on the Filioque, which implies an eternal relationship between the Spirit and the Son. In response, he went as far as to affirm repeatedly the Spirit's eternal independence of origin from the Son, as I show in Chapter 5. Moreover, during Lossky's time, most theologians accepted as normative Théodore de Régnon's theory that the Eastern doctrine of the Trinity emphasizes person over nature and Trinity over unity, whereas Western theology gives priority to nature over person and unity over Trinity. (Théodore de Régnon, *Études de théologie positive sur la Sainte Trinité*, 3 vols. (Paris: Retaux, 1892–1898).) Later on, John Meyendorff encouraged Orthodox theologians to challenge the traditional model according to which the East is more concerned with the trinitarian persons, while the West with the divine essence. (John Meyendorff in Meyendorff and Fahey, *Trinitarian Theology East and West*, 36.) Moreover, Congar showed that de Régnon's theory is not completely true, although he did not dismiss it totally. He stated that the trinitarian theologies that start from the persons were continuously present in the West, even if as minor traditions. Yves Congar, *I Believe in the Holy Spirit* 1, 85–92.

53  According to Congar and de Halleux, Lossky considered that the Filioque has several ecclesiological consequences, among which one can mention: "the people of God are subjected to the body of Christ, the charism is made subordinate to the institution, inner freedom to imposed authority, prophetism to juridicism, mysticism to scholasticism, the laity to the clergy, the universal priesthood to the ministerial hierarchy, and finally the college of bishops to the primacy of the Pope." Congar, *I Believe in the Holy Spirit* 3, 208.

because of the Filioque, Zizioulas (a "hawk" that Ware does not mention) further adds that in Catholic theology "God is implicitly identified with being as neutral substance rather than with being as communion." As Zizioulas sees it, the stage was set in the West for the Church as communion to dissolve into the Church as juridical institution, for the Church, too, came to be conceived of first as a neutral substance and only subsequently as a place for cultivating relationships.[54]

On the other hand, Ware refers to the moderate position, or the "doves," who point out that only in the twentieth century have theologians noticed a connection between the Filioque and papacy, so they question the existence of a real connection between the two.[55] Without naming them, Ware probably refers here to Sergey Bulgakov and Paul Evdokimov.[56] Somewhere in the middle, Nikos Nissiotis[57] is closer to Lossky, while Ware[58] is closer to Bulgakov.

Staniloae is much harder to categorize as a "dove" or as a "hawk" because he was not always consistent. On the one hand, Staniloae wrote that, because of the Filioque,

> in the West ecclesiology has become an impersonal juridical system, while theology, and in the same way the whole of Western culture with it, has become strictly rational. The character of a juridical society has been imprinted upon the Church, a society conducted rationally and in absolutist fashion by the Pope while neglecting both the active permanent presence of the Spirit within her and within all the faithful, and also the presence of Christ bound indissolubly to the presence of the Spirit. The Pope, the bishops, the priests occupy the place of the absent Christ

---

54  See Dennis M. Doyle, *Communion Ecclesiology: Vision and Versions* (Maryknoll, NY: Orbis Books, 2000), 160.

55  Meyendorff made the same observation. John Meyendorff and Nicholas Lossky, *The Orthodox Church: Its Past and Its Role in the World Today* (Crestwood, NY: St Vladimir's Seminary Press, 1996), 190.

56  See Congar, *I Believe in the Holy Spirit 3*, 210–11.

57  Nissiotis affirmed that, although not a heresy, the Filioque is a practical deviation with ecclesiological consequences. See Bernard Dupuy, "Nikos Nissiotis (1925– 1986), théologien de l'Esprit-Saint et de la gloire," *Istina* 32, no. 3 (1987): 228.

58  Ware writes that "the divergence between East and West over the Filioque, while by no means unimportant, is not as fundamental as Lossky and his disciples maintain. The Roman Catholic understanding of the person and work of the Holy Spirit . . . is not basically different from that of the Christian East; and so we may hope that in the present-day dialogue between Orthodox and Roman Catholics an understanding will eventually be reached on this thorny question." Ware, *The Orthodox Church*, 214–18.

who is not present through the Spirit in the hearts of the faithful (the vicarial theory).[59]

In my judgment, Staniloae was not writing at his best here, to say the least. He extended what he considered the logical consequences of the Filioque to the point of caricature, such that Catholic theologians would certainly not recognize them as their own positions. Then Staniloae applied these reductive conclusions to the life of the Church, taking what I have termed the reflective model to an extreme.

On the other hand, especially when Staniloae wrote in an ecumenical context, or after he had become exposed to what recent Catholic theologians actually affirmed, he adopted a more reconciliatory position.[60] He admitted that he had sometimes criticized not what these Catholic theologians stated, but the theoretical consequences of their theology, which, in practice, are not manifested in the life of the Catholic Church. I consider this to be Staniloae's final position: the Filioque might lead to unfortunate logical consequences if taken to an extreme but, in reality, the Catholic Church did not take the Filioque to that extreme, and these logical consequences do not apply to its practice. This is certainly a more balanced position than the one presented above.

Another major protagonist in the debate over the ecclesiological consequences of the Filioque was Yves Congar. He pointed out that, after their initial schism, Photios accepted to be in communion with the West without solving this issue; it is a theological opinion as opposed to dogma; and it is no longer obligatory for Byzantine Catholic Churches.[61] He also answered Lossky's (and indirectly Staniloae's) accusations that the Filioque leads to subjecting the charism to the institution, prophetism to juridicism, laity to clergy, the college of bishops to the primacy of the Pope. Based on the observation that the Filioque did not have the same consequences in several of the Reformed Churches that include it in their Confessions of Faith, Congar responded that "the whole body of consequences to which Lossky drew attention is too much his own reconstruction

---

59  Staniloae, *Theology and the Church*, 107. Staniloae actually referred here to P. Sherrard's *The Greek East and the Latin West*.

60  Staniloae affirmed that Orthodox and Catholic churches share in the same trinitarian and christological faith, even though there are differences between them, such as the Filioque. However, only the dogmas of papal primacy and infallibility are obstacles for communion, but not the Filioque. (Staniloae, *Spirituality and Communion*, 401–02.) Moreover, as mentioned in the previous chapter, Roberson mentions Staniloae's belief that Orthodoxy and Catholicism "are not divided by essential differences." Roberson, "Dumitru Staniloae on Christian Unity," 113.

61  Congar, *I Believe in the Holy Spirit 3*, 195–206.

to be really precise." Moreover, he referred to Orthodox theologians such as Evdokimov and Bulgakov who would disagree with Lossky and actually added that, because the Filioque has no practical consequences (quite significant for the study at hand), it is not a real dogmatic difference between the East and the West. This is why Congar concluded with the memorable words, "in the final analysis, then, the quarrel about the ecclesiological consequences of the Filioque is of doubtful value."[62]

Congar's words resonated with me for a long time. They still do. For a while, I believed that the Filioque has no consequences in the life of the Church and that this was also the intention of another memorable recommendation of the North American Orthodox-Catholic Theological Consultation: "that those engaged in dialogue on this issue distinguish, as far as possible, the theological issues of the origin of the Holy Spirit from the ecclesiological issues of primacy and doctrinal authority in the Church, even as we pursue both questions seriously together."[63]

I now think that Congar's statement is somewhat exaggerated. I also think that the above recommendation of the Consultation does not propose to separate the theologies of the Trinity and of the Church completely as if there were no connection between the two, but only the Filioque and the papacy, so that the polemic about the Filioque would not extend to the area of ecclesiology as well, and thus make it almost impossible to resolve. I agree that we should solve the problem of the Filioque first as a trinitarian question, and not as an ecclesiological issue. Yet, the Church is filled with the Trinity, so a genuine Triadology must have ecclesiological consequences.

## The Four Models: Theological and Practical Perspectives

There is a creative tension between Congar's position and the Trinity-Church continuum, which I will not attempt to resolve. This tension also prevents a clear-cut position on whether the Filioque has ecclesiological consequences or not. The Filioque is simultaneously related and not related to Church organization (the papacy), depending on the perspective from which this subject is addressed: practical/historical or theological/logical.

Is papal primacy an automatic *theological/logical* consequence of the Filioque? In my opinion, the Filioque *does not* automatically result in papal primacy and the other consequences that Lossky enumerated. I will refer to the four models

---

62   Ibid., 210–11.
63   Consultation, "The Filioque: A Church-Dividing Issue?" IV.

that I proposed in this chapter to support this affirmation, but I qualify them with a discussion of some *practical/historical* ways in which the Filioque and the papacy *are* interrelated in the life of the Church.

I disagree with Lossky and (sometimes) Staniloae's application of the first, reflective model to the Filioque. Although such methodology has its own merits, seeing the Church simply as a reflection of the Trinity risks pushing the logical consequences of trinitarian theology to conclusions that were not initially intended, and then reflecting them in an inaccurate description of the life of the Church. Lossky's description of the ecclesiological consequences of the Filioque does not correspond to the reality of present-day Catholic and Reformed churches, as Congar pointed out. Moreover, Lossky affirmed that "the Filioque was the primordial cause, the only dogmatic cause, of the breach between East and West. The other doctrinal disputes were but its consequences."[64] If this is the case, then solving the issue of the Filioque would automatically result in solving all the other differences between the Orthodox and Catholic churches, including the papacy. But since the papacy remains a Church-dividing issue, even after reaching agreement on the Filioque, it cannot be reduced to an automatic consequence of the Filioque. For these reasons, I suggest that if the reflection model is the basis for criticism, it should be abandoned. Rather, theologians should strive to find a continuum between Triadology and ecclesiology, and this is where the other three models can be applied.

Because the Church is the iconic, sacramental presence of the Trinity and the locus of *theosis*, the Filioque has no automatic consequences in the life of the Church. Trinitarian relationships are at work in the Church irrespective of our understanding of the procession of the Holy Spirit. The theology of the Filioque does not affect the direct manifestation of intratrinitarian relations in the Church; it is God's uncreated energies that manifest these relations.

Hence, the Filioque has ecclesiological consequences only from the perspective of the reflective model (which I do not condone in this case), not from the perspective of the Church as icon, sacrament, and divinization. Shifting the discussion from a theological/logical to a *practical/historical* perspective, it is necessary to acknowledge that, in history, the Filioque has crossed paths with Church life.

Without claiming to provide an exhaustive list of historical facts that show the consequences of the Filioque in the life of the Church, I briefly provide several examples. First, the theologians at Charlemagne's court accused the Greeks of reciting the Creed without the Filioque,[65] so the addition caused animosity

---

64    Vladimir Lossky, *The Mystical Theology of the Eastern Church*, trans. Fellowship of St. Alban and St. Sergius (Crestwood, NY: St Vladimir's Seminary Press, 2002), 56.
65    Ware, *The Orthodox Church*, 51.

within the Church. Second, the Filioque became an issue during the German mission in Bulgaria, where the Byzantine missionaries were also present; one would preach the Filioque, while the other would reject it. Thus, this thorny question affected the mission of the Church that was still united at that point. Third, for the Filioque to become authoritative teaching of the Catholic Church, it needed the approval of the Pope.[66] Thomas Aquinas affirmed that new explanations or additions to the Creed do not involve changing the old confessions of faith, and that the Pope had the authority to add the Filioque to the Creed commonly agreed upon at an ecumenical Council.[67] In Aquinas's mind, at least from a practical perspective, the Filioque and the papacy were interrelated. While still connecting the Filioque with issues of Church authority, Mark of Ephesus considered that a commonly agreed-to Creed could not be changed unilaterally, without the consultation of both parties.[68] Fourth, it is important to set the chronology straight: the Filioque appeared in the West long before official papal

---

66   In 1014, the Creed, including the Filioque, was sung for the first time at a papal Mass, so the Filioque was now generally assumed in the Latin Church to have the sanction of the papacy. The North American Orthodox-Catholic Consultation explains: "The Orthodox tradition sees the normative expression of that faith to be the Creeds and canons formulated by those Councils that are received by the Apostolic Churches as 'ecumenical' . . . The Catholic tradition also accepts conciliar formulations as dogmatically normative.... However, in recognizing the universal primacy of the bishop of Rome in matters of faith and of the service of unity, the Catholic tradition accepts the authority of the Pope to confirm the process of conciliar reception, and to define what does and does not conflict with the 'faith of Nicaea' and the Apostolic tradition. So while Orthodox theology has regarded the ultimate approval by the Popes, in the eleventh century, of the use of Filioque in the Latin Creed as a usurpation of the dogmatic authority proper to ecumenical Councils alone, Catholic theology has seen it as a legitimate exercise of his primatial authority to proclaim and clarify the Church's faith." Consultation, "The Filioque: A Church-Dividing Issue?," II.

67   Thomas Aquinas, *Summa Theologiae, Complete English Edition in Five Volumes*, trans. Fathers of the English Dominican Province (Allen, Texas: Christian Classics, a Division of Thomas More Publishing, 1981), 1172–73.

68   The opening remarks of Mark Eugenikos of Ephesus (1392–1444) at the council of Ferrara-Florence leave the impression that the Filioque, and not papal papacy, is the dividing issue between East and West. He addressed Pope Eugenius as the "most holy Father," asking him to receive "his children coming from the East" and "seeking his embrace." But, as Meyendorff points out, Mark "also stressed the minimum condition for true unity: the removal of the *interpolation introduced unilaterally by the Latins into a common creed*." [Emphases mine.] (Meyendorff, *Byzantine Theology: Historical Trends and Doctrinal Themes*, 111–12.) While Mark obviously condemned the theology of the Filioque, he also pointed to the ecclesiological aspect of the Filioque, namely its unilateral insertion into a creed commonly approved by both East and West, without the consultation of the East.

claims to universal jurisdiction[69] and infallibility.[70] Thus, papal authority cannot be the automatic theological consequence of the Filioque, or these consequences would have been manifested much earlier.

Without venturing to give a clear-cut answer as to whether the Filioque has ecclesiological consequences or not, especially in regard to the papacy, I consider that, although these two have been historically connected, the papacy and the "isms" listed by Lossky are not automatic consequences of the Filioque. Theologians should avoid polemics based solely on the reflection model, but strive to establish a direct relationship between the Trinity and the Church to inform their ecclesiological organization and Church life. From this perspective, Staniloae's considerations about the relationship between the Trinity and the Church provide a methodology for advancing the ecumenical dialogue on the ecclesiological consequences of the Filioque, even though he did not apply this methodology consistently.

## Conclusion

Staniloae's understanding of the relationship between the Trinity and the Church can be systematized in four models: the Church as a reflection of the Trinity, or the analogical relationship between the two; the Church as icon of the Trinity, where, just as in the icon the type points to its archetype because the icon is a presence of grace of the archetype, so the Church is a presence of the Trinity by grace, pointing toward the Trinity; the Church as the "third sacrament" of the Trinity in the world, as instrument and revelation of God; and the ecclesiological consequences of *theosis*, in which creation becomes god by grace, though not God by nature. These models result in Staniloae's affirmation that the same intratrinitarian relationships are manifested in the Trinity and in the Church,

---

69  One of the first occurrences of such pretensions appeared in Pope Nicholas's letter of 865 as part of the Photian Schism: the Pope is endowed with authority "over all the earth, that is, over *every* Church." Quoted in Ware, *The Orthodox Church*, 53. The East was not ready to grant the Pope universal jurisdiction, but only primacy of honor. It is important to mention, however, that earlier on in history, John the Faster (d. 595), Patriarch of Constantinople, assumed the title Ecumenical, which implies universal jurisdiction, although the Patriarch denied such claims. Pope Gregory I (590–604) responded by pointing out that there was no universal bishop and by assuming the title, *Servus Servorum Dei*, the Servant of the Servants of God.

70  In the Catholic Church, this claim became authoritative teaching only in 1870, with Vatican I's *Pastor Aeternus* 4, even though it can be traced earlier in history. It is also important to note that specific limitations describe the circumstances in which a papal teaching is considered infallible.

which is "filled with the Trinity." To further the ecumenical dialogue on the ecclesiological consequences of the Filioque (especially the papacy), I have suggested that only the last three models provide a better understanding of Church life based on Triadology.

Thus, the relationship between the Trinity and the Church as encapsulated in the four models that I have proposed based on Staniloae's theology supports my larger argument that the Church shares in the communion that exists within the Trinity. Trinitarian relations are both a model for the relationships that exist among humans and within Church, as well as the power that produces and deepens these relationships: "The life of the Trinity is interwoven in the life of the Church."[71]

To see concretely how the Trinity is present among us, in the second part of the book I discuss the relationship between each person of the Trinity and the Church.

---

71	Dumitru Staniloae, "Sinteza ecclesiologica [Ecclesiological Synthesis]," *Studii Teologice* 7, no. 5–6 (1955): 270–71.

# PART II

# FILLED WITH THE TRINITY

# Chapter 3

## ADOPTIVE CHILDREN OF THE FATHER:
## THE RELATIONSHIP BETWEEN THE FATHER AND THE CHURCH

In the previous pages I have attempted to show that ecclesiology is a chapter of Triadology and that each person of the Trinity is present in the Church. Sadly, many self-proclaimed trinitarian ecclesiologies are de facto monistic or binitarian understandings of the Church,[1] content with treating the relationship between the Church and the Son and the Holy Spirit. The Father is rarely mentioned. And yet, to support the affirmation that ecclesiology is ultimately a chapter of Triadology, one needs to first prove that ecclesiology is a chapter of the theology of the Father.

In light of Staniloae's theology describing the relationship between (1) the Son and the Father and (2) the Spirit and the Father, as they are both manifested in the Church, I analyze the relationship between the Father and the Church, concentrating on the biblical motif of adoption or sonship (*uiothesía*), which Staniloae defined as "the maximum loving relationship with God."[2] I conclude with the assertion that (3) adoption is both a present and an eschatological reality, closely connected to the Kingdom of God.

In previous chapters, I was able to compare Staniloae with many other Eastern and Western theologians; in this present chapter—with very few exceptions—Staniloae mostly stands alone. This is very surprising since there are many ecclesiological aspects involved in the discussion of adoption in New Testament texts such as these:

> For you did not receive a spirit of slavery to fall back into fear, but you have received a spirit of adoption (Rom. 8.15),
>
> And not only the creation, but we ourselves, who have the first fruits of the Spirit, groan inwardly while we wait for adoption, the redemption of our bodies (Rom. 8.23),

---

1 The terms monistic and binitarian are probably too strong, since, in reality, it is a matter of priority (at worst) or emphasis (at best).
2 Staniloae, *Jesus Christ, the Light of the World*, 102.

[God sent his Son] so that we might receive adoption as children. And because you are children, God has sent the Spirit of his Son into our hearts, crying, 'Abba! Father!' So you are no longer a slave but a child, and if a child then also an heir, through God (Gal. 4.5-7), [and]

[The Father] destined us for adoption as his children through Jesus Christ, according to the good pleasure of his will, to the praise of his glorious grace that he freely bestowed on us in the Beloved (Eph. 1.5).

Moreover, to give just an example from the early Church, Cyprian of Carthage made the connection between the Father and the Church when he affirmed that whoever does not have the Church as his mother could not have God as his Father.[3] Contemporary systematic theologians, however, do not discuss this relationship between the Father and the Church, or at least not to the same extent that Staniloae did. His is a major contribution toward a fully trinitarian ecclesiology.

### The Father and the Son in the Church

*The General Sense of Adoption*

I have contended that Staniloae extended the relations manifested within the Trinity to the world in general and the Church in particular. Applying this principle to our adoption, he wrote:

> Only because a triune God exists does one of the divine persons—namely the one who stands in relationship as Son vis-à-vis the other and, as man too, can remain within this affectionate relationship as Son—become incarnate, placing all his human brothers within this relationship as sons to the heavenly Father, or indeed placing his Father within a paternal relationship to all men.[4]

In other words, the Son places in a filial relationship with the Father all his human brothers and sisters with whom he shares the same human nature. In turn, the Father extends his paternal relationship with the Son to encompass the

---

3  Cf. Cyprian, *On the Unity of the Church* #6 and *Epist. LXXIII (To Pompey, Against the Epistle of Stephen About the Baptism of Heretics)*, #7. See the *Ante-Nicene Fathers* collection, vol. 5.

4  Staniloae, *The Experience of God 1*, 248.

entire humanity assumed in the incarnation. Staniloae added that the eternal love between the Father and the Son represents the basis for human relationships of paternity and sonship in general, which now are not simply carnal (blood lineage), but also spiritual. Just as the Father-Son relationship is fulfilled in the Holy Spirit, so human paternal-filial relations receive a spiritual quality through the Spirit of God. And yet, this comparison is limited, as intratrinitarian relations incomparably transcend human interaction.[5]

Another way to differentiate between the Father's relationship with humankind and with the Son is to affirm that the Son is begotten from the Father by nature, whereas we are adopted children by grace.[6] As Staniloae affirmed:

> By having a Son from eternity, the Father has from eternity the capacity to make us his children, too, though not through birth from his nature, . . . but through the Incarnation and, after the sin, through the cross of his Son, through the [Son's] descent to us with brotherly love even unto our death, and through his resurrection in his humanity for eternity. Saint Apostle Paul affirms this same idea: "just as he chose us in Christ before the foundation of the world to be holy and blameless before him in love. He destined us for adoption as his children through Jesus Christ, according to the good pleasure of his will" (Eph. 1.4-5, 9).[7]

At this point, it is important to acknowledge the originality of Staniloae's understanding of adoption. There are two senses in which he approached this concept. First, in a general sense, all humankind, recapitulated in Christ's human nature, was adopted through the incarnation and placed in a filial relationship with the Father. In a second, special sense, those who are united with Christ through faith in him, Baptism, and the Eucharist experience this filial relationship to the fullest in the Church, the Body of Christ. Staniloae's twofold understanding of adoption represents a significant contribution to anthropology and interreligious dialogue, even though only the special, ecclesial aspect of adoption is stated explicitly in the New Testament, while general adoption is only implicit. And since the two aspects of adoption cannot be separated, in the next section I transition from general adoption to a specific understanding of the relationship between the Father and the Son, as it is manifested in the Church.

---

5   Ibid., 246.
6   This is especially the case of baptized Christians. Ibid., 69–70.
7   Staniloae, *Spirituality and Communion*, 154.

*The Special Sense of Adoption*

In a broad sense, all people, from all times and all places, are children of God, through the act of creation. Because of the fall into sin, however, all are fallen children of God, who have been separated from their communion with God. According to Staniloae, the crucified Jesus expressed and experienced the state of the entire humankind, separated from and "abandoned" by God before redemption:

> being clothed in reality with human sin, which is so unpleasant to God, and having to suffer death, the distance that Christ feels between him and the Father is explicable. Here is where the great and fearful mystery of Jesus's "abandonment" by the Father comes in. His eternal bliss is represented by the loving intimacy with the Father, the love of the Father towards him. But this spiritual distance that he has to feel, since he bears the sins of the world, causes him the greatest pain.... This distance is infinitely more painful for the beloved Son of the Father than for any other human being who feels abandoned by God.... Jesus's "abandonment" by the Father is an abandonment that pertains to the sin that he bears, not to him personally, even though the person has to feel abandoned, as punishment for the sin.[8]

Thus, as the bearer of our fallen nature, Christ experienced the separation between humanity and the Father, even to the point of feeling abandoned and crying, "My God, my God, why have you forsaken me?" (Mt. 27.46; Mk 15.34, cf. Ps. 22.1). Christ feels this distance for the rest of the people. The Crucifixion is so tragic because it is the Son of God, eternally in communion with the Father, who ineffably experiences our separation from God.

The relationship between the Father and humankind will change dramatically with the Resurrection. Humankind will be granted communion instead of abandonment, and the baptized will become adopted children of the Father. Once again, the intratrinitarian relationships of paternity and sonship extend into the Church:

> The light of the Church represents the unity that the Son of God came to restore between humankind and him, after the model and power of the Holy Trinity. The glory that the Son of God received as man from the Father means that, just as he is united as human with the Father, he

---

8   Staniloae, *Jesus Christ or the Restoration of Humankind*, 294.

also makes humans one with the Father, as his children. Those disunited show that they are no longer brothers and sisters in Christ and children of the Father. In this sense Christ [says] "The glory that you have given me I have given them, so that they may be one, as we are one" (Jn 17.22). Because if he, the one who became human, is one with the Father and loved by [the Father], but dwells in [humans], then evidently they will be united with him and loved by the Father "that they may become completely one". (Jn 17.23)[9]

## The Effects of Adoption

It is now important to discuss the effects of our adoption. First, because we are adopted children of the Father united in Christ, Staniloae contended that the Son teaches us to love and obey the Father, emulating his love and obedience.[10]

Second, the Kingdom that Christ brought about is a Kingdom of love because the King is a Father who wanted to extend the paternal love that he has for the Son to other beings capable of receiving and responding to this paternal love. God is a merciful Father and we are his free children, not slaves. This is shown in the prayer, "Our Father," in which we ask for the Kingdom of the Father to come, for the will of the Father to be done, for the name of the Father to be blessed.[11] Staniloae's considerations of our status as free children of the Father were based on the work of his friend Jürgen Moltmann, who affirmed that the Son became a human being so that he could see the other human beings as his brothers and sisters.[12]

Third, Staniloae contended that the Eucharist reveals our adoption as a new ontological reality, far surpassing a mere new juridical relationship with the Father. In the Eucharist, we discover our quality as members of the Body of Christ. The Church as Body is sacrificed to the Father out of love, just as Christ's body was sacrificed on the Cross. The Church accepts being sacrificed both freely and with divine assistance. When we partake of the eucharistic sacrifice, Christ empowers us to present ourselves as spiritual sacrifices to the Father, united with the Son's sacrifice. This is the meaning of the Pauline words, "For as often

---

9    Staniloae, *Jesus Christ, the Light of the World*, 214.
10   Staniloae, *Spirituality and Communion*, 392.
11   Ibid., 145.
12   Staniloae referred to the German original, *Trinität und Reich Gottes* (München: Gütersloh, 1960). This book also exists in an English translation, Jürgen Moltmann, *The Trinity and the Kingdom: The Doctrine of God*, trans. Margaret Kohl (San Francisco: Harper & Row, 1981).

as you eat this bread and drink the cup, you proclaim the Lord's death until he comes" (1 Cor. 11.26).[13]

If in the Eucharist we are sacrificed to the Father with Christ, it means for Staniloae that we grow in the likeness of Christ, we are clothed with grace, and the love of the Father descends upon us. This is possible because, in Christ, we find ourselves in the presence of the Father. Staniloae reached this conclusion based on Cyril of Alexandria who, in *Worship in Spirit and in Truth* 10, commented on Heb. 9.24: "For Christ did not enter a sanctuary made by human hands, a mere copy of the true one, but he entered into heaven itself, now to appear in the presence of God on our behalf." Cyril contended that, through sin, we have fallen from the presence of God. In Christ, however, we have obtained the boldness to enter the heavenly Holy of Holies, in the presence of the Father. Christ did not need to bring himself in the presence of the Father—since the Son of God is always with the Father—but he did it for us, who are united with Christ and sanctified in him. Thus, in Christ, we can now be in the presence of the Father.[14] We offer ourselves as sacrifices in the Liturgy where, through the Holy Spirit, the eucharistic community is united with the sacrificed Christ in order to offer itself as a sacrifice to the Father, show its love for the Father, and be in the presence of the Father.[15] Additionally, Staniloae considered that our sacrifice implies not only participation in the Liturgy, but also living a virtuous life.[16]

These considerations about our sacrifice in Christ to the Father (with only a brief mention of the Spirit) could potentially give the impression of being another instance of binitarian ecclesiology, only this time the two divine persons in question are the Father and the Son. Nothing could be further from the truth: Staniloae's ecclesiology is fully trinitarian. In the next section, I present Staniloae's understanding of the relationship between the Spirit and the Father, as it is manifested in the Church.

## The Father and the Spirit in the Church

The Spirit dwells in the Church, which is the Body of Christ, because the Spirit rests from eternity in the Son. Moreover, the Holy Spirit represents the possibility

---

13  Staniloae, *Spirituality and Communion*, 373.

14  Ibid., 258.

15  Ibid., 145–46.

16  To support his affirmation, he quoted Rom. 12.1—"I appeal to you therefore, brothers and sisters, by the mercies of God, to present your bodies as a living sacrifice, holy and acceptable to God, which is your spiritual worship"—and Cyril of Alexandria's *Worship in Spirit and in Truth* 17: "for at all times and without ceasing, from the beginning to the end, we bring in Christ a sacrifice through virtue, in the holy tent, that is, in the church." Staniloae, *Dogmatics 2*, 146–48.

of extending the love between the Father and the Son to adopted human beings.[17] In this sense, Staniloae affirmed together with Moltmann that "the Spirit comes to us as bearer of the infinite love of the Father towards his Son."[18]

That is why our adoption is not dependent solely on the relationship between the Father and the Son, but also on the Spirit. Staniloae's account of adoption is fully trinitarian: "the preservation of the filial relation of the Son towards the Father together with the affirmation of the Spirit as Spirit of the Son . . . makes of the presence of the Son a source from which filial response, life and divine movement radiate upon men."[19]

These considerations are based on Staniloae's emphatic affirmation that the Spirit proceeds from the Father and rests in the Son. In this sense, the Son possesses the Spirit (since the Spirit rests in the Son), which explains the Pauline expression, the Spirit of Christ or of the Son. The Father sending the Spirit to the Son and the eternal resting of the Spirit in the Son manifests the paternal-filial relationship between the Father and the Son. Staniloae went on to argue that these intratrinitarian relationships extend to those united with the Son, i.e., to the Church. As a sign of the Father's love, the Spirit rests in the Church, even as the Spirit rests from eternity in the Son. At the same time, we could not be the Body of Christ without the Spirit, and this is why only in the Spirit are we united with Christ and, consequently, we rise to the Father.[20] Moreover, in the Spirit we gain the consciousness of being adopted children of the Father. In Staniloae's words:

> Possessing the Spirit, we have Christ himself within us together with his own awareness of himself as Son before the Father, a filial consciousness which we assimilate as our own.... A Christ without the penetration of his filial consciousness within us—without the Spirit—is impossible. At most we could theorize about such a possession of Christ. Moreover, a presence of the Spirit without Christ, if the Spirit is Christ's consciousness vis-à-vis the Father, is also impossible. [At this point Staniloae quoted extensively Rom. 8.14-17 and Gal. 4.6-7.][21]

The resting of the Spirit in the Son and its manifestation in the Church is only the first part of the equation. Staniloae also affirmed that the Spirit returns to the Father from the Son (in whom the Spirit rests), bearing the Son's loving response

---

17 Staniloae, *Theology and the Church*, 67. See more in the fifth chapter.
18 Quoted in Staniloae, *Dogmatics 2*, 200.
19 Staniloae, *Theology and the Church*, 106–07.
20 Staniloae, "The Procession of the Holy Spirit," 186.
21 Staniloae, *Theology and the Church*, 32–33.

to the love of the Father. The intratrinitarian relationships are then extended in the Church, so that, in the Spirit, the members of the Church respond to the paternal love of the Father and also gain the consciousness of adopted children of God. In this regard, Staniloae wrote about:

> how the Spirit descends through the Son in the temporal order and thereby manifests his eternal relation with the Son. When the Son becomes incarnate and unites men with himself, the love of the Father which is upon him and his own response to the Father's love are assimilated by all who are united with the Son. All are beloved of the Father in the Son and all respond to the Father in the Son with the Son's own love. This is the climactic moment of the condition of salvation: the union of all with Christ in the Spirit, and through the Spirit in the consciousness of the Father's love for them and of their own love for the Father. Hence salvation is recapitulation in Christ. All are loved in the Son by the Father and all respond in the Son with the Son's love, for inasmuch as all are found in the Son, the Spirit of the Father hovers over all and shines forth from all upon the Father.[22]

This is probably one of the best instances of Staniloae's theology of the Church raised into the Trinity. As stated in the previous chapter, the Church participates in the communion of the Trinity and manifests the eternal relations among the Father, Son, and Holy Spirit. First, Staniloae clearly delineated his methodology, that of applying intratrinitarian relationships into the Church. Then, he established a continuum between the Trinity and the Church through Christ, who is united with all human beings and thus puts them into a filial relationship with the Father and fills them with the Spirit. Again, adoption is used here in its general sense, referring to all human beings. The image of the Spirit hovering over all is quite illustrative in this sense, referencing the Spirit of God hovering over the waters of creation (Gen. 1.2). Along the same lines, but also indicating the special aspect of adoption in the Church as a new creation, Staniloae affirmed:

> The Spirit of the love between the Father and the Son breathes within the Church. This Spirit brings and implants in people the filial love towards the Father and the feeling of the Father's love towards the Son and, through him, towards those united with him in the body of the Church. The breath of this love, brought in us through the Spirit, has created the world and its breath re-creates it as Church.[23]

---

22  Ibid., 31–32.
23  Staniloae, *Dogmatics 2*, 147.

*Other Roles of the Spirit of Adoption*

Staniloae analyzed other ways in which the Spirit extends the paternal-filial relationship between the Father and the Son to the Church. Empowered by the Spirit, we have an active role in our filial relationship with the Father, just as the Son has an active role in his relationship with the Father, responding to his love. This synergy is only possible in the Spirit:

> The Son is not a passive object of the Father's love, as in fact we ourselves are not passive objects when the Holy Spirit is poured out upon us.... The Spirit of the Father penetrating within us as the paternal love kindles our own loving filial subjectivity in which, at the same time, the Spirit is also made manifest.[24]

Another role of the Spirit is that of spiritualizing our humanity, to make it fit for adoption after the model of the incarnation. Staniloae wrote in this sense that "the Holy Spirit makes spiritual the humanity assumed by the Son and deifies it, which is to say, makes it fit to participate in the love which the divine hypostasis of the Son has toward his Father."[25] In turn, we are all united in our humanity with Christ's deified humanity, so the Spirit deifies our humanity as well, making us fit to have a filial relationship with the Father. Commenting on Rom. 8, Staniloae affirmed that one of the consequences of our adoption is that we are capable of a certain conformity with God in the sense that we have a filial relationship with the Father and a brotherly relationship with the Son:

> The eternal, only-begotten Son of God came to put us too in the relationship that he has with the Father—even though we are created—and thus, in a brotherly relationship with him. This is also what he wanted to do through creation. Only in this sense, because the human being is capable of such a relationship, can be said that we have, or that we are capable of, a certain conformity with God.[26]

This is why, for Staniloae, being brothers and sisters with Christ, adopted children of the Father, filled with the Spirit, ultimately means divinization or

---

24  Staniloae, *Theology and the Church*, 31.
25  Staniloae, *The Experience of God 1*, 249.
26  Staniloae, *Jesus Christ or the Restoration of Humankind*, 69. For Staniloae's discussion of the role of the Spirit in our adoption resulting in a brotherly relationship with Jesus and among ourselves, see also Staniloae, *Theology and the Church*, 63–64.

*theosis*. To be precise, adoption is divinization. As Symeon the New Theologian put it in Hymn 25, "As a human being I know that I do not see any of the things divine, but through adoption I was made god."[27] Of course, divinization implies identification by grace between us and the Spirit, or being filled with the Spirit. This identification results in the elimination of the separation between the Father and us, giving us the boldness to pray to him or, more exactly, to let the Spirit pray in us. Staniloae's considerations resonate with several Pauline passages especially Rom. 8.15-16, 26: "For you did not receive a spirit of slavery to fall back into fear, but you have received a spirit of adoption. When we cry, 'Abba! Father!' it is that very Spirit bearing witness with our spirit that we are children of God.... Likewise the Spirit helps us in our weakness; for we do not know how to pray as we ought, but that very Spirit intercedes with sighs too deep for words." Based on Gregory the Theologian, Staniloae commented in this sense:

> Through the incarnate Son we enter into filial communion with the Father, while through the Spirit we pray to the Father or speak with him as sons. For the Spirit unites himself with us in prayer. "It is the Spirit in whom we worship, and in whom we pray.... Therefore, to adore or to pray in the Spirit seems to me to be simply himself offering prayer or adoration to himself."[28] But this prayer which the Spirit offers within us, he offers to himself in our name, and into this prayer we too are drawn. Through grace the Spirit identifies himself with us so that, through grace, we may identify ourselves with him. Through grace the Spirit eliminates the distance between our "I" and his "I," creating between us and the Father, through grace, the same relations he has by nature with the Father and the Son. If in the incarnate Son we have become sons by grace, in the Spirit we gain the consciousness and boldness that come from being sons.[29]

Thus, far from being an exclusively christological construct, our adoption as children of the Father is based on pneumatological grounds as well, making it fully trinitarian. We enter a filial relationship with the Father because of our union with Christ. This union is made possible by the Spirit and results in our identification with the Spirit, who prays within us. In this union of grace with the Trinity, our adoption becomes our divinization or *theosis*.

Is adoption in Christ, through the Spirit, the highest possible degree of union between the Father and the Church? I attempt to answer this question in the

---

27    Quoted in Staniloae, *Jesus Christ, the Light of the World*, 245.
28    Gregory the Theologian, *Oration* 31.12, PG 36.145C.
29    Staniloae, *The Experience of God* 1, 248.

following section, where I analyze both the present and eschatological aspects of adoption.

## Adoption as Both Present and Eschatological

### Present Adoption

For Staniloae, adoption is first of all a present reality. Our union with each person of the Trinity reaches in the Church its highest degree possible on this side of the eschaton. In his commentary on Rom. 8.17, Staniloae affirmed that suffering with Christ in order to become heirs together with him refers to our union with Christ, when our selfishness and inclination toward passions die, when we are filled with Christ's glory and become heirs of the Father's kingdom.[30] Adoption as freedom from sinful passions is thus attainable in the present world. This idea, however, does not exclude the understanding of adoption as something continuously in need of advancement both in this life and in the eschaton, when our filial relationship with the Father will be taken to a superior level. In Staniloae's words,

> Even those who have received in Christ the first fruits of the Spirit find themselves only in a strong hope of their future freedom as children, still not fully possessing adoption. Consequently we too still groan inwardly, as we await adoption as true salvation from under the slavery of depravity, as true freedom. "And not only the creation, but we ourselves, who have the first fruits of the Spirit, groan inwardly while we wait for adoption, the redemption of our bodies (from death)" (Rom. 8.23). We die with the body, although through the first fruits of the Spirit we have the hope that we will escape bodily death. Only full adoption brings us freedom from the laws of depravity and only in these are we going to truly live the redemption of the body from death.[31]

Staniloae affirmed here that on the one hand, we are already adopted children of the Father. On the other hand, we do not have the fullness of adoption until the eschaton, when we will be completely free from the fallen character of this world, particularly death. Shortly after this passage, Staniloae added that the Spirit of Christ cries in us, "Abba! Father!", representing the groaning that

---

30  Staniloae, *Spirituality and Communion*, 278.
31  Staniloae, *Jesus Christ, the Light of the World*, 104.

comes from not being completely free from the laws of depravity and lacking full adoption. At the same time, this cry illustrates the hope that the Spirit maintains in us, that we will become truly children of the Father.[32]

At this point, it is important to interject several remarks about Staniloae's biblical interpretation of adoption. (The reader has probably noticed a higher concentration of biblical references in this chapter, compared to the rest of the book.) Staniloae's considerations about the laws of depravity are justified, since Rom. 8 contrasts the spirit of adoption with the "deeds of the body." In this sense, the cry "Abba! Father!" refers to our liberation from the deeds of the flesh that enslave us, bringing us suffering. This cry, "Abba! Father!", is also reflective of suffering in a passage outside the Pauline corpus, namely in Mk 14.36, when Jesus prayed in the garden before he was sacrificed on the Cross: "Abba, Father, for you all things are possible; remove this cup from me; yet, not what I want, but what you want."[33] In his discussion of adoption, James Dunn affirms that, "like Jesus, believers cry 'Abba! Father!' and thus attest that they are children of God and joint heirs with Christ (Rom. 8.16-17)."[34] Thus, our adoption as liberation from passions is very significant for a discussion of the relationship between the Father and the Church. It refers to our union with Christ and the spiritual transformation that we undergo in this new filial relationship with the Father.

---

32   Ibid., 104–05.

33   The Gospel of Mark is a later document than Romans, although the gap in time is brief. However, a parallelism between Rom. 8.15 and Mk 14.36 could be grounded on (a) Jesus traditions that circulated in smaller collections from the beginning, (b) an oral tradition circulating at that time, according to which Jesus prayed using the appellative, "Abba," asking for the ease of his suffering, and (c) the early Church's usage of Abrahamic traditions, especially the sacrifice of Isaac, to understand the life and death of Jesus. The Church would cry together with Christ, "Abba!" and this cry most probably also found its way into the early Christian liturgy. See for example Joseph A. Fitzmyer, *Romans: A New Translation with Introduction and Commentary*, Anchor Bible Series (New York: Doubleday, 1993), 498. Regarding the Church's use of Abrahamic traditions, see Richard B. Hays, *Echoes of Scripture in the Letters of Paul* (New Haven, CT: Yale University Press, 1989), 112–17. Hays mentions several similarities between the Genesis story and Paul's accounts of adoption, especially the fact that both passages mention Isaac or the descendants of Isaac as inheriting their Father's estate (Gen. 21.10; Rom. 8.17–18; Gal. 4.30). To this, I would add the son addressing his father, and the cry, "Father" (Gen. 22.7, Rom. 8.15, Gal. 4.5).

34   James D. G. Dunn, "Spirit Speech: Reflections on Romans 8:12-27," in *Romans and the People of God: Essays in Honor of Gordon D. Fee on the Occasion of His 65th Birthday*, ed. Sven K. Soderlund and N.T. Wright (Grand Rapids, MI: Eerdmans, 1999), 84.

Additionally, Staniloae understands adoption as the transformation of interhuman relationships in Christ. He affirmed that Christ, by "exhorting us to call [God] 'our Father,' and not my Father, he taught us to consider ourselves as brothers, as together children of his Father and as together brothers of Christ."[35] As another consequence of our present adoption, we are all brothers and sisters among us and with Christ, since we are all children of the Father.

This new brotherly relationship is based on the Father's sanctification of our humanity, just as the Father sanctified the humanity of Jesus. Staniloae developed this affirmation in his exegesis of Heb. 2.11: "For the one who sanctifies and those who are sanctified all have one Father. For this reason Jesus is not ashamed to call them brothers and sisters." He contended that we are Christ's brothers and sisters because the Father bestows his holiness both on the humanity of Christ and on us. The Father's holiness comes to Christ in his humanity, since Christ offered himself as a sacrifice to the Father and since the Son and the Father are united in the same essence. This holiness also comes to Christians because they are brothers and sisters with the incarnate Son of God and join in his sacrifice. That is why—Staniloae continued in accordance to Rom. 8—Christians are together inheritors with the Son of the Father's Kingdom and of all its blessings. The Son will tell them at the Final Judgment, "come, you that are blessed by my Father, inherit the kingdom prepared for you from the foundation of the world" (Mt. 25.34).[36]

Of course, the larger context of Mt. 25.34, which Staniloae quoted above, refers to our philanthropic responsibilities toward those who are adopted children of the Father, or Christ's brothers and sisters. In this way, Staniloae considered another consequence of our adoption, referring to the love we need to have for one another, even as the Father loves the Son and us:

> We can and therefore must see the faces of our fellow men in the human face of Christ, just as in beholding his incarnate Son the Father sees and loves us all as sons and adopts us through the Incarnation of his Son, then it is plain that in the face of every man we must see and love some aspect of the face of Christ, indeed the very face of Christ himself.[37]

Thus, the Father loves us because he sees us in his beloved Son, and we should imitate the Father in loving our fellow human beings, in whom we find Christ.

---

35  Staniloae, *Spirituality and Communion*, 158–59.
36  Ibid., 175.
37  Staniloae, *Theology and the Church*, 206.

*Eschatological Adoption*

If the above considerations refer to adoption as a present reality preparing us for the eschaton, adoption is also an eschatological gift. At the end of time, Jesus

> will then perfect the communion among all the people from all times and he will change the image of the present world according to this perfect communion. The entire Church will resurrect in the new world together with the Lord. Then Jesus will subdue for the Father the world that would be saved and transfigured, and he will also subdue himself together with [the world], so that God would be all in all. Then will begin the day of perfect brotherhood among people and perfect sonship in relationship to the Father.[38]

If in the Church all are called to act as brothers and sisters toward each other, it will be even more so in the eschaton, when their communion will be perfected. All will live in perfect brotherly relationships with Christ and one another, and all will be perfected as children of the Father. This is possible because of the manifestation of the perfecting Spirit in the Church, and fully at the end of time. Because of its union with Christ, the Church already has the Spirit creating communion among its members and with Christ. But the Spirit will be fully manifested in the eschaton, when it will represent the fullness of the Father's gift to us, or the inheritance that the Father has promised us. As Staniloae wrote, "the Holy Spirit . . . unites us in Christ that we may rejoice together with Christ in what is his, and that we may become co-heirs with Christ in his inheritance from the Father, that is, the Spirit (Eph. 1.11-14)."[39]

This trinitarian understanding of adoption as children of the Father, united with the Son, in the Spirit also involves a liturgical aspect. We are united with Christ primarily in the Eucharist, and this union will be fulfilled in the eschaton or, more precisely, this union will be deepened eternally. Staniloae wrote that in the earthly Church we reach the highest step of our ascent to the Father when we unite ourselves with Christ, through the Spirit, in the Eucharist. He based his affirmation on Nicholas Cabasilas's *The Life in Christ*,[40] who contended that,

---

38  Staniloae, *Jesus Christ or the Restoration of Humankind*, 427.
39  Staniloae, *Theology and the Church*, 32.
40  Staniloae used the German translation, second edition, Vienna, 1966: 101, 104. This book is also available in English translation: Nicholas Cabasilas, *The Life in Christ*, trans. Carmino J. deCatanzaro (Crestwood, NY: St Vladimir's Seminary Press, 1974).

here on earth, our ascent ends when we receive the Eucharist as a foretaste of the Kingdom, after which there is nothing left for us to advance towards. What we need to do—continued Cabasilas—is to remain in the gift that we have been given: the mystery of the union between the Spirit of Christ and our spirit, of Christ's will with our will, of Christ's Body and Blood with our body and blood. As if slightly in disagreement with Cabasilas's contention that the Eucharist is the end of our ascent, Staniloae qualified this affirmation on an eschatological note: "But we can advance in the state of children [of God]. Because love has no end. Through this we have become inheritors of the Father's Kingdom together with his Son. But we can also advance eternally in partaking of the joy of the Kingdom."[41]

Staniloae's interpretation of Cabasilas's text is not at all forced. The affirmation of the eternal advancement in communion with God is a common thread in the Orthodox tradition, very similar to Gregory of Nyssa's considerations on *epectasis*. The Cappadocian bishop saw Moses as a proof that spiritual progress has no end, since there is always something new to be contemplated in the supreme Good. This desire for continuous growth cannot be satisfied even in eternity. At the same time, this progress is a standing still, since Scripture says, "You must stand on the rock" (Exod. 33.21). The ascent takes place by means of the standing, since the more one progresses in virtue, the more immovable that person remains in the Good.[42] Thus, in line with both Gregory of Nyssa and Nicholas Cabasilas, Staniloae affirmed that, even though in the Eucharist we reach the pinnacle of our adoption, we continue our progress in God's infinite love eternally. This discussion will continue in the next chapter, when considering the Liturgy as an anticipation of the eschatological kingdom.

---

41   Staniloae, *Spirituality and Communion*, 369.

42   Saint Gregory of Nyssa, *The Life of Moses*, trans. Abraham J. Malherbe and Everett Ferguson, *The Classics of Western Spirituality* (New York: Paulist Press, 1978), 30, 113–17. Along these lines, Staniloae adopted Maximus the Confessor's views on movement and *stasis*. Maximus emphasized the idea that even though in eternity we do not fluctuate between good and evil and we reach a certain stability (*stasis*), this does not mean that we will not continue our progress in good for eternity. However, this progress will be marked by stability in good. See for example Staniloae's "Preface" and note 419 to his translation of Saint Maximus the Confessor, *Ambigua: Tilcuiri ale unor locuri cu multe si adinci intelesuri din Sfintii Dionisie Areopagitul si Grigorie Teologul* [*Ambigua: Interpretations of Some Texts with Many and Deep Meanings from Saints Dionysius the Areopagite and Gregory the Theologian*], trans. Dumitru Staniloae, *Parinti si scriitori bisericesti 80* (Bucuresti: EIBMBOR, 1983), 34, 332.

### Conclusion

Staniloae's ecclesiology is neither monistic, nor binitarian, but fully trinitarian, where the Church is "filled with the Trinity." Summarizing the relationships existing between the Trinity and humankind in general and the Church in particular, Staniloae wrote about the "filial relationship of the faithful towards the Father, and of their intimate communion among themselves in Christ who is present within them through the Holy Spirit."[43]

More specifically, Jesus Christ, the Son incarnate, is the mediator of the communion between God and humankind, because he is both God and human in one hypostasis. In a general sense of adoption, Christ placed all humankind in a filial relationship with the Father. In a special sense, members of the Church are in a closer filial relationship with the Father, especially in the Eucharist, where the Church, united with Christ, brings itself as a sacrifice to the Father. In this context, we experience our special adoption as love, obedience to the Father, and life of virtue. Moreover, if in the incarnate Son we have become children by grace, filled with the Spirit we gain the consciousness and boldness that come from being adoptive children of the Father. And just as in the Trinity the Spirit is the bearer of love between the Father and the Son, so does the Spirit come to the Church bearing the love of the Father and empowering us to respond actively in love to the Father. Moreover, the Spirit divinizes our humanity to make it fit for such relationship with the Father, which ultimately results in *theosis*.

Approached from the perspective of union with Christ and the Spirit, morality, and participation in the Eucharist, adoption is a present reality. But this intimate filial relationship between the Church and the Father will be perfected in the eschaton. Because love has no end, we will eternally advance in the state of children of God, brothers and sisters with Christ and one another, and filled with the Spirit. More will be said in the following chapters, but it is safe to conclude now that ecclesiology is a chapter of the theology of the Father, while being ultimately a chapter of Triadology.

Staniloae's contribution toward a fully trinitarian ecclesiology is even more significant when considering the paucity of similar contributions among contemporary Orthodox theologians. Exceptionally, Evdokimov wrote about our adoption as an ascent that ultimately results in *theosis*.[44] Zizioulas affirms that

---

43    Staniloae, *Theology and the Church*, 107.

44    Evdokimov wrote that we move "from our pneumatophore [i.e., bearer of the Spirit] interiority, through our christological structure (members of the theandric Body of Christ) towards the bosom of the Father." This way, the soul is christified through the Spirit, and is pointed toward the mystical wedding with, and adoption in, the

"ecclesial fatherhood reflects Trinitarian Fatherhood in that membership in the Church requires 'generation' or 'birth'[45] or 'regeneration',[46] which is given 'from above' in an act or event (Baptism) of *sonship*, that is, our acceptance by the Father as his sons by grace through our incorporation into his only-begotten Son whom he eternally generates."[47] Among Western theologians, there is a similar infrequency of references to the Father and the Church although there is a great wealth of biblical scholarship, which I have applied here as an instance of open sobornicity (see Chapter 1).[48]

In this chapter, I focused on Staniloae's understanding of the relationship between the Father and the Church, which, of course, cannot be separated from the other two persons of the Trinity. In the next chapter, while maintaining a trinitarian perspective, I concentrate on the role of the Son in the Church.

---

Father. According to Evdokimov, ascent results ultimately in *theosis*. (Evdokimov, *L'Orthodoxie*, 111–12.) See also Nissiotis's brief mention of adoption and the Church as the People of God in Chapter 5.

45  The apostle, for example, is called "father" because he "gives birth" to the members of the community "in Christ Jesus" (1 Cor. 4.15).

46  1 Pt 1.3, 23; cf. Jn 3.3,7.

47  John D. Zizioulas, *Communion and Otherness: Further Studies in Personhood and the Church*, ed. Paul McPartlan (New York: T&T Clark—Continuum, 2006), 148. Moreover, Zizioulas writes about our adoption in terms of *theosis*. In both cases, he does not fully develop the ecclesiological implications of these affirmations. That is probably because he associates the God of the Old Testament with the Father, an idea that he adopts from Rahner and which does not take into account the richness of Orthodox early patristic writings, hymnology, and iconography that associate Old Testament theophanies with the Son (see for example Bogdan G. Bucur, "The Mountain of the Lord: Sinai, Zion, and Eden in Byzantine Hymnographic Exegesis," in *Symbola Caelestis: Le symbolisme liturgique et paraliturgique dans le monde chrétien*, ed. B. Lourié and A. Orlov (Piscataway, NY: Gorgias, 2009), especially 157–62.).

48  One such exception is Donald McLeod who presents a fully trinitarian theology from a Presbyterian perspective, emphasizing a direct relationship between each person of the Trinity and the Church. Based on the Pauline image of adoption he speaks of a forensical or relational change in our relationship with the Father, while the Johannine idea of rebirth suggests the ontological or transformational dimension of our change of status toward the Father. All are united among themselves in this new situation, even if "we may not always approve of God's policy on adoption or always be impressed by the new additions to the family. But he doesn't ask. He simply requires us to accept them." Donald McLeod, "The Basis of Christian Unity," in *Ecumenism Today: The Universal Church in the 21st Century*, ed. Francesca Aran Murphy and Christopher Asprey (Burlington, VT: Ashgate, 2008), 108.

## Chapter 4

## BODY OF CHRIST: THE RELATIONSHIP
## BETWEEN THE SON AND THE CHURCH

Is ecclesiology a chapter of Christology or of Pneumatology? These are the parameters within which most theologians tend to describe the relationship between the Trinity and the Church. First and most obvious, as argued in the previous chapter, few discuss the relationship between the Father and the Church—a necessary aspect of any sound trinitarian theology. Second, while analyzing the relationship between the Son or the Spirit and the Church, almost everybody tends to affirm the need to find a balance between the christological and pneumatological dimensions of the Church. However, theologians differ in the degree of success they have in finding such equilibrium. They tend to emphasize one to the detriment of the other, as I will show more thoroughly in the next chapter.

Having argued already that ecclesiology is a chapter of the theology of the Father, in this chapter I attempt to show in what sense Staniloae would agree that ecclesiology is also a chapter of Christology. In the following chapter I will present ecclesiology as a chapter of Pneumatology, as well. Thus, ecclesiology is ultimately a chapter of Triadology and Staniloae has indeed found a balanced relationship between ecclesiology and the theology of the Father, of the Son, and of the Holy Spirit.

What is the relationship between the Son and the Church? United with Christ, the Church has been raised within the bosom of the Trinity. To put it in more detail, according to Staniloae, the Church has been established by and united with Christ especially at the incarnation and crucifixion, and this unity is continually renewed and strengthened in the sacramental life of the Church. When he ascended into heaven with his humanity, Christ raised the Church and placed it at the right hand of the Father, brought it as a sacrifice to the Father, and filled it with the Holy Spirit. This thesis supports the larger argument of the book that the Church shares in the communion that exists within the Trinity, since the same relationships are manifested both within the Trinity and the Church.

In the following pages, I analyze the ecclesiological implications of Staniloae's Christology and soteriology, highlighting the ecumenical relevance of his understanding of (1) the Church as the Body of Christ and (2) the worshipping Church: the Church realized in the Liturgy. Thus, the reference to the Body of Christ in the title of this chapter refers to both the Church and the Eucharist, signaling that the chapter also deals with the sacramental life of the Church.

### The Church as the Body of Christ

The New Testament refers to the Church through a wealth of images, such as community of disciples, the reestablished Israel, the bride of Christ, the temple (or dwelling place) of God, and the pilgrim People of God.[1] Staniloae applied most of these New Testament images to the Church, but the one that he used most frequently and considered most adequate was that of the Church as the Body of Christ.[2] He occasionally added to this Pauline expression the term, "mystical," referring to the Church as "the mystical Body of Christ," or contending that "the Church, as mystical humanity of Christ, receives the Holy Spirit, in its capacity of Body of Christ."[3] He thus differentiated between the physical body of Christ and the Church. Before continuing this discussion, it is important to note other designations that theologians rarely (if ever) use for the Church.

In addition to the New Testament images enumerated above, Staniloae used the Old Testament image of the burning bush. He defined the Church as "the burning bush lit by the fire of Christ and guiding lamp towards the eternal Kingdom of God."[4] The Romanian expression, *rugul aprins*, is a poetical reference to the burning bush from which God spoke to Moses (Exod. 3.2-4). Between the two World Wars, this was also the name of a group of intellectuals who were interested in promoting Romanian cultural values. When they realized that Orthodoxy represents a constitutive part of Romanian identity, they sought Staniloae's presence at their gatherings.[5] Staniloae occasionally attended their meetings. Later on, the Communist regime labeled "The Burning Bush" as a "controversial" group and Staniloae's association with this group led to his incarceration for five years. Both these biblical and political meanings of the burning bush are relevant for Staniloae's theology of the Church.

---

1   Frank J. Matera, "Theologies of the Church in the New Testament," in *The Gift of the Church: A Textbook on Ecclesiology in Honor of Patrick Granfield, O.S.B.*, ed. Peter C. Phan (Collegeville, MN: Liturgical Press, 2000), 19–20.

2   Dumitru Staniloae, "Autoritatea Bisericii [The Authority of the Church]," *Studii Teologice* 16, no. 3–4 (1964): 183.

3   Staniloae, *Jesus Christ or the Restoration of Humankind*, 363.

4   Ibid., 213.

5   Radu Bordeianu, *Interview with V. Rev. Fr. Roman Braga, November 30, 2002* (Transfiguration Monastery, MI: unpublished audio material, 2002).

The first reason Staniloae used the Old Testament image of the burning bush in the definition of the Church is theological in nature. Christ is the true God who called Moses on the Mount Horeb, leading him and the Jewish people out of bondage, to the land of Canaan.[6] Christ is also the one who calls us to freedom from bondage (spiritually, as well as politically), and is the one who guides the Church to the eternal Kingdom of God, where there is freedom and peace. Moreover,

> The Church is the spiritual Kingdom . . . in which Christ the King is always present with his power. He enkindles and gives light to all the members of the Church as to a *burning bush* and as a chandelier made up of the believers who are united without confusion. The believers are enkindled and lit by the same light of the love of Christ and for Christ, as branches and candles. The burning bush that Moses saw represents the Mother of God and any saint filled with the fire of Christ's love. But the entire encompassing *burning bush* is the Church in which the fire of love unites all those who believe in Christ not only as individuals with Christ, but also among themselves. [emphases mine][7]

Without diminishing the theological aspect of Staniloae's definition of the Church, one could say that the second reason for Staniloae's use of the image of the burning bush points to the liberating presence of Christ in the Church and the liberating role of the Church in society. This was especially relevant for Romanian society, marked by communist oppression. Given these aspects and also Staniloae's association with the group, "The Burning Bush," it is not surprising that the book from which the previous passage was quoted, *Jesus Christ or the Restoration of Humankind*, was first published before the communist rule in 1943, and reprinted only in 1993, after the 1989 Revolution that marked the chute of Communism in Romania.

Another important aspect of this quote is that the burning bush represents both the Church and Virgin Mary. Staniloae thus implied that the Virgin Mary is an image for the Church. This text is the only instance that I have found in which Staniloae associated the Virgin Mary with the Church, and then only indirectly. This scarcity is rather surprising, given the potential that this imagery has for ecclesiology. The Theotokos is an image of the Church as the one who contained Christ within herself (in her womb) and who is a model of prayer. For

---

6   In this sense, see Bucur's analysis of several Orthodox hymns and their patristic background in Bucur, "The Mountain of the Lord," 136–41.
7   Staniloae, *Jesus Christ or the Restoration of Humankind*, 215–16.

this reason, in Orthodox churches she is depicted above the altar, as the fullest manifestation of the priestly function of the Church.

## The General Sense of Recapitulation

After this succinct overview of the biblical images for the Church, it is important to approach Christ's relationship with humankind and the Church. In the previous chapter, I argued that adoption has two senses: a general one, according to which all of humankind enters a filial relationship with the Father, and a special one, referring to the Church. In both cases, the incarnation made adoption possible by virtue of the unity of Christ's human nature with all human beings and, to a higher degree, with those who constitute his Body (the Church) and who partake of his Body and Blood in the Eucharist.

Because Adam's sin affected all of humankind, Christ's humanity had to encompass human nature in its entirety. His humanity was not that of an individual who possesses his or her nature primarily for him or herself. Rather, the hypostasis of the Son of God, who is equally close to all humans, assumed the human nature through which he is closer to each of us more than any other human, meaning that Christ is closer to each of us than we can be to each other. Thus, Jesus is "the central human being," or "humanity in its totality."[8]

This is, indeed, the general sense of Christ's recapitulation of all people who are now in a filial relationship with the Father and a brotherly relationship with Jesus. Hence, we have the duty to assist all our brothers and sisters in Christ, that is, (beyond the customary usage of this expression) all humans: "This self-identification of Christ with humanity, which represents the foundation of the dogma of redemption, makes us understand *literally*, not metaphorically, his words at the Final Judgment: 'just as you did it to one of the least of these who are members of my family, you did it to me' (Mt. 25.40)."[9]

To this charitable implication of the redemption of human nature in Christ's hypostasis, Staniloae added an interreligious aspect. The Church is called to live in the image of trinitarian communion, and this communion is to be lived on the level of Christian ecumenism and extended to all humankind:

> Only in Christ do we see revealed the universal unity of mankind and the design of mankind's "recapitulation" and resurrection to eternal life in God. For the Son did not become an individual human hypostasis, but

---

8    Ibid., 163–64, 272.
9    Ibid., 283.

the hypostasis of human nature in general, and so a kind of "hypostasis-head" of the whole of humanity, destined to become a theandric subject together with all human subjects and thus a subject in whom all human subjects converge, yet without the loss or confusion of their own identities.[10]

Based on the passage above, one could affirm that the Church extends to the entire world, transforming the world into the Church. The world becomes a communion of persons united—without confusion—in Christ. Hence, the mandate to realize communion internally becomes a mandate for the Church to extend this communion to the world, in order to bring salvation to the world.

Staniloae's affirmations about unity in Christ are relevant for both ecumenism and interreligious dialogue. The entire Christian family, united in one Church, needs to extend the unity of Christ to the rest of humanity, to bring the world to unity in Christ. And since the Church needs to find unity internally and then extend that unity to the rest of humankind, the mandate of ecumenism to realize unity in Christ becomes even more pressing. Moreover, by affirming the unity that extends from the humanity of Christ to all of humanity, Staniloae affirmed indirectly that interreligious dialogue already has an ontological basis in Christ. From this perspective, it is difficult to agree with the suggestion that interreligious dialogue needs to abandon inclusivism with its christocentric focus in favor of pluralism and its trinitarian perspective.[11] Staniloae offered a soteriology that relates all humankind to each and every person of the Trinity, without separating the Logos from the incarnation,[12] without separating the Son from the other two persons of the Trinity, and without abandoning the centrality of Christ for salvation.

The discussion of the relationship between the Son and all humankind will be enriched in the next chapter with several pneumatological considerations and will then continue in the chapter on natural priesthood. For the moment, it is important to return to the relationship between the Son and the Church—the Body of Christ.

---

10    Staniloae, *Theology and the Church*, 222.
11    A representative of this position is Konrad Raiser (*Ecumenism in Transition: A Paradigm Shift in the Ecumenical Movement?*, trans. Tony Coates [Geneva: WCC, 1991], especially 79–86.). See also a critical appraisal of Raiser's position in Geoffrey Wainwright, "Review of *Ecumenism in Transition* by Konrad Raiser," *Mid-Stream* 31, no. 2 (1992): 169–73.
12    See the discussion of Dupuis's proposition of *logos asarkos* shortly.

*Special Sense of Recapitulation*

Throughout his writings, Staniloae emphasized different aspects of the theology of the Church as the Body of Christ, such as the complementariness of the gifts of all the members who constitute the Body; the consequences of the affirmation that the Church is raised within the Trinity; the theanthropic character of the Church; and the Church as an extension of the Incarnation.

Staniloae affirmed that catholicity is understood today as communion, which implies complementariness. The unity of the Church is realized and maintained by the convergence, communion, and *complementarity of its members*, not through their confusion into a uniform unity. Consequently, the Church is a spiritual Body, a fullness that has everything it needs, and this fullness is present in each of its members, acts, and parts. This explains the biblical image of the Church as the Body of Christ and Paul's definition of the Church as Christ's "Body, the fullness of him who fills all in all" (Eph. 1.23).[13]

The complementarity of the members who form the Body of Christ implies that the faithful who make up the Church maintain their personal character, an idea that resurfaces constantly throughout Staniloae's writings.[14] This is primarily because the model and force of union in the Church is the community of the Trinity in which the persons are not lost in an impersonal nature. This communion became accessible to the Church when, united with Christ, *the Church was raised within the Trinity*, participating in God's communitarian life:

> Through the reality of the person of Christ, come down to the plane accessible to human beings and bringing the pressure of his self-evidence to bear upon us, the Trinity itself exerts its influence or reveals itself completely. Through himself, Christ makes visible the Father and the Spirit and, together with them, achieves the task of *raising humanity up to an*

---

13  Staniloae, *Dogmatics 2*, 186–87.
14  Similarly, Florovsky warned of the danger of referring to the Church as the Body of Christ without also specifying that each personality is maintained in the Church: "The idea of an organism when used of the Church has its own limitations. On the one hand, the Church is composed of human personalities, which never can be regarded merely as elements or cells of the whole, because each is in direct and immediate union with Christ and His Father—the personal is not to be sacrificed or dissolved in the corporate, Christian 'togetherness' must not degenerate into impersonalism. The idea of the organism must be supplemented by the idea of a symphony of personalities, in which the mystery of the Holy Trinity is reflected (cf. Jn 17.21, 23), and this is the core of the conception of 'catholicity' (sobornost)." Florovsky, "The Church: Her Nature and Task," 67–68.

*eternal communion with the Holy Trinity*, itself the *structure of perfect communion*. [emphases mine][15]

As shown previously, human communion does not merely mirror intratrinitarian communion. Rather, they are connected by a continuum of grace and, even more, by Christ. All humankind is united with the humanity of Christ and raised in the bosom of the Trinity, particularly at the Ascension, when our nature sat at the right hand of the Father.[16] This means that humans, who were created to share in the communion of the trinitarian persons but lost this capacity with the fall, are now restored to a life of communion with one another and with God. Indeed, this is characteristic of true humanity, lived to the fullest in Christ who was filled with the Spirit and in a loving relationship with the Father, both in his humanity and as the Son of God. In Staniloae's words,

> if salvation does not look for anything other than to raise the human being to likeness with the Son of God, making it also a child, and this is done through the sending of divine love, that is of the Spirit of adoption in the human being, then the divine model that stays at the foundation of creation and salvation, the divine model of the human being, or the "heavenly Human," would not stay in anything other than in the character of perfect subject of love in communion. And this is God because he is a Trinity of Persons. The foundation and model of creation and salvation would thus be God's mode of being in the Holy Trinity.[17]

Thus, Staniloae's affirmation that the Church as the Body of Christ is raised in the Trinity implies that the Church becomes an instrument of revelation for the Trinity and a sacrament through which intratrinitarian communion extends into the world. In the Church we share to the greatest extent in the fullness of Christ's humanity, so the Church presents true humanity as communitarian, or as living in a union of love. This communion comes from above: the Church

---

15   Staniloae, *The Experience of God 1*, 67.

16   Along these lines, Silviu Rogobete wrote: "In the reality of the participation of the divine 'subjects' lies the perfect model for our own participation. However, far from being just a simple model, through the consubstantial identification of Christ, one of the divine 'I's,' with our own nature, this communional participation became open for each one of us." Silviu Eugen Rogobete, "Mystical Existentialism or Communitarian Participation?: Vladimir Lossky and Dumitru Staniloae," in *Dumitru Staniloae: Tradition and Modernity in Theology*, ed. Lucian Turcescu (Iasi, Romania; Palm Beach, FL: Center for Romanian Studies, 2002), 205.

17   Staniloae, *Jesus Christ or the Restoration of Humankind*, 68, 76.

participates by grace in the same communion that the persons of the Trinity share by virtue of their common nature.

The *theanthropic character of the Church* is closely related to Christ's theanthropy (traditionally known as theandry) described above.[18] Staniloae affirmed that both the divine and human natures have been manifested in Christ in a way in which his divinity was shown through the humble image of his humanity. In support, he quoted Maximus the Confessor's affirmation that Christ "was suffering in a divine way, because he was suffering of his own will since he was not a simple man, and he performed miracles in a human way, because he performed them through his body, since he was not God fully apparent. His sufferings are miraculous . . . and his miracles are suffered. [PG 91, 105B]"[19] Staniloae wrote about the theanthropic character of the Church, itself an extension of the theanthropic union of Christ's two natures:

> The subject of the Church is divine-human; the divine will always has the initiative, and the wills of the people are, under its influence, a common will that follows the divine will. In fact, the two kinds of will are distinct only ontologically, but functionally they are one.... Thus, the center of the Church, its leader, the one who has the initiative, is Jesus Christ, whose divine-human will extends as central will of the Church in all the eras and in each one of its members.[20]

Thus, Staniloae applied the dogma of Chalcedon—referring to the union of the divine and human natures in Christ—to the Church, adding a Maximian perspective, in reference to Christ's two wills and their symphonic manifestation, in line with Maximus's rejection of monothelism and monoergism. He applied the Chalcedonian dogma also when he affirmed that Christ and the Church are united without confusion and without change. There is a perichoresis between them, similar to the relationship between Christ's humanity and his divinity. Just as Christ's humanity and divinity are not confused when united in his person,

---

18  While this term suggesting the divine-human reality of Christ is widely used in patristic writings, it would be more correct to use theanthropy, since *anthropos* means human being inclusive of man and woman, while *andros* means exclusively man.

19  Along the same lines, Gregory the Theologian affirmed that Christ "was not doing the divine things in a divine way, but through his body . . . united with him according to his hypostasis.... Nor did he do the human things in a human way, but he was doing them according to his will, unlimited in power." Both Fathers quoted in Staniloae, *Jesus Christ or the Restoration of Humankind*, 139–41.

20  Ibid., 381.

so the faithful are united with the person, will, and operation of Christ, while maintaining their personality. Each person moves around and in the other (etymologically, the meaning of perichoresis), becoming interior to the other. This perichoresis both safeguards their existence and develops it. And yet, there is a difference between Christ's theanthropy and that of the Church: in Christ, it refers only to the relationship between his two natures, while in the Church it refers, in addition to its divine-human constitution, to the personal relationships between the members of the Church and Christ.[21]

Other Orthodox and Catholic theologians applied the dogma of Chalcedon to ecclesiology, although from different perspectives. Paul Evdokimov, for example, contended that "we should avoid any 'ecclesiological monophysitism,' according to which the invisible is comprised of the elected ones, while the visible by the sinners. We should rather apply christological theandry."[22] From Lossky's point of view, the application of christological theanthropy to the Church is also a reaction to ecclesiological monophysitism and nestorianism:

> Ecclesiological monophysites seek only to preserve the Truth, and in the process have no hesitation in stifling church economy, that multifaceted and ever varied activity of the Church by which, in accordance with the needs of a given time or place, she nourishes the world. By contrast, ecclesiological Nestorians are prepared, for economy's sake, to lose sight of the immutable fullness of the truth abiding in the Church: instead of enriching the world by means of it, they look for the Church's nourishment to the outside world, to human creativity.[23]

When referring to ecclesiological monophysites, Lossky had in mind that fraction of Orthodoxy that still observes the Julian (old) calendar and rebaptizes converts to Orthodoxy, not recognizing the validity of Baptisms administered by other Christian denominations. Ecclesiological Nestorians are the chiliastic movements that strive to attain the kingdom of God and to fight for social justice in a worldly manner, without an emphasized religious character, as well as the ethnophyletists who declare the nation as the basis of the local Church. In

---

21   Staniloae, "The Authority of the Church," 187. Staniloae developed some of these ideas starting from the theology of Karmiris. Later on, however, Staniloae hesitated to use Karmiris's expression, "the theandric nature of the Church," so as not to imply that divinity and humanity are united in a monophysite sense, preferring "the theandric constitution of the Church" instead. Staniloae, *Dogmatics* 2, 137.

22   Evdokimov, *L'Orthodoxie*, 125.

23   Vladimir Lossky, "Ecclesiology: Some Dangers and Temptations," *Sobornost*, no. 4 (1982): 22.

response, Lossky proposed a theanthropic approach to the life of the Church, in which both the human and divine elements should coexist harmoniously.

Nikos Nissiotios, too, applied the Chalcedonian dogma to ecclesiology. He affirmed that any discussion of the sinfulness of the Church accentuates exclusively the sinful-human aspect of the Church, to the detriment of its holy-divine aspect. This, Nissiotis calls "monophysitic ecclesiology," in which the human absorbs the divine. Yves Congar employed the expression "ecclesial monophysitism or christomonism" in the opposite sense, i.e., the overemphasis on the divine element of the Church, with the exclusion of its human aspect.[24]

The authors mentioned above argue for a balanced approach to the divine-human character of the Church, which manifests the harmonious union of the two natures in Christ. When basing ecclesiology upon Christology, they all assume that, as Georges Florovsky wrote, the Church is *the extension of the Incarnation*, particularly through the sacraments:

> The Eucharist is Christ himself, acting still as the High Priest of the New Covenant. He abides sacramentally in the Church, which is his body.... The Church is the extension and the "fullness" of the holy Incarnation or rather of the Incarnate life of the Son.... The Incarnation is being completed in the Church and in a sense the Church is Christ himself in his all-embracing plenitude (cf. 1 Cor. 12.12).[25]

Staniloae was in full agreement with Florovsky. He, too, affirmed that the ascended Jesus is present in the Church through the sacraments, so the church represents "the extension of the new reality of Jesus Christ."[26] Staniloae added that the Church is the extended Body of Christ[27] or an "extension of the mystery of Christ" not in the sense of replacement of Christ, but as an actualization of the potential for perfected union between God and humankind, which the incarnation has initiated.[28] In other words, the hypostatic union experienced by Christ is extended to the Church, where we, too, can experience union with God. This is a union of grace, not of nature, as Christ's humanity was united with his

---

24  Yves Cogar, in Bradford Hinze, "Ecclesial Repentance and the Demands of Dialogue," *Theological Studies* 61, no. 2, June (2000): 226.

25  Georges Florovsky, "The Historical Problem of a Definition of the Church," in *Ecumenism II: A Historical Approach, Collected Works* 14 (Belmont, MA: Nordland Pub. Co., 1989), 29.

26  Staniloae, *Jesus Christ or the Restoration of Humankind*, 392–93. See also Staniloae, "Ecclesiological Synthesis," 267–68.

27  Staniloae, *Dogmatics* 2, 148.

28  Ibid., vol. 3, 13.

divinity. And just as the Spirit dwelt fully in the humanity of Christ, so is the divine grace manifested in the Church, particularly through the sacraments.[29]

And yet, the previous affirmation of the theanthropic character of the Church and this imagery of the Church as an extension of the incarnation need to be complemented with that of the union between husband and' wife. On the one hand, this latter image implies the union between Christ and the Church, as do the previous two categories. But Christ's presence in the Church does not result in the perfection of the Church as fully divine institution. This is why, on the other hand, this marital image shows that the Church yearns for Christ, calling him in its prayers, just like the bride in the Song of Songs. "The Church is pilgrim and unceasingly praying, an uninterrupted epiclesis."[30] In a sense, the Church is praying for what it already has: Christ. But Christ continues to stand above the Church. As Berger points out, this union between Christ and the Church needs to be further qualified as a limitation of the Church's authority. "The Church's teaching, for example, cannot contradict Christ' teaching. When the Church teaches, it participates in the teaching of Christ. But the Church is also itself *taught* by Christ, who '... advises, commands and comforts, as one who is higher than her.'[31]"[32] This application of marital imagery to the Church is based on an archaic understanding of the dynamics within marriage. It certainly sounds very patriarchal. And yet, when applied to the Church, it means that the Church is not an exclusively divine, irreformable institution, as the image of the Body of Christ might suggest. Moreover, this imagery points to the fact that the Church is under Christ's authority, even as it truly represents the extension of Christ.

In this section I have presented different biblical images that Staniloae used to describe the Church and its relationship with the Son. In a general sense, Christ has assumed human nature in order to reestablish the communion between God and all of humankind, for which we were created. In a special sense, however,

---

29  Staniloae, "Ecclesiological Synthesis," 267.
30  Staniloae, "The Authority of the Church," 188.
31  Ibid., 185.
32  Calinic (Kevin M.) Berger, "Does the Eucharist Make the Church? An Ecclesiological Comparison of Staniloae and Zizioulas," *St Vladimir's Theological Quarterly* 51, no. 1 (2007): 41. Similarly, Ratzinger, von Balthasar, and Susan Wood consider that the representation of the Church as Virgin Mary and bride imply that the Church is distinct but not separate from Christ, it is a "who," not only a "what," as the image of the Body of Christ would suggest. See Francesca Aran Murphy, "De Lubac, Ratzinger and von Balthasar: A Communal Adventure in Ecclesiology," in *Ecumenism Today: The Universal Church in the 21st Century*, ed. Francesca Aran Murphy and Christopher Asprey (Burlington, VT: Ashgate, 2008), 55–56.

recapitulation implies a most intimate degree of communion between God and the members of the Church, the Body of Christ, which has multiple implications, such as the complementariness of the members who, united, form the Church; the Church is raised within the Trinity, thus realizing the maximum degree of communion between God and humankind; the Church is a theanthropic reality, based on Christ's theanthropy; and the union between Christ and the Church is so intimate, that the Church—particularly through its sacraments—represents the extension of the incarnation.

All these considerations support the first part of the thesis of this chapter, that the Church is united with Christ, being raised in the Trinity. These elements will prove very valuable in the larger argument of the book, that the Church is filled with the Trinity and the implication that the Church is communion, according to the structure of the Trinity. For now, however, it is important to delve deeper into the last of these considerations, namely Christ's manifestation through the liturgical life of the Church.

### *The Worshipping Church: The Church Realized in the Liturgy*

Kallistos Ware recognizes the importance of the Church's worship in Staniloae's theology: "Underlining as he does the integral connection between dogma and prayer, he certainly regards all dogmatic theology as liturgical and mystical."[33] In fact, Staniloae dedicated an entire book to the explanation of the Divine Liturgy,[34] namely *Spirituality and Communion in the Orthodox Liturgy*. This book is part of a trilogy that Staniloae wrote, together with his *Orthodox Dogmatic Theology* and *Orthodox Spirituality*. The Liturgy is certainly one of the major sources of his theology.

In this section, I analyze the relationship between the liturgical life of the Church and Staniloae's ecclesiology. As I hope to show, the worshipping Church

---

33 Ware, "Foreword," xviii. Looking at the larger context from which this passage is extracted, Ware actually criticized Staniloae for making little explicit reference to liturgical books in the first volume of *The Experience of God*. Ware's comment refers only to this book and, in all fairness to Staniloae, he does make several references to the Liturgy such as those on pages 251 or 269, although, granted, less than characteristic of his overall work.

34 The exact translation of the Romanian *Sfânta Liturghie* that Staniloae generally used would read "The Holy Liturgy," but I translate it as "The Divine Liturgy," since this is both more commonly used in English and closer to the Greek, *I Theia Leitourgia*. Moreover, Romanians also refer to the Liturgy as "The Holy and Divine Liturgy," so the expression, "The Divine Liturgy" is not foreign to Romanian Orthodoxy and to Staniloae.

is raised within the Trinity, united with Christ in the Holy Spirit, and brought as sacrifice to the Father. I begin by defining the Liturgy in a general sense, to include all aspects of Christian life. I continue more specifically with an analysis of Staniloae's sacramental theology, particularly the Eucharist, and their constitutive role for the Church, offering a preliminary answer to the question, "Does the Eucharist make the Church?" I end with the relationship between the Trinity and the Liturgy, emphasizing the Eucharist as the Kingdom of the Trinity; this Kingdom is simultaneously present in the Liturgy and an eschatological reality, thus rendering *theosis* as both liturgical (communitarian) and never-ending.

When Staniloae referred to the presence of Christ in the Liturgy, he had in mind primarily the Divine Liturgy, or the Eucharistic service, but not exclusively. He also used the term liturgy in its broad sense. He affirmed that Christ is present in the worship of the Church in several different ways:

> a) in the Eucharistic sacrifice; b) in the other Sacraments; c) in sacramentals, in other Church services (Lauds), in the prayers and blessings of the priest; d) in the word of the Holy Scripture as read by the priest in the church; e) in the proclamation of the priest; f) in the prayers said and sung by the faithful in the church, in the dialogue between them and the priest in worship; g) in the readings of the faithful from Holy Scripture outside the church sanctuary, in their prayers and readings of other books of Orthodox teaching and spirituality; h) in the faithful conversations of the believers about God and in their good and pure deeds coming out of faith. Thus, the whole life of the faithful is a worship given to God, or a liturgy in the broad sense of the word.[35]

Staniloae's assertion that Christ is present in the worship of the Church in different ways and to different degrees, thus making the entire Christian life a form of worship, should sound familiar to Catholic ears. As a footnote to the text quoted above, he referred to the Second Vatican Council, *Constitutio Liturgica* art. 7, which enumerates the degrees of Christ's presence in worship: liturgical presence, presence in the sacraments, in word and Holy Scripture as read in the Church, and in the community that prays and sings.[36] Thus, all aspects of Christian life are a liturgy, manifesting Christ in the world. More fully, Christ is present in the sacraments.

---

35   Staniloae, *Spirituality and Communion*, 81–82.
36   Ibid., 82.

*Christ in the Sacraments*

One could say that, for Staniloae, the sacraments make the Church and the Church makes the sacraments:

> On the one hand, the Church is constituted and maintained through the sacraments and through the other means to obtain and maintain the presence of Christ. On the other hand, all these means have the Church as a premise. Christ comes in the Church . . . through all its forms of prayer, proclamation, and accomplishing his will. And yet he is in the Church through his Holy Spirit, making the prayers, proclamation, and the good and pure deeds of the faithful into means of his perpetually renewed coming.[37]

Staniloae's view of the organic relationship among all aspects of Church life is noteworthy. Unlike scholastic theology, he does not separate clearly between the sacraments and the other prayers, the proclamation, or the good deeds of the Church. It would not be a stretch to refer to the sacramentality of all these means of obtaining and manifesting grace. Christ is already present in them and sustains the Church in its celebration of these liturgical acts. At the same time, the purpose of the Church is to make Christ ever more present among his people, through his Holy Spirit in all aspects of its life, but primarily in the sacraments. There is a mutual relationship between the Church and the sacraments: the Church is constituted and continues to exist through the sacraments, while the sacraments can only take place in the Church.

For Staniloae, sacraments are at the core of the reality of the Church. One is a member of the Church only by partaking of the grace imparted in the sacraments. Following up on his definition of the Church as burning bush, Staniloae affirmed that all the members of the Church

> are branches of the same bush, branches lit by the love of the same Christ, or of his Spirit, received through sacraments. Christ himself said that he will be in those who will be baptized in the name of the Holy Trinity, being born again from his Holy Spirit (Mt. 28.19; Jn 3.5), and are nourished with his Body and Blood in the Holy Eucharist (Mt. 26.26-27), thus being capable to keep the teaching that Christ gave to his Apostles. The successors of the Apostles—who have received the same Spirit of teaching through the successive ordinations from the Apostles and their successors—will proclaim this teaching until the end of the ages.[38]

---

37  Ibid.
38  Staniloae, *Jesus Christ or the Restoration of Humankind*, 215.

The grace imparted through the sacraments marks the beginning of the spiritual journey of the faithful (Baptism), assists them and empowers them to continue this journey (Eucharist, Ordination, and the other sacraments), and leads them to the highest stages of their spiritual ascent (*theosis*). A few remarks are necessary about Baptism, while other sacraments will be addressed later on.

## Baptism

I prefer to approach Baptism through a relational, communitarian prism. That is because the fall was primarily an interruption or impoverishing of the paradisiacal communion between God and humankind. This communion was objectively reestablished in Christ through the hypostatic union of the divine and human natures. We appropriate subjectively this communion through Baptism, when we die with Christ and resurrect with Christ, when we are clothed with Christ (cf. Rom. 6.3-5, Gal. 3.27), meaning that we unite ourselves with the divine-human Christ, as members of his Body. In the Church we become children of the Father and receive the Spirit who rested in the Son, thus living in communion with God. If the original (or ancestral) sin is indeed an impoverishment of communion, then that sin is undone in Baptism as it provides entry into the Church.

This communitarian understanding of Baptism has the advantage of explaining infant Baptism—a reality that was not emphasized enough in early patristic literature, when most people were baptized as adults. It was easier then to explain Baptism as forgiveness of sins, meaning primarily personal sins. The contemporary Orthodox service of Baptism is reflective of this perspective, making it slightly less relevant in the case of infant Baptism, which is the norm, rather than the exception today. (A separate study should address the abundance of references to the devil acting in the catechumens' lives prior to Baptism and the meaning of exorcisms in the case of infant Baptisms.)

The East never spoke of Baptism as forgiveness of original sin in the sense of guilt and deserving eternal punishment. Emphasis on forgiveness of personal sins is irrelevant in the case of infant Baptism. Describing Baptism as a change in our moral character in the case of infants is neither verifiable nor—as the father of three wonderful children I am inclined to say—realistic. In the case of adults, the moral change most likely takes place before Baptism. This change is, of course, fulfilled by the grace of Baptism and needs to be continually renewed by a constant commitment to a life in Christ.

Thus, most references to forgiveness of sins in the service of Baptism should be read from the perspective of reestablishing communion with God. Baptism is primarily union with Christ in his Body—the Church, which is obviously the case when infants also receive Chrismation (Confirmation in Western parlance) and their first Communion. Infants are full members of the Church even from a sacramental perspective. Baptism is primarily churching or incorporation into Christ, receiving of the Spirit, placing into a filial relationship with the Father, or reentering in prelapsarian communion with God. This means undoing the ancestral sin of Adam and Eve, which resulted in the interruption of our communion with God. Baptism and the other sacraments make one a member of the Church and renew their belonging to the Body of Christ. Indeed, the sacraments make the Church, while the Church makes the sacraments.

## The Eucharist Makes the Church[39]

The Eucharist occupies a primary place among the sacraments that are constitutive for the Church. In this sense, Staniloae wrote that "the Church takes shape as a body formed from believers to whom Christ gives himself fully in the Eucharist. Then they, through the power Christ gives of himself, give themselves to one another in a movement of continual convergence and unification."[40] Staniloae was emphatic in his affirmation that the Church is realized in the Eucharist as a liturgical sacrifice, which unites the faithful among themselves and with Christ.

Given that the Church is the eucharistic union of the faithful among themselves and with Christ, the practice of rare communion, widespread in the East, is simply inexplicable. Schmemann reacted most vehemently against this situation.[41] His writings had a significant impact upon Orthodoxy in the West, where most faithful currently practice frequent communion. Eastern Europe, however, is only slowly receiving Schmemann's work. Staniloae, too, affirmed the need to receive Communion "not too rarely," although his tone was rather reserved.[42] Elsewhere, Staniloae drew closer to Schmemann, when he lamented the absence of the faithful from Communion, thus supporting the practice to receive the Eucharist every time it is offered.[43]

The pioneer of this liturgical renewal within Orthodoxy was Nicholas Afanassieff. He pointed out that ever since the beginning, receiving the Eucharist manifested one's belonging to the Church. Those who refused to take communion

---

39 This phrase was consecrated by Henri de Lubac and John Zizioulas; see Paul McPartlan, *The Eucharist Makes the Church: Henri de Lubac and John Zizioulas in Dialogue* (Edinburgh: T&T Clark, 1993).

40 Staniloae, "Creation as Gift and the Sacraments," 18. Miller's translation.

41 See for example Alexander Schmemann, *The Eucharist: Sacrament of the Kingdom* (Crestwood, NY: St Vladimir's Seminary Press, 1988).

42 Staniloae, *Spirituality and Communion*, 413.

43 Dumitru Staniloae, "Iisus Hristos, Arhiereu in veac [Jesus Christ, Eternal High Priest]," *Ortodoxia* 31, no. 2 (1979): 228.

were threatened with excommunication. Later on, however, Christians started to receive Communion less and less often, out of a wrongly understood humility. They implied that the person is not worthy to receive Communion, so, in order to become worthy, they would need to go through a very strict regime of preparation. This understanding, however, is in contradiction with the unanimously affirmed idea that we are never worthy to receive Communion, but that Christ still chooses to offer himself to us, the unworthy, just as he offered himself to Judas.[44] This situation determined twelfth-century canonists to take a stance against these rules, against this misunderstood humility.[45] And yet, I would add, the less-than-conducive, strict rules of preparation before Communion continued to be enforced. They were never imposed upon the clergy who had the obligation to commune every time they liturgized. This double standard created a divide between the clergy and the people. On a regular basis, only the clergy had access to the full manifestation of the Church in the Eucharist, while the people participated fully only several times a year.

In light of this regrettable eucharistic decline, the shift that occurred primarily in Orthodoxy in the West is salutary. One can only hope that this renewal will reverberate into Orthodoxy in the East, and thus all Orthodox will reaffirm (theoretically and practically) that one's belonging to the Church is conditioned by receiving the Eucharist. I come back to this issue in Chapter 8, where I analyze Afanassieff's eucharistic ecclesiology in light of Zizioulas and Staniloae's comments. I will show

---

44    It is not the place here to address this issue extensively, but some fragments from the prayers before Communion are welcome: "How shall I, who am unworthy, enter into the splendor of Your saints? If I dare to enter into the bridal chamber, my clothing will accuse me, since it is not a wedding garment.... Receive me today, Son of God, as a partaker of Your mystical Supper. I will not reveal Your mystery to Your adversaries. Nor will I give You a kiss as did Judas. But as the thief I confess to You: Lord, remember me in Your kingdom." Saint John Chrysostom, *The Divine Liturgy*, trans. Members of the Faculty of Hellenic College/Holy Cross Greek Orthodox School of Theology, Third ed. (Brookline, MA: Holy Cross Press, 1985), 30. Elsewhere, Chrysostom makes the argument that, on the one hand, none is worthy to commune. On the other hand, however, by being among the participants at the entire Liturgy (as opposed to being dismissed with the penitents and catechumens), Christians are worthy to receive the Eucharist. Saint John Chrysostom, "Third Sermon on Ephesians 1:15-20," in *Nicene and Post-Nicene Fathers, Series 1*, ed. Philip Schaff (Grand Rapids, MI: Eerdmans, 1988), 63–65.

45    Afanassieff, *The Church of the Holy Spirit*, 50–56. For more on the significance of Afanassieff's eucharistic renewal, see Radu Bordeianu, "Nicholas Afanasiev, *The Church of the Holy Spirit*. Translated by Vitaly Permiakov, edited with an Introduction by Michael Plekon, foreword by Rowan Williams (South Bend, IN: Notre Dame University Press, 2007). Pp. xx + 327 [Review Essay]. " St Vladimir's Theological Quarterly 54, no. 2 (2010): 245–47.

that the affirmation "the Eucharist makes the Church" needs to be qualified with the constitutive role of the other sacraments (which I discussed above), the role of the bishop, and the importance of communion of teachings as factors of unity. Before moving on to the next subject, several practical considerations are necessary here. Having lived in communist Romania and having traveled recently to India, I am inclined to question the absoluteness of claims such as "the sacraments make the Church" or "the Eucharist makes the Church."

Staniloae described the eucharistic nature of the Church despite the forced non-eucharistic context in which he lived. During his 5 years of incarceration, one must assume that he did not participate in many, if any Liturgies (prisoners sometimes managed to get the necessary wine and bread for the eucharistic service and there, in prison, live the fullness of the Church gathered in the Eucharist). Romanians in particular and people living under Communism in general, attended church with great risk, and many were deprived of the eucharistic aspect of their Church membership. And yet, for Staniloae, the Church remains fundamentally eucharistic. What is the meaning of his claim? That even when the faithful commune very rarely or attend the Liturgy irregularly, they still have the consciousness that the fullness of the Church is eucharistic and a non-Eucharistic life represents a diminishment of that fullness? Or does it mean that, when deprived of the Eucharist because of external factors such as persecution, the fullness of the Church is accomplished other than directly in the Liturgy? That second option would put in a different light the situation in places such as India, where there is an anti-conversion law. There, missionaries cannot baptize those who embrace the faith in Jesus, and cannot offer Communion. The consequences of overt conversions would be devastating for future missionaries or for the converts who would be ostracized by their families, as is the custom in traditional Indian society. And yet, missionaries there are content to change someone's heart and are assured that this is the will of Christ for his Church, and theologians should ponder this thought.

## The Trinity in the Liturgy

Staniloae affirmed that, even though the Divine Liturgy is christological because it presents mysteriously the saving work of Christ and in it we are united with Christ through the Eucharist, it is also trinitarian, since through the Liturgy we are led by Christ into the Kingdom of the Holy Trinity.[46] That is because Christ is the Son incarnate, one of the Trinity, whose work is always united with that of the Father and of the Spirit.

---

46   Staniloae, *Spirituality and Communion*, 177.

> The Holy Trinity is present throughout the entire Liturgy, as supreme structure and source of love, which represents the foundation of the Incarnation of the Son of God, of his sacrifice and resurrection for our reconciliation with the Father, for our salvation, adoption, and resurrection. When Christ is talked about, when his saving acts are re-actualized, he is seen as one of the Trinity. All that he has done before and is actualized in the Liturgy has its foundation and explanation in the Holy Trinity, in the fact that he is one of the loving Trinity.[47]

Besides the Son being one of the Trinity, working inseparably with the Father and the Spirit, Staniloae emphasized the role of each of the three persons in the Liturgy. He affirmed that, similar to the incarnation from the Virgin Mary and the Spirit, the work of Christ in the Liturgy is not separated from that of the Holy Spirit, even though the bread and the wine become Christ's Body and Blood. It is actually the Father who initiates this consecration, but the Father accomplishes it through the Holy Spirit.[48] However—Staniloae added in a slightly polemical and also critical tone—Western Churches almost see Christ alone at work in the Liturgy: the Protestants in the proclamation of the word and the Catholics in the act of transubstantiation through the simple repetition of the words of institution.[49]

A very important word that Staniloae used here is "almost": Protestants and Catholics see Christ "almost" without the Spirit at work in the Liturgy. He noted the diminished insistence of Western theologies on the theology of the Holy Spirit, either because of excessive emphasis on the homiletic aspect of the Liturgy, or because of the exclusion of the epiclesis from some variants of Roman Catholic Liturgies. Concerning the latter, as I show momentarily, Kasper affirmed the epiclectic character of the entire Liturgy, and thus the work of the Spirit in the eucharistic worship of the Church. And yet, an explicit *epiclesis* in the Orthodox understanding of the term is still missing in Catholic liturgies, despite the relatively recent (four decades ago) revision of the Eucharistic Prayer I and the addition of the other three Eucharistic prayers, the latter being more explicitly pneumatological. Could these revisions have gone further to satisfy the Catholics and non-Catholics who wanted a more prominent role of the Spirit? Madathummuriyil intimates that such endeavor is limited first by the understanding of the priest reciting the words of institution as the moment of transubstantiation, which does not confer a prominent role to the *epiclesis*. Second, the Catholic position that, at the moment of consecration, the priest

---

47   Ibid., 257.
48   For an excellent Orthodox account in this sense, see Kallistos Ware, *The Holy Spirit in the Liturgy of St John Chrysostom, Holy Spirit Lecture and Colloquium 3* (Pittsburgh, PA: Duquesne University Press, 2007).
49   Staniloae, *Spirituality and Communion*, 103.

acts exclusively *in persona Christi*, does not leave enough room for a communal, pneumatological understanding of the Eucharist.[50] If this is the case, Staniloae's remarks about the role of the Spirit in the liturgical sacrifice of Christ to the Father shift the discussion of the consecration toward pneumatological or, indeed, trinitarian grounds. Furthermore, the considerations in the last chapter about the priest acting both *in persona Christi* and *in persona ecclesiae* will prove valuable not only toward a recovery of the communitarian aspect of the Liturgy, but also of its pneumatological and ultimately trinitarian character.

Back to Staniloae's reference to Western liturgies. Without taking away from the essence of his criticism, his reference to Protestantism is rather general and does not apply to Pentecostal churches, to give just one example. Nor is it fully reflective of Catholic theology, represented here by Walter Kasper, whom Staniloae quoted at times. In fact, the two theologians are very similar in their understanding of the trinitarian character of the Liturgy. According to Kasper, the two movements "from above" and "from below" meet in the event of the Eucharist as *epiclesis*, where the self-offering of God takes the form of the offering of the human self to God. The same Spirit who makes Christ present in the Eucharist is also the one who prays in the faithful gathered for in the Liturgy. In other words, Christ is present in the Eucharistic community through the Spirit, and the Eucharistic community is in communion with Christ through the same Spirit, being filled with the Spirit.[51] In the Liturgy, as in the economy of salvation, "our way in the Holy Spirit through Christ to the Father corresponds therefore to the movement from the Father through Christ in the Holy Spirit to us."[52]

How is Staniloae similar to Kasper? Staniloae wrote about the presence and action of the Trinity in the Liturgy: in the Eucharist, Christ offers himself as a sacrifice to the Father. At the same time, Christ offers himself to the faithful who, united with Christ in the Eucharist, offer themselves as a sacrifice both to the Father and to each other. This is possible because of the presence of the Holy Spirit in the Eucharist and the irradiation of the Holy Spirit from it.[53] United with one another in Christ through the Spirit and as sacrifices to the Father, the members of the Church are united "with the Holy Trinity as well, strengthening their status of together-inheritors with Christ of the Kingdom of the Father, having the Holy Spirit rest upon them."[54] Thus, both Kasper and Staniloae write about the ascent of the faithful to the Father, in Christ, through the Spirit, and

---

50 Sebastian Madathummuriyil, *Sacrament as Gift: A Pneumatological and Phenomenological Approach* (Leuven: Peeters, 2011): 281-290. See also Kevin W. Irwin, *Models of the Eucharist* (Mahwah, NJ: Paulist Press, 2005), 263–90.

51 Kasper in Badcock, *Light of Truth & Fire of Love*, 164.

52 Walter Kasper, *Jesus the Christ*, trans. V. Green (New York: Paulist Press, 1976), 171.

53 Staniloae, *Spirituality and Communion*, 106.

54 Ibid., 6.

the descent of the Spirit upon the Body of Christ, in the context of the Liturgy. Despite Staniloae's warranted criticism of the insufficient place of the Spirit in Catholic Liturgies, Kasper's theology represents a felicitous counter-balance.

Continuing in the same trinitarian tone, Staniloae wrote about the transformation of the faithful into the likeness of Christ[55] and their incorporation into the Body and Blood of Christ. In the prayer of the epiclesis, the Father is asked: "Send down your Holy Spirit upon us and upon these gifts here presented and make this bread the precious Body of Your Christ."[56] Since the Father sends the Spirit upon both the gifts and the community, Staniloae contended that we are incorporated in the Body and Blood of Christ, the liturgical sacrifice. We are in this state of sacrifice because of our union with the sacrificed Christ. In this union, the Son imprints upon the community both his image and his feelings toward the Father. At the same time, the Father looks favorably both upon the Son who is sacrificed, and upon the community that brings the sacrifice and also brings itself as a sacrifice in Christ.[57]

Thus, while being christological, the Liturgy is essentially trinitarian: through the descent of the Spirit, we are united with the eucharistic sacrifice of Christ and brought as sacrifice to the Father.


## The Eucharist as Kingdom of the Trinity

In the Liturgy, the Church finds itself in the bosom of the Trinity, experiencing here and now the Kingdom of the Trinity. It is a Kingdom of communion, unity, love, and sacrifice. As foretaste and instrument of the Kingdom, the Church is the dwelling place of the Trinity, or the temple of the Trinity. Staniloae considered that in the Church

> we build ourselves as a dwelling place for the Holy Trinity: "In him the
> whole structure is joined together and grows into a holy temple in the

---

55  To these considerations, Staniloae also added the idea that the faithful, who are united with Christ in the sacraments, are made into the likeness of the sacrificed Christ: "The presence of Christ dwells more durably in those who receive the sacraments, or even forever through some of the sacraments.... [Through the prayer of the priest, which becomes the prayer of the whole Church, the faithful] express their desire to offer or sacrifice themselves totally to God [i.e., the Father], and through the descent of the Holy Spirit, the sacrifice is received and sanctified, because the Spirit who descends is the Spirit of the sacrificed Christ, who wants to make us—if we agree—after his likeness." Ibid., 94–95.

56  John Chrysostom, *The Divine Liturgy*, 22.

57  Staniloae, *Spirituality and Communion*, 296–97.

Lord; in whom you also are built together [in the Spirit[58]] into a dwelling place for God" (Eph. 2.21-22). This is the Kingdom of the Holy Trinity: a divine intimate dwelling place that includes all of us. The Liturgy takes us deeper into it through the loving sacrifice of Christ, [a dwelling place that] gives birth to love and sacrifice within us.[59]

Staniloae's considerations about the Church as a temple or a dwelling place of the Trinity imply that "in the Divine Liturgy, the Holy Trinity is most descended to the believers."[60] They complement the previous assertion about the ascent of the Church into communion with the Trinity, or the raising of the Church in the bosom of the Trinity. Staniloae took the ascent-descent motif further, to imply that the Church gathered in the Liturgy "is the anticipated Kingdom of the Holy Trinity. And the place in which this foretasted Kingdom of the Holy Trinity is strengthened is the Divine Liturgy. It is the fountain that waters the life of communion of the faithful with the Holy Trinity and among them."[61]

While the Kingdom of God is already here, it is not yet present in its fullness. Staniloae developed this idea in his explanation of the Divine Liturgy. In the Orthodox tradition, while the royal doors[62] are open, the priest begins the Divine Liturgy with the words, "Blessed is the Kingdom of the Father and the Son and the Holy Spirit." In Romanian practice, the priest closes the doors after this exclamation, but he does not pull the curtain.[63] There is

---

58   The NRSV reads, "spiritually," but Staniloae's text reads, "in the Spirit," as in other English translations (e.g., RSV) and closer to the Greek, *en pneúmati*.

59   Staniloae, *Spirituality and Communion*, 374–75.

60   Ibid., 6.

61   Ibid. Staniloae's affirmation is in line with the Syriac tradition after Theodore of Mopsuestia, which has developed the consideration of the Liturgy as an anticipation of the Kingdom. Irénée-Henri Dalmais, "Place de la Mystagogie de saint Maxime le Confesseur dans la Théologie Liturgique Byzantine," in *Studia Patristica V* (Berlin: Akademie-Verlag, 1962), 283.

62   In the Orthodox churches, the nave and the altar are delimited by the icon screen, or iconostasis, which has two doors on the sides (diaconal doors) and a set of two doors in the middle (royal doors). The side doors are used for exiting and entering into the altar and for small processions, while the middle doors are used for some of the most important processions. These doors are called royal because Byzantine emperors used to enter into the altar through them, so as to receive Communion. When the royal doors are closed, the priest can also pull the curtain (reminiscent of the Old Testament temple), so that there would be no more visual access inside the altar.

63   This is also the case in Slavonic Orthodox traditions. However, in the Greek-American Orthodox tradition, as well as in all Orthodox traditions when the bishop is present, these doors remain open until the end of the Divine Liturgy.

visual contact between the faithful and the altar, but not fully, as when the royal doors are open. Staniloae interpreted this liturgical element to mean that, even though we have been invited into the Kingdom of the Trinity, in this earthly life our union with Christ is not perfected yet. However, Staniloae pointed to the fact that the royal doors will be open several other times during the Divine Liturgy and they will remain open from the moment when the faithful receive Communion until the end. This means that, by receiving Communion, the faithful have entered in the Kingdom of the Trinity. Thus, the Divine Liturgy is the anticipation and prefiguration of the heavenly Kingdom, after the faithful have gradually ascended toward it in their lives.[64]

These considerations are important for ecclesiology, since they show that the Church, especially when gathered in the Liturgy, prefigures and at the same time represents the Kingdom of heaven. If the Kingdom is already here but not yet, the Church represents the "already here." This is not to identify the Kingdom with the Church. Hans Küng argues that the word "Church" appears only twice in the Gospels, in passages whose authenticity exegetes dispute. On the other hand, the notion of the "Kingdom of God" occurs about one hundred times in the Synoptic Gospels. As Alfred Loisy has written, "Jesus proclaimed the kingdom of God, and what came was the Church."[65] Küng acknowledges that Loisy's statement has oftentimes been interpreted as ironic, when Loisy intended it in a positive sense. The fact remains, however, that the preaching of Jesus concentrated mostly around the idea of the Kingdom of God, or as Küng prefers to put it, the Reign of God,[66] a notion that is more inclusive and does not have sexist and political connotations. For the same reason, some prefer to speak about the Commonwealth of God.

The Church and the Kingdom should not be confused. The Kingdom extends beyond the Liturgy into all other aspects of Church life,[67] beyond the Church's charity and fight for justice, or even beyond the canonical boundaries of the Church, as the following chapters will show. But nor should the Kingdom and

---

64    Staniloae, *Spirituality and Communion*, 137.

65    Alfred Loisy, *L'Évangile et l'Église* (Paris: Picard, 1902), 111.

66    Hans Küng, *The Church* (Garden City, NY: Image Books, 1976), 69–71.

67    Based on the parable of the marriage feast in Mt. 22.1-14, Staniloae affirmed that the Kingdom of God "is the union of those who believe in the Holy Trinity, through the marriage between the faithful humankind and the Son of the heavenly King, followed by the feast of an eternal love.... One enters [the Kingdom] through the sacrament of Baptism and Chrismation, and reenters after the fall from it through the sacrament of Confession and maintains life in it through Holy Communion. This is why the Divine Liturgy begins with the promise of this full union with the Holy Trinity and of this eternal feast of love, towards which the faithful advance through the Eucharist, as union with Christ." Staniloae, *Spirituality and Communion*, 138–39.

the Church be separated. As shown above, the Church gathered eucharistically remains a manifestation and anticipation of the Kingdom. Another aspect of the Church's manifestation and anticipation of the Kingdom is its spirituality.

## Theosis

Staniloae explored the intrinsic connection between spirituality and the liturgical (communitarian) aspect of the Church throughout his work, but primarily in *Orthodox Spirituality*.[68] "Man's ascent to God begins in the Church and ends there,"[69] he wrote. Personal spirituality needs to be complemented by the communitarian, liturgical aspect of the Church. At the same time, the reverse is true. The more each faithful grows in relationship with Christ, the more this personal spiritual progress creates communion in the Church, especially in the Liturgy.

> Spirituality and communion are necessarily interrelated. Each person's life grows in relationship with the others, it comes from the others. This living spirituality, which encompasses the whole human being and is nourished by the communication with the others, creating communion, is maintained in Christianity by the Divine Liturgy.[70]

Spirituality is particularly connected with the liturgical life of the Church. Based on Symeon the New Theologian, Staniloae affirmed that divinization did not come through the efforts of the saint, but through sacraments in general[71] and the Eucharist in particular. We reach the fullness of our belonging to the Body

---

68 See Bordeianu, "Orthodox Spirituality [Book Review]," 414–16.

69 Staniloae, *Orthodox Spirituality*, 353.

70 Staniloae, *Spirituality and Communion*, 5. For an analysis of several patristic precedents pertaining to the interrelatedness between spirituality and communion, see Golitzin, "Hierarchy Versus Anarchy?," 148–50, 57–64.

71 In his 29th Hymn, Symeon expanded on the Pauline words, "it is no longer I who live, but it is Christ who lives in me" (Gal. 2.20):
   "God, the one double according to nature,
   Being one according to hypostasis,
   Made me double, as well.
   But making me double, notice the difference:
   I am human through nature, but god through grace . . .
   The union that I have received through Him,
   I refer to it as coming sensibly through sacraments." Quoted in Staniloae, *Jesus Christ or the Restoration of Humankind*, 253.

of Christ in the Eucharist, in which we become members of Christ and Christ becomes us in the sense that he dwells in us and us in him:

> In this sense we can understand the words of Saint Apostle Paul, that we are members of Christ . . . (1 Cor. 12.12; Rom. 7.5), but also the word of the same Apostle, "it is no longer I who live, but it is Christ who lives in me." This, because of our love for him, "I have been crucified with him," "who loved me and gave himself for me" (Gal. 2.20). One could also understand in this sense Christ's word that the one who gave food to the one who was hungry and visited the sick, did these to Christ himself (Mt. 25.35).[72]

Here Staniloae showed the maximum extent to which we are united with Christ in the Church through the Eucharist. He emphasized the change that happens in the members of the Church who now become Christ according to grace. The Son is manifested directly in the Church through the faithful. What appears to be a human action—Symeon and Staniloae would say—is actually Christ working through the Church, in the people united sacramentally with him, and in the poor. In the sacraments in general and the Eucharist in particular, the Church is united with the Son or, as stated in the second chapter, it is incorporated in the Trinity and is filled with the Trinity. In a rather difficult text, Staniloae wrote:

> Observing the movement of those who are gathered together in Christ for the actualization of the various potencies of their nature from the humanity of Christ—humanity that is integral, fully actualized, and united through Christ with the Father and reaching its maximum potentiality through the Holy Spirit—it must be noted that the same thing that happened eternally within the Holy Trinity with their common divine nature, happens now with the humanity of the human persons. Just as in the Holy Trinity each person has actualized as its own the powers of the divine nature of all the three persons from eternity, so also will each human person in Christ have actualized as its own the potencies of all the human persons, or of the entire human nature. But in this, the presence of the Trinity among humans is more clearly revealed. The unity given eternally in the Holy Trinity is a target for the unity towards which we move in Christ. This is also an ascension equivalent with its [i.e., our unity] full penetration by the Triune God. In Christ, human happiness consists in the joy given by the experience of all human potencies actualized for all in Christ. He also has as his own all the potencies of the divine nature actualized from

---

72   Staniloae, *Spirituality and Communion*, 375–76.

eternity, together with the Father and the Holy Spirit, and he imprints his unity according to his divinity with the Father and the Holy Spirit, in the unity according to his humanity with the other people gathered in him.[73]

Immediately after these words, Staniloae added that humans will advance eternally in their unity infused with the unity of the Trinity, in love, and in knowledge both of God and of the entire creation, since creation is rooted in the Trinity.[74]

Staniloae's works are not easy to read. His style is very complicated, with long sentences and countless parentheses, very similar to that of Maximus the Confessor, the Father whom he loved most and translated extensively. The text extensively quoted above is no exception. Because of its importance, I chose to translate it in its entirety and stay true to Romanian syntax. But a second translation, into simpler terms, is necessary.

Staniloae affirmed that in Christ, human nature has been elevated to its maximum potentiality. That is because the subject of the incarnation is the Son, who took on humanity. The relationship that the Son has with the other persons of the Trinity transfers to his humanity, resulting in the union of Christ's human nature with the Father and its perfection by the Spirit. United with Christ in the Church through the sacraments, each person experiences Christ's perfected humanity as his or her own. This is similar to what happens eternally in the Trinity, in which the Father, Son, and Holy Spirit share in the same nature and experience the fullness of the divinity possessed by each divine person. Our union with Christ and with his perfected humanity is actually a gradual process of greater and greater union with God. God communicates his grace to our humanity in a continuous process of perfection. And because the persons of the Trinity are in perfect unity from eternity, our unity is strengthened as we receive the grace of the Trinity. Grace is also the force that attracts all human beings in unity with each other and with God. Of course, this advancement in the unity of the Trinity is a process that will continue for eternity.[75]

These considerations on the perfected nature of our humanity, in union with Christ through the sacraments of the Church, relate to some of the arguments already presented above. They come as a complement to the discussion in the beginning of this chapter on the restoration of human nature in general. They also relate to the models presented in Chapter 2. Staniloae applied the reflection model when he referred to our union as being similar to the unity within

---

73  Ibid., 376–77.
74  Ibid., 377.
75  The affirmation of the eternal advancement in communion with God is very similar to Gregory of Nyssa's considerations on *epectasis* and Maximus's understanding of movement and stability, presented in Chapter 3.

the Trinity, the model for our unity. He also applied the other models when he affirmed the direct connection between union in the Church and union in the Trinity as well as the presence of the Trinity in the Church, which portray the Church as a sacrament of the Trinity. When he wrote about the Church's "full penetration of the Triune God," Staniloae applied the *theosis* model. By affirming that Christ imprinted "his unity according to his divinity with the Father and the Holy Spirit, in the unity according to his humanity with the other people gathered in him," Staniloae alluded to the infusion of the Son's experience of intratrinitarian unity into the unity of the Church. Thus, the same relationships apply in the Trinity and the Church. Staniloae was very successful in explaining the direct relationship between the Trinity and the Church as the Body of Christ.

### Conclusion

Ecclesiology is a chapter of Christology, but only to the extent to which it is also a chapter of Triadology. In a general sense, Christ united humankind with God, reestablishing the communion lost with the fall. More specifically, this communion is experienced fully in the Church, which has been established by and united with Christ, and this unity is continually renewed and strengthened in the sacraments. In light of the union between Christ and the Church, Staniloae affirmed that, when he ascended into heaven with his humanity, Christ raised the Church and placed it at the right hand of the Father, brought it as a sacrifice to the Father, and filled it with the Holy Spirit.

In the Body of Christ, which is the extension of the incarnation, the members of the Church maintain their personalities and achieve their maximum potential, offering themselves as living sacrifices. This is possible because of the presence of the Trinity in the Church and its sacraments—especially the Eucharist—where the Church is raised in the Trinity to experience the same kind of communion that the persons of the Trinity share eternally. This communion then needs to be extended outside the Church, to include the entire world, thus fulfilling the missionary nature of the Church, transforming the world fully into the Kingdom of God, and resulting in the perfection (*theosis*) of all creation now become Church.

In the next chapter I analyze the relationship between the Spirit and the Church, hoping to show that ecclesiology is a also chapter of Pneumatology and ultimately a chapter of Triadology.

# Chapter 5

## FILLED WITH THE SPIRIT: THE RELATIONSHIP BETWEEN THE HOLY SPIRIT AND THE CHURCH

Is institution superior to charism, or is charism above institution? Another way to put this question is to ask: Is the unified hierarchical structure of the Church above the diverse charisms manifested in the Church or do charisms take precedence over the hierarchy? Institution and hierarchy are generally associated with the manifestation of Christ (the High Priest) in the Church. At the same time, theologians tend to regard charisms exclusively as manifestations of the Spirit, without reference to Christ. Thus, the practical problem of the relationship between institution and charism, or between the hierarchy and the rest of the faithful, becomes also a theoretical problem: how is the relationship between the Son and the Spirit manifested in the Church?

Most theologians try to find a balance between the christological and pneumatological aspects of ecclesiology. However, they have found such equilibrium with different degrees of success, and the relationship between the Trinity and the Church is still being reduced to binitarian terms: Is ecclesiology a chapter of Christology, or a chapter of Pneumatology?

I have previously outlined Staniloae's understanding of ecclesiology as a chapter of the theology of the Father and of Christology. In this chapter, I hope to show the sense in which ecclesiology is a chapter of Pneumatology and ultimately of Triadology because the Church is filled with the Holy Spirit, the manifestation of love both within the Trinity and in the Church. In order to prove this thesis, I analyze the ecclesiological implications of Staniloae's Pneumatology, highlighting his theology of (1) the Spirit of communion; (2) the Spirit of Christ and the balance between Pneumatology and Christology, with implications for (3) the relationship between the institutional and charismatic aspects of the Church.

Throughout the chapter, I discuss the role of the Spirit in the immanent Trinity and then apply it to the Church. I also compare Staniloae's position to that of other prominent theologians, especially Orthodox and Catholic, in order to emphasize his ecumenical contribution.

## The Spirit of Communion

The role of the third person as the Spirit of communion is based on the eternal relations of generation in the Trinity. With the exception of modalism, the status of the Father as unoriginated remained largely unchallenged throughout history. However, many treatments of the relationship between the Son and the Spirit were written in a polemical context, surrounding the issue of the Filioque. By way of example, one of the most important Eastern figures, Photius, affirmed that the Spirit proceeds from the Father alone, intimating only a temporal, not an eternal relationship between the Son and the Spirit. Such position is extreme and Catholic theologians after the Council of Lyons critiqued the East for not seeing an eternal connection between the Spirit and the Son as the basis of their collaboration in the economy. Involved in this polemic, some theologians adopted very rigid positions, while others, such as Gregory the Cypriot and Gregory Palamas, kept an open mind and saw the validity of the other side's arguments.[1] Building upon their work as well as on other patristic writings (including by Photius), Staniloae described the Spirit's eternal resting in, and shining forth from, the Son.

Staniloae quoted John Damascene's affirmation that "we believe also in the Holy Spirit who proceeds from the Father and reposes in the Son," which implies that the Son is the Treasurer of the Spirit.[2] This means, on the one hand, that the Spirit is breathed forth toward the Son, resting in the Son. On the other hand, the Son has an active role in the procession of the Spirit, because he is the Treasurer of the Spirit, sending the Spirit back to the Father as a response of love. Staniloae developed both of these themes.

### The Spirit's Resting in, and Shining Forth from, the Son

The New Testament and the Fathers of the Church speak about the "coming to rest of the Spirit" upon the Incarnate Son and about Christ sending out the Spirit. Because there is an intrinsic connection between the immanent and the economic Trinity, Staniloae concluded that the same "resting" of the Spirit upon the Son and shining forth of the Spirit from the Son in the economy of salvation, also take place from eternity, in the immanent Trinity. The term "rest" is not used here as opposed to weariness, but as the end of all-further departing, as an abiding of the Spirit in the Son.[3]

---

1   Staniloae, "Le Saint Esprit," 661.
2   *Dogmatics (Concerning Orthodox Faith)* 8, in Staniloae, "The Procession of the Holy Spirit," 181–82.
3   Staniloae, *Theology and the Church*, 21.

The breathing forth of the Spirit is complete only "when" the Spirit rests in the Son. This does not mean that the Spirit is only partially constituted as a person when the Father breathes him forth, but that his resting in the Son marks the fulfillment, or achievement of the end for which the Spirit exists.[4] The Son then responds to the love of the Father in the Spirit, so the Spirit shines forth from the Son eternally, which is then reflected in the temporal order when the Son sends the Spirit upon the Church. These lines should be read apophatically. The temporal expressions used here only show the limited character of human language describing the distinctions of origin within the Trinity, when in fact there is neither temporal succession, nor separation between the generation of the Son and the breathing forth of the Spirit. "Consequently, the person of the Son and the person of the Spirit also remain united, or interior, to one another."[5]

Staniloae thus brought an important contribution to the discussion of the Son's active role in the eternal procession of the Holy Spirit. The Spirit "is manifested" or "shines forth" through the Son, in the loving dialogue within the Trinity. The Spirit produces communion, manifesting the love between the Father and the Son, both of whom love each other in the Spirit as the third in their relationship.

### The Spirit as "The Third": Bond of Joyous Love

As "the third" in the relationship between the Father and the Son, the Spirit represents the bond of love between them.[6] Staniloae quoted Gregory Palamas who accentuated the way in which the Father loves the Son in the Spirit and the Son responds to the paternal love also in the Spirit, rejoicing in each other:

> And the Spirit of the supreme Word is like an inseparable love on the part of the One who begets the Son, who is born in an unspeakable way. In him the beloved Son and Word of the Father rejoices looking towards him who engenders, and having him as if coming forth from the Father with him and resting in him by the unity of the nature.... And by [ the Spirit] the Son rejoices together with the Father who rejoices in the Son.[7]

Thus, the Spirit can be separated neither from the Father, as the Father's love, nor from the Son, as the resting place and response to paternal love. He is "the

---

4   Ibid., 184.
5   Staniloae, "The Procession of the Holy Spirit," 183.
6   Ibid., 185.
7   Gregory Palamas, *Capita theologica*, in Staniloae, *Theology and the Church*, 186.

Spirit of the supreme Word" from eternity. It is as if the Spirit carries the Father to the Son and the Son to the Father, in a dialogue of love and the Spirit represents their union or bond of love.[8]

Staniloae explained that the way in which the Spirit unites the Father and the Son does not imply that he ceases to be a distinct person: "the Spirit is not himself the joy. He is the one who, by participating in the joy which the Father has in the Son and the Son has in the Father, shows forth in its fullness the joy which one has in the other, or the joy which all three have in all three."[9] Thus, as the third person, the Spirit fulfills the joy between the Father and the Son, revealing the Trinity as a communion of joyous love.

We know from Revelation that God is triune, but why is this the most suitable way for God to exist? Starting from Hugh of Saint Victor's *De Trinitate* III (although Gregory of Nyssa and Basil the Great espouse a similar position[10]), Staniloae showed how a love between two persons is enclosed in its own selfishness and is not fully communitarian. The Spirit avoids these dangers and makes perfect the love between the Father and the Son.[11] This is another instance of open sobornicity, in which Staniloae adopted elements of Western theology.

## The Church as the Third: in the Spirit

The Spirit as the bond of joyous love between the Father and the Son, or the third who fulfills the love between the first two, has significant ecclesiological ramifications for Staniloae:

> Only through the Holy Spirit, therefore, does the divine love radiate to the outside. It is not to no purpose that created "I's" are brought forward

---

8   For a comparison between Palamas and Augustine on the Spirit as the bond of love in the Trinity, see Reinhard Flogaus, "Inspiration—Exploitation—Distortion: The Use of St Augustine in the Hesychast Controversy," in *Orthodox Readings of Augustine*, ed. George E. Demacopoulos and Aristotle Papanikolaou (Crestwood, NY: St Vladimir's Seminary Press, 2008), 63–80.

9   Staniloae, *The Experience of God 1*, 276. Same basic idea in Staniloae, "Le Saint Esprit," 677.

10  Lossky referred extensively to select *Orations* by Gregory of Nyssa and the treatise *On the Holy Spirit* by Basil the Great, in which they show that the number three is the most appropriate for God (although they do not attempt to explain it as a rational necessity, but as an explanation of what we already know from Revelation) and that human understanding of numbers is insufficient to describe the supra-rational Trinity. Lossky, *Mystical Theology*, 46–48.

11  Staniloae, *The Experience of God 1*, 266–67, 70.

and raised to the level of being partners in dialogue with the Father and Son through the Holy Spirit. The Holy Spirit represents the possibility of extending the love between Father and Son to other subjects, and at the same time he represents the right which a third has to a part in the loving dialogue of the two, a right with which the Spirit invests created subjects.[12]

Staniloae implied here that God manifests his love outside the intratrinitarian communion through the Spirit. He is the Spirit of love both within and outside the Trinity. The Spirit penetrates the Church and raises it up within the Trinity, where it, too, represents "the third" who participates in the loving dialogue between the Father and the Son. The Church is so permeated by the Spirit (the third) that it does not constitute "the fourth" in the divine communion of love, similar to how the Church was portrayed in the previous chapter as the Body of Christ, or the extension of Christ, distinct but not separated from Christ. Without introducing multiplicity in the nature of the Spirit, but while affirming a union by grace, one might even say that the Church is included in the Spirit and thus raised in the Trinity. This ascent happens in conjunction with the descent of God upon the Church through the Holy Spirit. As Staniloae put it:

Through the Spirit as his gift, God dwells in us (1 Cor. 12.3-11). Saint Athanasius declares: "But we apart from the Spirit are strange and distant from God, and by participation of the Spirit we are knit into the Godhead; so that our being in the Father is not ours, but is the Spirit's which is in us and abides in us, which by the true confession we preserve it in us."[13] . . . To participate as person and to make himself participated in as person, these belong to the Spirit. He is the expression of the generosity of God, of God's forgetfulness of himself as he "goes out" towards creatures. The Spirit is the joy God finds in them and they in God.[14]

Several elements stand out in this quote. First, the Spirit is the gift of God to us. As in the service of Chrismation, where the newly baptized is sealed with "the gift of the Holy Spirit," so the Church receives not only the gifts of the Spirit, or charisms, but the Spirit himself, as gift. Second, Athanasius implied the idea mentioned above, namely that the Church is united with the Spirit, participates in the Spirit, and its being is the being of the Spirit (by grace, of course). Third,

---

12  Ibid., 268.
13  *Against the Arians* 3.24, PG 26.373B–C; ET Newman/Robertson: 407.
14  Staniloae, *The Experience of God 1*, 277–78.

Staniloae suggested that while the Church is not united with the Spirit according to nature, it is united with the person of the Spirit. The theanthropic nature of the Church presented in the preceding chapter takes on a new, pneumatological aspect. Fourth, if the Spirit has been portrayed above as the love manifested outside the Trinity, now Staniloae introduces the Spirit as the bond of joy between God and the Church, as God generously goes out to creatures.

This is why Staniloae affirmed elsewhere that the Holy Spirit "is the power of communication between the Holy Trinity and us, power that . . . realizes between us and God and among ourselves the true communion, or the Church."[15] The Spirit effecting communion between God and the Church, and also among the faithful, captures the meaning of the Pauline expression, "the communion of the Holy Spirit be with all of you" (2 Cor. 13.13).[16]

## The Spirit and the Church: Union without Separation, without Confusion

The relationship between the Spirit and the Church as Staniloae described it here represents a perfect balance between the human and divine elements of the Church, united without separation or confusion, to borrow from Christological, Chalcedonian language. On the one hand, the Spirit and the Church are so united, that Tertullian called the Church, *Ecclesia Spiritus Sancti*,[17] and Irenaeus affirmed that "where the Church is, there too is the Spirit of God, and where the Spirit of God is, there is the Church and all grace: and the Spirit is Truth."[18] On the other hand, the union between the Spirit and the Church preserves the identity of both and maintains the distinction between them. Nissiotis considered that, if the sanctifying work of the Spirit is ignored, the Church becomes anthropomorphic and is reduced to a social institution. Instead, we participate in the Spirit, so the Spirit sanctifies us, transforming us into the Body of Christ and adoptive children of God. At the same time, the human element cannot be ignored, since the Church is the "People of God" and "Body of Christ"; both expressions prevent us from falling into the dangers of abstraction when speaking about the Church as purely spiritual.[19]

---

15  Staniloae, *Spirituality and Communion*, 169.

16  Staniloae, "Le Saint Esprit," 677.

17  Quoted in Afanassieff, *The Church of the Holy Spirit*, 1–2. While supporting this expression, Afanassieff disagreed with the rest of Tertullian's argument that the Church belongs exclusively to the "pneumatics."

18  *Adversus Haereses* III 24:1. Quoted in Staniloae, *The Experience of God 1*, 58.

19  Nissiotis, "Pneumatological Christology as a Presupposition of Ecclesiology," 244, 50.

One way to maintain the distinction between the Spirit and the Church without separating them is to refer to the Church as the temple or dwelling place of the Spirit.[20] If Christ is the temple of the Holy Spirit and if our bodies are temples of the Spirit (1 Cor. 6.19), then the Body of Christ, or the Church, is a temple of the Spirit. This is especially true since, by definition, a temple is a dwelling place of God and of his Spirit, where the two are neither confused, nor separated. Thus, the Church is intimately united with the Spirit, while they each maintain their identity.

Having presented the Spirit as the third through whom the Church is raised in the Trinity where it experiences the intratrinitarian relationships, it is important to look more closely at the relationship between the Spirit and the Son as they are manifested in the Church.

### The Spirit of Christ: Balance between Pneumatology and Christology

The material presented thus far is a clear indication that, for Staniloae, the Spirit and the Son are closely interrelated both in the immanent Trinity and in their work *ad extra*. Most importantly, one does not have priority over the other. Staniloae was adamant in regard to this issue, which was and still is hotly debated among Catholic and Orthodox theologians.

I first offer some brief remarks about the inseparability of the three divine persons' works *ad extra* and the positions of several representative Catholic and Orthodox theologians who wrote on the relationship between the Spirit and the Son in the Church. Then I highlight Staniloae's understanding of this relationship, continuing in the following section with the way it informs the interaction between institution and charisms. Thus, I hope to show Staniloae's contribution to ecumenical dialogues on the Holy Spirit.[21]

---

20  Bouyer and Groppe explain that the faithful become living stones within the Body of Christ understood as temple of the Spirit. Each member becomes a stone that contributes with their charism to the beauty of the temple. Louis Bouyer, *The Church of God: Body of Christ and Temple of the Spirit*, trans. Charles U. Quinn (Chicago: Franciscan Herald Press, 1982), 248–64, 307–13. Elizabeth T. Groppe, *Yves Congar's Theology of the Holy Spirit* (Oxford, NY: Oxford University Press, 2004), 130–35.

21  While I address primarily the issue of balance between the works of the Son and the Holy Spirit in the Church, Jeffrey Vogel focuses on the reasons for which various Orthodox theologians (including a brief discussion of Staniloae) describe the Spirit's hiddenness: either as an act of pulling back in order to show Christ, or as kenosis, or as being constantly outpoured and enabling us to see Christ. Jeffrey A. Vogel, "How the Spirit Hides: Rival Conceptions in Recent Orthodox Theology," *St Vladimir's Theological Quarterly* 53, no. 1 (2009): 99–122.

Most Western and Eastern theologians agree that the operations of God *ad extra* should be regarded as one. The presence of one person of the Trinity in the Church cannot be separated from the work of the other divine persons since, in Irenaeus's apt phrase, the Father always works with his two hands, the Son and the Spirit. Of course, this does not mean that the works of each person cannot be distinguished from that of the others, in what classical theology called appropriation.[22]

Based on John Damascene, Staniloae affirmed that *perichoresis* among the three divine persons is more than the motion of each person around the others, as etymology suggests; it is their reciprocal interiority. The Spirit passes through the Son as one who proceeds from the Father and returns to the Father. The Son passes through the Spirit as one who is begotten by the Father and returns to the Father.[23] Based on their *perichoresis*, the trinitarian persons act together in their work *ad extra*, especially in the Church:

> On account of these interior relations with the others [*perichoresis*] no divine Person is ever, either in the Church as a whole or in the individual believer, without the other divine Persons or without the particular characteristics of the others. "The Church is filled with the Trinity," said Origen,[24] and the faithful too, for according to St. Maximus the Confessor the purpose of the saints is "to express the very unity of the Holy Trinity."[25] Christ and the Spirit work together to make us sons of the Father.[26]

To give just one example in this sense, Staniloae placed one of the most Christocentric subjects, namely the Crucifixion, in a trinitarian context. He affirmed that, just as the Spirit participated in the descent of the Son to our

---

22 Manastireanu appreciates Staniloae's concern to have a balance between Christ and the Spirit, but he considers that Staniloae went too far with his concern to maintain a balance between the christological and pneumatological aspects of ecclesiology. Staniloae should have found more effective ways to express their specific roles, without "leveling" out the specificity of Christ and the Spirit. (Manastireanu, "Dumitru Staniloae's Theology of Ministry," 131.) I think that Manastireanu is right to consider that balance should not mean leveling out the roles of the Son and the Spirit in the Church. However, in light of the material presented above, I think that Staniloae was successful in presenting the specific roles of Christ and the Spirit, understood as appropriation.

23 Staniloae, *Theology and the Church*, 38–39.

24 Origen. *Selecta in Psalmos* 23, 1 PG 12,1265B.

25 Maximus the Confessor, *Ambigua*, PG91, 1193C–1196C.

26 Staniloae, *Theology and the Church*, 39.

fallen humanity in the incarnation, so does the Spirit participate in the continuation of this descent to the level of the Cross, as well as in the ascent into heaven. Actually, Staniloae added, since this happens by the will of the Father, the entire Trinity participates in oikonomia in general, and in crucifixion in particular.[27] Consequently, the missions of the Father, Son, and Holy Spirit in the world cannot be separated or given priority, one over the other. Still, in practice, the issue of the relationship between the Spirit and the Son remains a difficult one, as a brief survey of recent theology suggests.

### Status Quaestionis

A detailed survey of contemporary Catholic and Orthodox theology is impossible here, but several brief remarks will suffice to show how the roles of the Spirit and the Son in the Church have been addressed recently. While this question was not posed explicitly before Vatican II, Catholic ecclesiology was predominantly Christocentric. The most notable exceptions were Heribert Mühlen, who is credited to have reactualized the biblical and patristic theme of the anointing of Jesus by the Spirit and thus Spirit Christology,[28] and the early Johann Adam Möhler's pneumatological ecclesiology, even though he later preferred an institutional, christological approach.[29] But the one who had a decisive influence on the Catholic understanding of Spirit Christology and its ecclesiological repercussions was Yves Congar.

---

27  Staniloae, *Spirituality and Communion*, 154. De Beauregard comments: "Although still very Christocentric in line with St. Maximus, his master, Father Dumitru Staniloae, however, underlines the fundamental place of the Giver of Life in the veritable experience of the Cross, both on a personal and cosmic plan. The Cross signifies the victory of the Spirit," because only in the Spirit can the Son accomplish the Father's will. Without the Spirit, human will would not be capable of choosing the divine will. On the Cross, Christ is filled with the Spirit, as he was all along his ministry. Marc-Antoine Costa de Beauregard, "Le Cosmos et la Croix," in *Dumitru Staniloae: Tradition and Modernity in Theology*, ed. Lucian Turcescu (Iasi, Romania; Palm Beach, FL: Center for Romanian Studies, 2002), 165.

28  Badcock, *Light of Truth & Fire of Love*, 145. Staniloae was aware of Mühlen's work. See also Kasper's "Christology in a pneumatological perspective," or other variants of this construction, such as "pneumatologically oriented Christology," "pneumatologically defined Christology," and "spiritual Christology." Kasper, *Jesus the Christ*, 267, 49, 52 and *Theology and Church*, trans. Margaret Kohl (New York: Crossroad, 1989), 94.

29  See Michael J. Himes, *Ongoing Incarnation: Johann Adam Möhler and the Beginnings of Modern Ecclesiology* (New York: Crossroad, 1997), 198–99, 209–15.

In his earlier writings, Congar gave priority to Christology and the institutional aspect of the Church over Pneumatology and charisms.[30] A shift was
soon to occur. When present as a *peritus* at the Second Vatican Council, he
shared a meal with two Orthodox observers, Nikos Nissiotis and Alexander
Schmemann. They said: "If we were to prepare a treatise *De Ecclesia*, we would
draft a chapter on the Holy Spirit, to which we would add a second chapter on
Christian anthropology, and that would be all."[31]

This conversation made a lasting impression upon Congar who, especially
after this point, stressed the pneumatological aspect of ecclesiology. He started
using the expression "pneumatological ecclesiology" and went as far as to write
that "Ecclesiology is a function of pneumatology."[32] By this he meant that the
Holy Spirit empowers the sacraments and the doxology of the Church; builds up
the Church with charisms; and makes the Church one, holy, catholic, and apostolic.[33] As a reaction to pre-Vatican II ecclesiology, which regarded the Church
as a preexisting, Christologically constituted Church, Congar affirmed that the
Spirit co-institutes the Church together with the Son. Congar thus implied that
the Church was not instituted whole at the Last Supper, but that there is place
for change and development under the guidance of the Spirit. The Church is
not the perfect, absolute, divine society in which the Spirit functions ontologi-
cally as its soul, amounting to ecclesiological monophysitism. The Spirit is not
simply the guarantor of magisterial decisions who enables the faithful to obey
these hierarchical pronouncements, but charisms have their proper role in the
Church, in communion with the hierarchy.[34] This communion is rooted in a
sound relationship between Christology and Pneumatology: "no Christology
without Pneumatology and no Pneumatology without Christology."[35]

---

30   Elizabeth T. Groppe, "The Contribution of Yves Congar's Theology of the Holy
     Spirit," *Theological Studies* 62, no. 3 (2001): 461, 68–73.

31   Yves Congar, *I Believe in the Holy Spirit: He is Lord and Giver of Life*, trans. David
     Smith, vol. 2 (New York: Seabury Press, 1983), 66. As a reaction to these lines, John
     Zizioulas later commented with irony that the Orthodox know very little about the
     Church, since their response to Congar was strictly pneumatological and anthropo-
     logical. John D. Zizioulas, *Being as Communion: Studies in Personhood and the
     Church*, Contemporary Greek Theologians; no. 4 (Crestwood, NY: St Vladimir's
     Seminary Press, 1985), 123.

32   Congar, *I Believe in the Holy Spirit* 2, 46.

33   See Groppe, *Yves Congar's Theology of the Holy Spirit*, 85–114.

34   Congar, *I Believe in the Holy Spirit* 1, 153–57. See also the section entitled, "The
     'Two Missions': The Spirit as the Co-instituting Principle of the Church" in Congar,
     *I Believe in the Holy Spirit* 2, 12ff.

35   Yves Congar, *The Word and the Spirit*, trans. David Smith (San Francisco: Harper
     & Row Publishers, 1986), 1.

Most contemporary Catholic theologians who benefit from Congar's journey would agree that there is a healthy tension between the pneumatological and christological aspects of the Church. This polarity sustains a healthy balance between charism and office, where the Holy Spirit indwells all ministries of the Church, both ordained and not. The charismatic element is not parallel to the institution, since both are means of grace in which the Word and the Spirit act together.[36]

Similar to Congar's journey, modern Orthodox theologians tried to find a balance between Christology and Pneumatology with their ecclesiological implications. Lossky was the first to write about "a twofold divine economy: the work of Christ and the work of the Holy Spirit"[37]:

> The work of Christ concerns human nature which he recapitulates in His hypostasis. The work of the Holy Spirit, on the other hand, concerns persons, being applied to each one singly.... Thus, the work of Christ unifies; the work of the Holy Spirit diversifies. Yet, the one is impossible without the other.... Christ creates the unity in His mystical body through the Holy Spirit; the Holy Spirit communicates Himself to human persons through Christ.[38]

Although affirming that the works of Christ and the Spirit are interrelated in the economy, Lossky introduced a separation by narrowly associating the work of the Son with nature and unity, while the Spirit pertains to diversity and persons. This separation becomes explicit in the immanent Trinity, where the Spirit is independent from the Son.[39] Staniloae criticized Lossky for being too polemical and deemphasizing the eternal relation between the Son and the Spirit. Moreover, Lossky should not associate the work of the Son with nature without involving the Spirit, nor should he associate the work of the Spirit with person, without the Son having a role; union with Christ is possible through

---

36  Avery Dulles, *A Church to Believe In: Discipleship and the Dynamics of Freedom* (New York: Crossroad, 1983), 19–40. Walter Kasper, *The God of Jesus Christ*, trans. Matthew J. O'Connell (New York: Crossroad, 1987), 206. Denis Edwards, *Breath of Life: A Theology of the Creator Spirit* (Maryknoll, NY: Orbis, 2004), 91–94. Groppe, *Yves Congar's Theology of the Holy Spirit*, 137–47.

37  Lossky, *Mystical Theology*, 156.

38  Ibid., 166–67.

39  Ibid., 169, 243–44. As mentioned in the first chapter, Lossky's exaggerated position is a polemical reaction to the Filioque, which presupposes an eternal relationship between the Son and the Spirit. Lossky was influenced by de Régnon's theory that the East starts from person and Trinity, whereas the West gives priority to nature over person and unity over Trinity.

the Spirit and our union with Christ accentuates our growth as persons. Lastly, there is no separation between nature and person, as if nature could exist by itself.[40] Thus, Lossky affirmed the eternal independence of the Son and the Spirit, which resulted in two economies: that of the Son paired with the recapitulation of human nature and Church unity, and that of the Spirit, directed toward personal sanctification and ecclesial diversity.

Florovsky believed exactly the contrary, namely that it is Christ who maintains the personal character of the members of the Church, concluding that "we should prefer a christological orientation in the theology of the Church rather than pneumatological. For, on the other hand, the Church, as a whole, has her *personal center* only in Christ, she is not an incarnation of the Holy Spirit, nor is she merely a Spirit-being community, but precisely the Body of Christ, the Incarnate Lord."[41] Consequently, for Florovsky the christological aspects of ecclesiology take priority over Pneumatology, and ecclesiology is a chapter of Christology.[42]

Florovsky's disciple, John Zizioulas, initially adopted the same idea that "ecclesiology ceases to be a separate chapter for theology and becomes an organic *chapter of Christology*."[43] After 1974,[44] Zizioulas distanced himself from his mentor and argued that, even though Christology is the starting point of ecclesiology, it is inconceivable without Pneumatology: "to the Christomonistic tendencies of the West, Orthodox theologians tend to answer with a Pneumatomonistic tendency in ecclesiology; we became 'specialists in Pneumatology,' but we should actually present a synthesis between Pneumatology and Christology."[45] Another

---

40   Staniloae, "Le Saint Esprit," 671. Staniloae, *Theology and the Church*, 27.

41   Florovsky, "The Church: Her Nature and Task," 67–68.

42   Georges Florovsky, "Le corps du Christ vivant," in *La sainte église universelle: Confrontation oecuménique* (Neuchâtel: Delachaux et Niestlé, 1948), 12. Zizioulas contends that this statement—ecclesiology is a chapter of Christology—is a reaction to Khomiakov who saw the Church as a "charismatic society" rather than the Body of Christ. Zizioulas, *Being as Communion*, 124. See also Jerry Zenon Skira, "Christ, the Spirit and the Church in Modern Orthodox Theology: A Comparison of Georges Florovsky, Vladimir Lossky, Nikos Nissiotis and John Zizioulas" (Doctoral dissertation, University of St. Michael's College in Toronto, 1998) 173–74.

43   John D. Zizioulas, *Eucharist, Bishop, Church: The Unity of the Church in the Divine Eucharist and the Bishop During the First Three Centuries*, trans. Elizabeth Theokritoff (Brookline, MA: Holy Cross Orthodox Press, 2001), 15.

44   On Zizioulas's evolution, see Gäetan Baillargeon, *Perspectives orthodoxes sur l'Église-Communion: l'oeuvre de Jean Zizioulas* (Montréal: Éditions Paulines, 1989), 101–02.

45   John D. Zizioulas, "The Pneumatological Dimension of the Church," *Communio* 1 (1974): 143–44. See also Zizioulas, *Being as Communion*, 110–11, 23.

departure from Florovsky is Zizioulas's adoption of the principle that the Spirit makes Christ relational and a corporate personality, proposed by Lossky.[46] And yet, he later abandoned Lossky's two economies by affirming that "the Spirit not only diversifies, he also unites (1 Cor. 12.13; Eph. 4.4), and Christ unites not via *nature* but 'hypostatically', i.e., via *personhood*."[47]

Zizioulas's success in finding a balance between Christology and Pneumatology is only partial. Like Lossky, he continues to treat the missions of the Spirit and of the Son if not separately, then at least with a certain priority. He distinguishes between the Son's economy of becoming history and the Spirit's economy of liberation from history, allowing one to take priority over the other, even though he assigns the question of priority to the realm of *theologoumenon*.[48] This principle is best illustrated in his eucharistic theology.

The Church is epiclectic by nature. The Spirit descends upon it from the eschaton, so the Church becomes again and again the corporate Christ that it will be in the future. For this reason, Skira accuses Zizioulas of ruling out the presence of the Spirit in history, and thus giving the Son a "temporal priority" over the Spirit.[49] Similarly, Berger appreciates Zizioulas's contribution concerning the eschatological character of the Eucharist, implying the need of institutions to reflect the kingdom, and the epiclectic existence of the Church, which lacks any sort of self-sufficiency but depends on the Spirit.[50] But he criticizes Zizioulas for giving primacy to the Eucharist, the exclusive event in which there is a synthesis between christological and pneumatological, between historical and eschatological.[51] This synthesis is only momentary; it is "acquired only to be lost again" and leads to what McPartlan calls a "rhythmic" Christian existence.[52] If this is the case, Zizioulas is unable to explain the presence of the Spirit outside the Eucharist, which calls into question the spiritual character of the other aspects of Church life, especially its institutions.[53]

---

46    Zizioulas, "The Pneumatological Dimension of the Church," 146.
47    Zizioulas, *Communion and Otherness*. Zizioulas also refers here to his *Being as Communion*, pp. 124–25.
48    Zizioulas, *Being as Communion*, 129–30.
49    Skira, "Christ, the Spirit and the Church" 181.
50    Zizioulas, *Being as Communion*, 138, 85–87.
51    While Berger is largely accurate in his description of Zizioulas's theology, there are some exceptions (even inconsistencies) in Zizioulas's work. In one instance he affirms that the institution of the Church "constantly depends on the Spirit and it exists only epiclectically." Zizioulas, "The Pneumatological Dimension of the Church," 150–52.
52    McPartlan, *The Eucharist Makes the Church*, 266–72, 87.
53    Berger, "Does the Eucharist Make the Church? An Ecclesiological Comparison of Staniloae and Zizioulas," 49–50.

Another Orthodox theologian who tried to maintain a balance between a christological and a pneumatological perspective on ecclesiology was Paul Evdokimov. He affirmed that Christ and the Spirit are inseparable since Christ is manifested by the Spirit and the Spirit is communicated by Christ.[54] In line with Lossky, he considered that Christ recapitulates and integrates humanity, while the Spirit gives personal gifts to each of the member of the Church. Similar to Zizioulas, he also attributed to the Spirit the role of uniting charisms in the Church.

And yet, Evdokimov affirmed that the action of the Spirit precedes that of Christ: the Spirit hovered over the waters of creation, the prophets predicted the Incarnation, the Spirit descended over Virgin Mary and sanctified her, the Spirit rested upon Christ at Epiphany and upon the Apostles in order to give birth to the Church at Pentecost, and the same happens now in the sacraments.[55] Thus, despite his intention to find a balance between the two, Evdokimov gave Pneumatology priority over Christology.

This is also the case of Nikos Nissiotis. Even though he affirmed that there should be a balance between Pneumatology and Christology, in his considerations of "Pneumatological Christology," "Pneumatological Ecclesiology," and "Ecclesiological Pneumatology," he emphasized the role of the Spirit as being the "decisive element" in the economy. Similar to Evdokimov, Nissiotis portrayed the Spirit as present in the world before being the Spirit of Christ in the Church and as having a role in creation and providence even before the Christ event.[56] Similar to Lossky, he referred to the qualitative equality of all the members of the Body of Christ, while the Holy Spirit makes a hierarchical distinction among them.[57]

In summary, Congar sealed the departure of Catholic theology from Christomonism to an emphasis on the role of the Spirit in the Church, attempting to find a balance between the roles of Christ and the Spirit. Lossky overemphasized the distinction between the missions of the Spirit and the Son in the Church, which led to the discussion of whether one has priority over the other. In varying degrees, Florovsky and Zizioulas gave priority to

---

54   Paul Evdokimov, *Présence de l'Esprit-Saint dans la tradition orthodoxe* (Paris: Cerf, 1977), 55, 59.

55   Evdokimov, *L'Orthodoxie*, 127, 43–48.

56   Nikos Nissiotis, "La pneumatologie ecclésiologique au service de l'unité de l'Eglise," *Istina* 12 (1967): 329–31. See also Nissiotis, "Pneumatological Christology as a Presupposition of Ecclesiology," 237–50.

57   Nikos Nissiotis, "The Charismatic Church and the Theology of the Laity," *Laity*, no. 9 (1960): 32–34.

Christology, while Evdokimov and Nissiotis preferred the pneumatological aspects of ecclesiology. All these theologians intended to offer a balanced position[58] but, as Zizioulas noted, the debate continues: "the problem *how* to relate the institutional with the charismatic, the christological with the pneumatological aspects of ecclesiology, still awaits its treatment by Orthodox theology.... It is probably one of the most important questions facing Orthodox theology in our time."[59]

In the next section, I propose that Staniloae was able to achieve this much-needed balance between the Son and the Spirit in both immanent and economic Trinity, as well as in its application in the life of the Church.

*Staniloae: Immanent and Economic Trinity*

In my estimation, the main reason for Staniloae's success in avoiding the dangers of prioritizing the presence of Christ and the Spirit in the Church was that his ecclesiology was deeply rooted in a very solid Triadology. His discussion of the Spirit of the Son in the immanent Trinity determined his understanding of the Spirit of Christ in the economy of salvation.[60] The eternal relationship between the Spirit and the Son represents the basis for their manifestation in the world, this principle having already been developed in the second chapter. According to Staniloae, because the Father breathed the Spirit upon the Son in the immanent Trinity, the Father also gave the Spirit to the incarnate Son, invisibly at the virginal birth and visibly at his Baptism by John.[61] Consequently, "the Holy Spirit makes spiritual the humanity assumed by the Son and deifies it, which is to say, makes it fit to participate in the love which the divine hypostasis of the Son has toward his Father."[62] As shown in the previous chapter, the humanity of Christ is united with our humanity, so the Spirit rests upon us, too. Our humanity is transformed and raised in an intimate relationship with God. The Church, as the Body of Christ whose members

---

58 Skira, "Christ, the Spirit and the Church," 204–05. See also Jerry Zenon Skira, "The Synthesis between Christology and Pneumatology in Modern Orthodox Theology," *Orientalia Christiana Periodica* 68, no. 2 (2002): 435–65.

59 Zizioulas, *Being as Communion*, 125–26.

60 For example, on page 149 of the second volume of his *Dogmatics*, Staniloae used the expression "Spirit of Christ" six times.

61 Staniloae, *Chipul evanghelic al lui Iisus Hristos* [*The Evangelical Image of Jesus Christ*], 270.

62 Staniloae, *The Experience of God 1*, 249.

bear Christ in their hearts, represents the mystical humanity of Christ upon which rests the Holy Spirit.[63]

Thus, trinitarian relationships are not forcefully applied to economy, but they presuppose and are accompanied by a change in human nature, the latter being made fit to participate in trinitarian relationships. Staniloae wrote about both the Spirit resting in the Son and his shining forth from the Son as manifested in the Church:

> There is a special reciprocity between the Son and the Spirit which is *reflected in their contact with the world* [emphases mine]. The Son by himself transmits the Spirit to those who believe in him. But only through the Spirit is the Son known by those who believe. The Spirit shines out from the Son above all after the Resurrection and since the day of Pentecost. But it is exactly on account of this that the face of the Son gains its radiance, and its divine reality (visible or invisible) is intensely felt through the Spirit, or in the measure that the Spirit is communicated by the Son. Thus one can say that the Son makes the Spirit accessible to us, but that the Spirit in his turn makes the Son accessible in his divine interiority, where by the Spirit, we know the Son and rise to the Father in a pure life and in prayer.[64]

Here Staniloae applied both the reflection model and the other models that establish a continuum between the Trinity and the Church. On the one hand, because the Spirit rests eternally in the Son, the Spirit also rests in those who believe in the Son; their faith in the Son is made possible by the Spirit; through the Spirit, the Son's humanity reveals his divinity, and this divinity is accessible to us. We thus ascend to the Father, in the Son, through the Spirit. On the other hand, because the Spirit shines forth eternally from the Son, Christ manifests the Spirit into the world primarily at his Resurrection and at Pentecost, thus making the Spirit accessible to us, just as the Spirit brought Christ closer to us. The Spirit and the Son are inseparable both in the immanent and economic Trinity, in a perfect reciprocity.

Having established not merely a reflection, but a continuum between the eternal and temporal Spirit-Son relationship, it is time to see how the resting of the Spirit in the Son and the shining forth of the Spirit from the Son are manifested in the economy of salvation. As in the preceding two chapters, this economy is understood in a general sense as referring to all humankind and in a special sense in reference to the Church.

---

63   Staniloae, *Jesus Christ or the Restoration of Humankind*, 363.
64   Staniloae, "The Procession of the Holy Spirit," 186.

*The Spirit Rests in the Son and Leads to Christ*

The Spirit proceeds eternally from the Father toward the Son, resting in the Son. Staniloae described a similar movement in the economy of salvation, where the Spirit rests upon those united with the Son, that is, humankind in general (by virtue of the union of our human nature with Christ's humanity) and the Church in particular, as the Body of Christ. He wrote:

> the sending of the Spirit by the Son to men rather signifies that the Spirit rests in those who are united with the Son, since he rests in the Son. The Spirit does not go beyond the Son, . . . even when we say improperly that he is sent to men. The Son is the only and ultimate resting place of the Spirit. The Spirit dwells in us insofar as we are raised up in the Son.[65]

Staniloae implied here that the same intratrinitarian relationships are manifested in the Church. And yet, one cannot help but notice that the Trinity remains a mystery and that (unlike Rahner's principle) economic Trinity is not entirely similar to immanent Trinity. Eternally, the Spirit rests upon the Son when he is sent by the Father. When the Spirit rests upon the Church (the Body of Christ), however, he is sent by the Son, not the Father. Moreover, in the immanent Trinity the Son sends the Spirit back to the Father, while in the economy of salvation the Spirit is sent by the Son upon those united with the Son. These qualifications do not necessarily challenge the essence of the principle that the same relationships apply in both the immanent and economic Trinity, but they serve as a reminder that the presence of the Trinity in the world remains a mystery, which should be approached apophatically. The examples that follow attempt to dive deeper into this mystery, to present more fully the role of the Father in the economy of salvation, and thus resemble more closely the relationships in the immanent Trinity.

Both the Son and the Spirit are directly present and active in the world. Their works complement each other and presuppose each other. According to Staniloae, Christ did not depart from the world completely at his ascension into heaven, leaving the Holy Spirit to replace him and continue his work in his absence. When Christ ascended into heaven, he did not separate himself from the people, but took us with him into heaven, at the right hand of the Father, and close to the Theotokos and the saints. Thus, Christ remains

---

65 Ibid., 179. Similarly, Staniloae wrote that "The Spirit 'comes to rest' (alights) upon the Church and in the Church because he comes to rest upon Christ, its head, and because the Church is united with Christ." Staniloae, *Theology and the Church*, 27.

faithful to his promise, "And remember, I am with you always, to the end of the age" (Mt. 28.20).[66]

Christ is present in the world primarily through the Eucharist, in which he continues to work for our salvation together with the Spirit. The bread and the wine are changed into the Body and Blood of Christ through the descent of the Holy Spirit. Hence, Christ's work is not separate from that of the Holy Spirit or of the Father who sends the Holy Spirit. Staniloae wrote:

> The entire Trinity is at work in the Divine Liturgy because the Eucharistic sacrifice is brought to the Father, by the Son, who also brings us together with him, and the bread and the wine are changed through the descent of the Holy Spirit, who remains in the Body and Blood of Christ. Thus the faithful will unite through Communion not only with Christ, but also with the Father, to whom [Christ] offers himself as a sacrifice, uniting us also with himself, and through himself with the Father (as sacrifice), and with the Holy Spirit. Only united with the Holy Trinity, are the faithful also united among themselves: "And unite us all to one another—the priest prays after the gifts have been changed—who become partakers of the one Bread and Cup in the communion of the one Holy Spirit."[67] The Holy Spirit is in a special way the unifying factor, the factor of communion, because he is in God both of the Father and of the Son, and in humans he is both of the one and of the other.[68]

Staniloae assumed here that in the Eucharist we are united with each of the persons of the Trinity, an idea that I have presented in the previous two chapters. Additionally, he showed how our union with each person reflects the eternal relations in the Trinity. The Spirit constitutes us into the Body of Christ understood both as sacrifice and as Church. United with Christ in the Spirit, we are brought as a loving sacrifice to the Father, just as the Spirit shines forth from the Son as a response to the Father's love. We are united not only with the sacrifice of Christ, but also with the Spirit, and brought to the Father. The Spirit thus unites us both with the Son, since he is the Spirit of the Son, and with the Father, since he is the Spirit of the Father. The Spirit is the bond of love within

---

66  Staniloae, *Spirituality and Communion*, 380–81.
67  Saint Basil the Great, *The Divine Liturgy*, trans. Members of the Faculty of Hellenic College/Holy Cross Greek Orthodox School of Theology (Brookline, MA: Holy Cross Orthodox Press, 1998), 31.
68  Staniloae, *Spirituality and Communion*, 391. Staniloae affirmed the same idea in his commentary on Eph. 2.18: through Christ, all humankind has "access in one Spirit to the Father." Staniloae, *Spirituality and Communion*, 258.

the Trinity, as well as between the Trinity and us. Moreover, each of us, united eucharistically with the Son, in the Spirit, as sacrifices to the Father, find a new identity in God. And since we all find the same God-like identity, we are united to one another in God. Therefore, the Holy Spirit, or "the unifying factor, the factor of communion," is the one who unites us with one another and ultimately brings us in communion with the Trinity.

To Staniloae's considerations on the roles of the Son and of the Spirit in the economy of salvation, I would add that the mission of the Church to proclaim Christ to the nations is based on the work of the Holy Spirit who dwells in the Body of Christ. The Apostles had to be "clothed with power from on high" (Lk. 24.49), that is, with the Holy Spirit, before leaving Jerusalem to spread the Gospel. Acts 1.8 makes this connection even more clearly: "But you will receive power when the Holy Spirit has come upon you; and you will be my witnesses in Jerusalem, in all Judea and Samaria, and to the ends of the earth." The gift of the Holy Spirit received by the Church is not supposed to be used only within the Church, for the building up of the community, but also to bring the world to Christ. Better stated, the receiving of the Spirit for the building up of the community has a missionary implication, namely to preach Christ to the nations. At the same time, as I show next, the Church fulfils the presence of the Spirit in the world by manifesting the Spirit in its sacraments and mission.

### The Spirit Shines forth from the Son and Is Made Known by Christ

The Son manifests the Spirit in relation to both the Father and creation. As the Son sends the Spirit to the Father, so Christ makes known the Spirit to all humankind.[69] The Son sends the Spirit fully upon the Church and, through the Church, in the world, so all humans in general and the Church in particular know the Spirit through Christ.

Staniloae based these affirmations on Maximus the Confessor who showed that the Son can bestow the gifts of the Holy Spirit upon the Church because he possesses the Spirit from eternity, according to his nature.[70] Thus, the Son is not the absolute source of the Spirit. The Father is the one who gives him the Spirit from eternity, so the Son possesses the Spirit from the Father and is able to send the Spirit upon the Church, which, in turn, has the Spirit from the Son—its head. The Church is not the absolute source of the Spirit. It has the Spirit as a gift both for

---

69  Staniloae, *Theology and the Church*, 21.
70  Saint Maximus the Confessor, *Raspunsuri catre Talasie* [*Answers to Thalasius*]. Translated by Dumitru Staniloae. Second ed. Vol. 3 of the Romanian *Philokalia* (Bucharest: Harisma, 1994), 63/371.

the sanctification of its members and for the world. As Staniloae put it, inasmuch as the faithful are united with Christ, the Spirit irradiates from the Church too.[71]

Based on the distinction between full participation in the life of the Trinity of the divine persons and the participation by grace of human persons, Staniloae explained how the Spirit irradiates from the Church. He referred to the mystical writings of Symeon the New Theologian who wrote about saints as covered with the divine light and the mind which is "filled with irradiation and becomes light," similar to God's glory.[72] Staniloae concluded that there is a difference between "irradiation" and "shining forth," the first one pertaining to the saints, and the second to the Son. Still, he acknowledged that Gregory of Cyprus used "shining forth" when he referred to the saints, too,[73] a fact that points to the poverty of human language to express the divine mystery.

Terminology aside, the above considerations suggest that the Church makes the Spirit manifest in the faithful who make the work of the Spirit more transparent in their lives. I would add that the Church manifests the Spirit in its sacraments as outpourings of grace upon creation and in its proclamation of the Gospel to the nations. This is not to say that the Spirit is absent outside the Church. The entire Trinity is present in creation in general and humankind in particular. The Church is called to manifest this presence more fully and to bring the world closer to the Trinity, as I show in the next chapter.

## The Spirit, Christ, and Missions

In the previous two chapters I attempted to explain how the Father and the Son are present in a general sense in all humankind and in a fuller, special sense in the Church. The Spirit is no exception. In a general sense, the Spirit is present in all creation, especially in each and every human being, regardless of their religious affiliation, and the Spirit leads them to the Son. Corresponding to the eternal resting of the Spirit in the Son, Staniloae wrote about the role of the Spirit to draw the world toward the Son, since "no one can say 'Jesus is the Lord' except by the Holy Spirit" (1 Cor. 12.3).[74] This means that, just as the Spirit is breathed forth in order to rest in the Son, so the people who are filled with the Spirit are directed toward Christ, whom they experience more and more fully. Humankind becomes fully united with the humanity of Christ in the Church, where the Spirit is fully manifested. Thus, in an imperfect way, the entire world is filled with the

---

71  Staniloae, "The Procession of the Holy Spirit," 179.
72  Symeon the New Theologian. *Hymns of the Divine Love* 24 and 39.
73  Staniloae, *Theology and the Church*, 27–28.
74  Ibid., 14.

Spirit and waits to be led to the Son. These considerations are very relevant in discussions of the missionary task of the Church and of interreligious dialogue.

The East has a longstanding history of missionary activity, represented for example by the evangelization efforts of Cyril and Methodius among the Slavs and Russian missions to Alaska. It is thus surprising to note Zizioulas's affirmation that in the Orthodox Church, mission is still possible "here and there" and it is always centered on the Eucharist, since mission starts with the building of a new Church. He then states that in Orthodoxy there is "more care for the glorious liturgy than for the social problems and mission."[75] Even more surprisingly, Zizioulas supports his statement with his understanding of the relationship between the Spirit and the Son. He considers that there are two types of Pneumatology in the New Testament. According to the first, *missionary-historical* type, the Spirit is the power that Christ gives to the Church for its mission, so the Spirit is an agent of Christ. According to the second, *eucharistic-eschatological* type of Pneumatology, the Spirit leads to Christ's birth, baptism, and resurrection, to which corresponds the Spirit's work of building up the Church as communion, without empowering individuals for mission. This is Christology conditioned by Pneumatology.[76] Zizioulas seems to embrace exclusively the second model, but does not justify ignoring the first, even though it is biblical and patristic. Staniloae was much more successful in presenting a balance between Christology and Pneumatology, between the Spirit resting in the Son and the Son sending the Spirit, so Staniloae's trinitarian foundation of missiology is much more solid. Elsewhere Zizioulas drew closer to Staniloae's position:

> On the one hand the Spirit creates a centripetal movement by drawing the Church towards unity in and through a given structure. On the other hand, the same Spirit makes the Church *ek-static*, relational, and all-embracing towards everything not strictly enclosed by the given structures, even towards the whole of creation.[77]

Kasper is more consistent than Zizioulas in his theology of missions as an application of his pneumatologically defined Christology:

> A Christology in a pneumatological perspective is therefore what best enables us to combine both the uniqueness and the universality of Jesus Christ.

---

75   John D. Zizioulas, "Implications ecclésiologiques de deux types de pneumatologie," in *Communio Sanctorum: Mélanges offerts à Jean-Jacques von Allmen*, ed. Boris Bobrinskoy and Yves Congar (Geneva: Labor et Fides, 1982), 149–50.

76   Ibid., 141–45.

77   Zizioulas, "The Pneumatological Dimension of the Church," 156–58.

It can show how the Spirit who is operative in Christ in his fullness, is at work in varying degrees everywhere in the history of mankind, and also how Jesus Christ is the goal and head of all humanity. The Body of Christ, the Church, is greater and wider than the institutional boundaries of the Church; it has existed since the beginning of the world and to it belong all who allow themselves to be led by Christ's Spirit in faith, hope, and love.[78]

It is very important to emphasize that, in Kasper's opinion, the Spirit is related to Christ who is the Son incarnate, and not a *Logos asarkos*, as in the theology of Jacques Dupuis.[79] The Spirit leads humankind to the incarnate Christ, its goal and head. However, what is intriguing about Kasper's affirmation is precisely the last four words, "faith, hope, and love." Kasper means to say, and I agree with him, that non-Christians can have, in Christ's Spirit, faith, hope, and love. Does he mean explicit faith/hope/love in the Triune God? Kasper sheds more light on this issue in the following lines, where he uses language close to Rahner's "anonymous Christian":

> The Spirit of Christ is indeed at work everywhere where men seek to transcend their life towards an ultimate meaning of their existence and where, in the hope of being finally and absolutely accepted, they seek to accept themselves and their fellow men. But all these anonymous ways to Christ attain their ultimate clarity and fulfillment only in an explicit encounter with him.[80]

Here, Kasper affirms the superiority of explicit Christian proclamation to the "anonymous ways to Christ," and presents the Spirit as the one who leads to Christ. In other words, the good ways of living one's life, empowered by the Spirit, lead to and find their fulfillment in the explicit proclamation of Christ.

The Church has the mission to make more and more effective the Spirit who already exists in the world so that all the human beings are drawn to the Body of Christ, in which the Spirit is present in its fullness. This is a theanthropic activity, where the human efforts of evangelization are joined with the Holy Spirit who empowers the Church for missions and is present in the entire world, drawing it to the Son. As with the Father and the Son, the Spirit is present in a general way in all of humankind, and in a special, fuller sense, in the Church.

---

78  Kasper, *Jesus the Christ*, 267–68.

79  Jacques Dupuis, S.J., *Toward a Christian Theology of Religious Pluralism* (Maryknoll, NY: Orbis Books, 1997).

80  Kasper, *Jesus the Christ*, 268. See also John Paul II's *Redemptoris Missio* no. 29 in William R. Burrows, ed., *Redemption and Dialogue: Reading Redemptoris Missio and Dialogue and Proclamation* (Maryknoll, NY: Orbis Books, 1993) 19.

The role of the Spirit in the world and the Spirit's activity in bringing the world to the Son are also relevant for interreligious dialogue. On the one hand, these principles reinforce the need for the Church to accomplish its missionary task to bring all the nations to Christ (Mt. 28.19). On the other hand, they value the presence of God in the followers of non-Christian religions, which is an absolute condition for having a constructive interreligious dialogue.

The same relationships between the Spirit and the Son are relevant for the discussion of charisms and institution in the Church.

## Institution and Charisms

No one in the West should ever forget the Inquisition and its exaggerated emphasis on the unity (indeed, uniformity) of faith and administration. Charisms were violently quieted down. No one in the East should ever forget the great number of theologians—ordained, as John Chrysostom, or not, as Maximus the Confessor—who were exiled for the "good," "peace," and "unity" of the Church, seen exclusively as institution. These theologians were persecuted by their own Church, which later canonized them and now venerates them as saints.

The relationship between charism and institution is of course a much older issue. Without going into a detailed biblical discussion, at the minimum one can affirm that, in the New Testament, charisms are meant for the common good of building up the Church,[81] while offices are seen as ordering the charismata.[82] There is a concern here to maintain diversity (represented by the multitude of gifts) in unity (safeguarded by the institution), concern that stayed with the Church throughout its history and will remain until the eschaton.[83]

These examples show that sometimes the institutional character of the Church takes precedence over its charismatic aspects, even when the vessels of the charisms are ordained representatives of the institution. Simultaneously—and this is generally the danger in Protestant churches—the charisms can at times

---

81  "When you come together, each one has a hymn, a lesson, a revelation, a tongue, or an interpretation. Let all things be done for building up" (1 Cor. 14.26).

82  "Be eager to prophesy, and do not forbid speaking in tongues; but all things should be done decently and in order" (1 Cor. 14.33, 39–40).

83  Golitzin compares Pseudo-Dionysius's emphasis on the institutional character of the Church with Symeon the New Theologian's insistence on the charismatic aspects of ecclesiology. Golitzin concludes that the tension between charisms and institution represents "one of the fundamental antinomies of Christian existence *in statu via* . . . [and] does not appear to admit of any resolution this side of the eschaton." Golitzin, "Hierarchy versus Anarchy?" 175.

take precedence over the institution by refusing an ordering of these charisms and rejecting some forms of institutional authority.

Staniloae discussed the relationship between charism and institution first as a response to the slavophiles who opposed the institutional character of the Church to a life of grace and communion in love. Second, he addressed the overemphasis of the institutional character of the Church in Catholicism.[84] And third, he responded to Barth's criticism that sacramental churches are excessively institutional and not event-oriented, the latter placing more emphasis on the Spirit's movements in the hearts of those who hear the word of God.[85]

## *The Association Christ-Institution, Spirit-Charisms*

Because ordained ministers are commissioned by Christ to teach, liturgize, and lead the Church in his name, institution is generally associated with the work of Christ in the Church. Similarly, because the Holy Spirit bestows charisms upon the faithful—ordained and nonordained alike—the charismatic aspect of the Church is paired with the work of the Spirit. Staniloae, however, did not adopt these associations to the point of separating Christ from the Spirit and their works in institution and charisms. He affirmed the christological character of charisms and the pneumatic character of the institution. He is one of the most convincing Orthodox theologians to explain the intimate connection between charism and institution.

Staniloae noted that both institution and charisms strive to accomplish a common goal, namely to build up the Body of Christ (cf. Eph. 4.12). Given the eternal relationship between the Son and the Spirit and its manifestation in the Church, there is diversity in the institution and unity in the gifts that have their unique source in the Spirit of Christ.[86]

In light of these considerations and having 1 Cor. 12.4-6[87] in mind, the association of Christ with the institution and unity, or of the Spirit with charisms and diversity is very limited—partly justified, but limited. Staniloae insisted on the Spirit as factor of unity. He affirmed that "the Spirit active in the Church through Christ not only imparts the variety of charisms but also creates unity

---

84    Staniloae, "Ecclesiological Synthesis," 275–77.
85    Staniloae, "Sacramental Aspect," 531–34.
86    Staniloae, *Theology and the Church*, 53.
87    "Now there are varieties of gifts, but the same Spirit; and there are varieties of services, but the same Lord; and there are varieties of activities, but it is the same God who activates all of them in everyone" (1 Cor. 12.4-6).

among those who have been given these gifts in Christ."[88] Staniloae based his affirmations on the many patristic instances that attribute to the Holy Spirit the role of creating unity. For example, Gregory Nazianzen[89] and Gregory of Nyssa regarded Pentecost as a reversal of the confusion of languages at the tower of Babel (cf. Gen. 11.9), since the Spirit established a common understanding among the faithful who speak different languages in the Church.[90] Hence, the Spirit gives diverse gifts, but these are unified in being gifts of the one Spirit, for the building up of the Body of Christ, which is both unified and made up of diverse members.[91] These remarks complement Lossky and Florovsky's imbalances presented above, as well as a strict association between Christ and institution or the Spirit and charisms.

## Charismatic Institution and Institutional Charisms

Staniloae argued that "institutional" and "charismatic" are inseparable emphases of the same ecclesial life, since the institution is also charismatic and the charisms are made effective in the institution. The explanation lies in the eternal relationship between the Son and the Spirit.

Staniloae commented on the document produced by the Faith and Order Commission of the World Council of Churches in Montreal (1963), whose main point was that "all members of the Church are gifted for the common good." Reflecting upon this affirmation and also upon the rest of the document, Staniloae concluded that an exclusively institutional depiction of the Church denotes a poor spirituality and that charisms cannot accomplish their purpose outside of the institution:

> If the variety of gifts derives from the same Spirit who is at work in all and is revealed in the service of the common good, then we can conclude

---

88   Staniloae, *Theology and the Church*, 40. This understanding reflects the Pauline words: "All these [gifts] are activated by one and the same Spirit, who allots to each one individually just as the Spirit chooses" (1 Cor. 12.11).

89   *In Pentecostem*, Oratio 16, PG 34, 448.

90   Staniloae, "The Theological Foundations of Hierarchy and Synodality," 166–67.

91   Afanassieff would support Staniloae's affirmation that the Spirit is not a factor of anarchy, but of unity in the Church. He wrote: "it is the Spirit who serves as the guiding principle of organization and order in the Church.... For this reason it is hard to imagine anything that would contradict the basic principles of ecclesial life as much as the hypothesis that distinguishes charismatic from non-charismatic ministries." Afanassieff, *The Church of the Holy Spirit*, 5. Similarly, Ware considers that the Spirit unites and diversifies at the same time because there is only one Spirit who bestows many charisms. Ware, *The Orthodox Church*, 242.

that the institution is not devoid of spirituality while spirituality on the other hand is not inevitably lacking in structure and institutional order. An institution with a weakened spiritual life would give proof of a weakening of the actual presence of Christ as well, while a disordered spirituality which does not maintain ecclesial unity would indicate in turn a weakening of the true presence of the Holy Spirit. The true Church is christological *and* pneumatological, institutional and spontaneous at the same time, or rather it is christological because it is pneumatological and vice-versa.[92]

Given Staniloae's understanding of the eternal relationship between the Son and the Spirit, in which the Spirit rests in the Son and then returns to the Father from the Son, and in which the begetting of the Son and the procession of the Spirit from the Father are so closely related, it is not surprising that he did not separate the economies of the Son and of the Spirit. He disagreed both with Lossky's pairing of nature with Christ or person with the Spirit, as well as with the association between institution and Christ or charism and the Spirit:

> It is inadmissible to say . . . that the institutional priesthood is christological while the non-institutional priesthood is pneumatological. Nor can it be said that Christ unifies us within a unity of nature while the Spirit distinguishes us as persons within this institutional or pantheist[93] unity (Lossky). All that Christ achieves, he achieves through the Spirit.[94]

---

92  Staniloae, *Theology and the Church*, 39–40.
93  Staniloae's term "pantheist" cannot be taken in its proper sense. He meant it as an impersonal created nature penetrated by an impersonal divine nature. Staniloae was too harsh in this instance, since Lossky would not have taken the logical consequences of his ecclesiology that far. And yet, Staniloae pointed to a danger inherent in Lossky's theology, namely the logical possibility of a christological, institutional Church that is not at the same time a charismatic community. Staniloae's criticism of pantheism started early in his career, when he saw the threat of the infiltration of pantheistic ideologies in the writings of Orthodox theologians such as Berdiaev and especially Bulgakov. Probably only later on, when he noticed that these two Russian theologians did not have the expected influence upon Orthodox theology, Staniloae stopped referring to them. But he did not cease to criticize pantheism. In my view, during this time Staniloae was in fact subtly criticizing communist pantheist-like ideology, which proposed union without the preservation of personal characteristics. Paradoxically, if Communism theoretically advocated equality among people, in reality it led to the subordination of the masses (devoid of personal characteristics) to their leaders.
94  Staniloae, *Theology and the Church*, 39.

Thus, Staniloae affirmed the equal presence of the Spirit upon both the ordained and the rest of the faithful, when he underlined the pneumatological character of institutional priesthood, or when he contended that, because the special grace of priesthood is given at Ordination, this does not mean that the Spirit rests "more" upon the clergy than upon the rest of the believers; it just means that they have a special grace.[95] Along the same lines, Afanassieff considered that the plenitude of grace (*omnis gratia*) was given to the Church, so the Church is a charismatic organism. Not only those possessing certain extraordinary gifts, but all ministers and laics are charismatics.[96]

Zizioulas, too, argues that sacraments and ministry should not be seen as strictly christological, since they are also pneumatological, in the sense that every Ordination is a new Pentecost. He actually contends that "one of the greatest and historically most inexplicable misfortunes for the Church came when, I do not know how, the most charismatic of all acts, namely ordination into the ministry, came to be regarded as a non- or even anti-charismatic notion."[97] Thus, extraordinary ministries are wrongly called "charismatic," as if the ordinary ministries would not be charismatic. On the contrary, the institution is "a charismatic demand of the communion created by the Spirit . . . it constantly depends on the Spirit and it exists only epiclectically."[98] These remarks on the institutional and charismatic aspects of ecclesiology are intrinsically connected to the idea that communion implies unity in diversity of ministries.

## Unity in Diversity

The union of the faithful without the loss of each person's characteristics and the free manifestation of their charisms takes place primarily in worship, which I discuss next. But first, a few explanatory liturgical notes.

At the Preparation Service (*Proskomide*), the priest prepares the gifts of bread and wine to be consecrated during the Liturgy. After preparing the Lamb (the piece of bread that will become the Body of Christ), the priest also takes some small pieces of bread and puts them around the Lamb. These pieces represent the Theotokos, nine categories of saints and angels, as well as the living and departed members of the Church. Right there, on the paten, stands the entire

---

95  Dumitru Staniloae and M. A. Costa de Beauregard, *Mica dogmatica vorbita: dialoguri la Cernica [Brief Spoken Dogmatics: Dialogues at Cernica].* Translated by Maria-Cornelia Oros. (Sibiu: Deisis, 1995), 31.

96  Afanassieff, *The Church of the Holy Spirit*, 2–3.

97  Zizioulas, *Being as Communion*, 192.

98  Zizioulas, "The Pneumatological Dimension of the Church," 150–52.

Church, heaven and earth gathered around Christ, all being prepared for the bloodless sacrifice.

Toward the end of the Divine Liturgy, after the faithful have received the Eucharist, the priest pours into the chalice the pieces for the living and the dead praying: "Wash away, Lord, by Your holy Blood, the sins of all those commemorated through the intercessions of the Theotokos and all Your saints."[99] Staniloae regarded this succession of liturgical events as unifying the entire Church, showing the continuity between the Church militant and triumphant. He considered that the Blood of the Lord creates solidarity both among the Church in heaven (the Theotokos and the saints) and between heaven and earth. All are united in prayer through the Blood of the liturgical sacrifice, as all these pieces of bread are poured into the chalice.[100] Staniloae continued:

> The solidarity or the sobornicity indicated among them through the positioning of their pieces on the same disc, around the Lamb that will become the Body of Christ, becomes more accentuated through the introduction of the parts for all in the unconsumed Blood of Christ, as infinite reserve of life. The blood is the principle of life of the organism. The Blood of Christ, in which there is also the power of the Holy Spirit, is more so the principle of unitary life of all those who are introduced in it through their pieces [of bread taken at the Preparation Service].[101]

Thus, Staniloae affirmed clearly the unifying role of the Liturgy, which brings together Christ and the faithful (both living and departed, now purified through the Eucharist), the angels, and the saints. All are united in the Spirit of Christ, represented by the Blood of the sacrifice, so both the Spirit and Christ create unity.

This unity is not uniform. When distributing Communion, the priest mentions the name of each communicant, making them part of the Body of Christ or the Church, without the loss of personal characteristics. This safeguards the role that each member accomplishes in the Church, according to the Pauline words, "For just as the body is one and has many members, and all the members of the body, though many, are one body, so it is with Christ.... If all were a single member, where would the body be?" (1 Cor. 12.12-19). Staniloae continued:

> So the indication of the name does not imply a right to individualistic affirmation, but the call to the fulfillment of a service in conformity with

---

99    John Chrysostom, *The Divine Liturgy*, 33.
100   Staniloae, "Ecclesiological Synthesis," 276.
101   Staniloae, *Spirituality and Communion*, 366.

one's own characteristics.... Because only by accomplishing a specific service, does one serve the others and help the harmony of the entire Body of Christ or of the Church.... Saint Maximus the Confessor goes even further, saying that each person receives from the Body of Christ what is fit for that person, or according to the stage in which that person is. It could be said that each person receives the entire Body of Christ, but actualizes only those works or powers of the Body of Christ that are more in tune with that person's characteristics, ascending on one's own path, but in solidarity with all, from one stage to the other.[102]

It is important to stress Staniloae and Maximus's affirmation that, even though the faithful receive the entire Body of Christ in the Eucharist, they actualize only those powers that are in tune with their characteristics. Looking deeper into Staniloae's sources, it is significant that elsewhere Maximus described these powers as "the grace of adoption which was given through holy baptism in the Holy Spirit and which makes us perfect in Christ."[103] Juan Miguel Garrigues interpreted this Maximian text to mean that the divine form that Christ communicates to us in Baptism is an ontological disposition that empowers our nature to respond actively to the vocation that solicits us personally to be children of God and to enter into Christ's "mode of life."[104] The predisposition instilled in the faithful at Baptism is activated in the Eucharist, when the members of the Body of Christ accomplish their specific charismatic roles within the organism of the Church, according to their capacities. Thus, Staniloae's argument does not rest exclusively on the Eucharist, but on all the sacraments and the other charismatic manifestations in the life of the Church.

---

102　Ibid., 337–38. Staniloae based these affirmations on Maximus's *Ambigua (Romanian)* 124a, 309. See the same idea in Maximus's "Chapters on Knowledge II, 56." In *Maximus Confessor: Selected Writings* Translated by George C. Berthold (New York: Paulist Press, 1985), 159: "The one who prays to receive his daily bread does not exactly receive it as the bread is in itself but as the one who receives it is capable. For the Bread of Life because he loves men, gives himself to all who ask but not to all in the same way; rather to those who perform great works of righteousness in a fuller way, to those who do less in a smaller way—to each in accordance with his spiritual capacity."

103　Saint Maximus the Confessor, "The Church's Mystagogy in Which Are Explained the Symbolism of Certain Rites Performed in the Divine Synaxis," in *Maximus Confessor: Selected Writings*, ed. George C. Berthold, *Classics of Western Spirituality* (New York: Paulist Press, 1985), 24, 211.

104　Juan Miguel Garrigues, *Maxime le Confesseur: La charité, avenir divin de l'homme, Théologie Historique 38* (Paris: Beauchesne, 1976), 118–20.

Berger considers that Staniloae's description of the Church as "an uninter-rupted *epiclesis*"[105] made possible by his treatment of Baptism and Chrismation, offers a significant advantage over Zizioulas's exclusively eucharistic approach to the presence of the Spirit in the Church. Staniloae did not limit the presence of the Spirit to the Eucharist, but affirmed a perpetual abiding of the Spirit in the Body of Christ, manifested in all aspects of Church life, and particularly in the sacraments.[106] In light of these remarks, I would add that Staniloae went beyond Zizioulas's "rhythmic Christian existence," toward a Church that resembles the hesychast model of unceasing prayer. The Father, Son, and Holy Spirit are per-petually present in the Church, through their continual invocation in all facets of ecclesial life.

## Conclusion

In this chapter I continued the discussion of the Church as a reflection, icon, sac-rament of, and union with, the Trinity. I first analyzed Staniloae's understand-ing of the Church as it is filled with the Spirit of communion, manifestation of love both in the Trinity and in the Church. I continued with the ecclesiological implications of Staniloae's Pneumatology, highlighting his understanding of the specific roles that the Son and the Spirit have within the Church, as well as the balance between these roles, with implications for the relationship between the institutional and charismatic aspects of the Church. Staniloae had a major contribution in this sense, since he succeeded in finding the balance between the roles of the Son and the Spirit in the Church or, in fact, a balance among the theologies of all three persons of the Trinity.

In this second part of the book I attempted to show that ecclesiology is a chapter of the theology of the Father, of Christology, and of Pneumatology. Ecclesiology is ultimately a chapter of Triadology. I have not separated the works of the Father, Son, and Holy Spirit in the Church, not even when, for reasons of systematization, I emphasized the role of each person in a distinct chapter. Staniloae's theology would not permit such separation, since his eccle-siology is fully trinitarian.

---

105   Staniloae, "The Authority of the Church," 188.
106   Berger, "Does the Eucharist Make the Church?" 51. On the same page, Berger adds in regard to the Spirit's continual rest in the Body of Christ: "The Church is thus seen as an *epiclectic*, eschatological and *koinonic* reality in its *totality*, in all its activities and in the life of every believer, and not exclusively in its Eucharistic celebration. Through its continual *epiclesis*, the Church is being *continually trans-formed* into the Body of Christ."

In the final section of the book, I attempt to address the ways in which the theological considerations presented thus far impact the life of the Church. In the discussion of the various aspects of priesthood and the relationships among local churches, I present the Church as a communion in the image of the Trinity, while engaging Staniloae with different aspects of Catholic communion ecclesiology.

# PART III

# COMMUNION ECCLESIOLOGY

# Chapter 6

## PRIESTHOOD TOWARD CREATION

In the previous chapters I contended that each person of the Trinity is present in a general sense in all creation, human and nonhuman alike. In a special sense, the Trinity is fully manifested in the Church. It is now important to present God's priestly work toward creation both in a general and special sense, as God's acts are mediated through natural priesthood and the priesthood of the Church. Such a discussion is particularly relevant for ecology.

In today's ecological crisis, we, humans, are the consumers of a creation that we treat as ours to possess and even abuse for our own, anthropocentric, interests. Through our attitudes, we question God's presence in the world, the purpose and sacramentality of creation. In response, Staniloae referred to the human being as priest of creation, a designation that was in turn rooted in the theology of Maximus the Confessor.[1] Rather than being the consumer, the human person sanctifies and reestablishes the Godward movement of creation, regarding it as God's presence, gift, and sacrament. This is possible because we share in Christ's priesthood toward creation.

### Christ's Priesthood toward Creation

Adam was created as priest of creation but, with the fall, he greatly impoverished his natural priesthood.[2] Several cosmological, anthropological, and soteriological observations support this affirmation. Provided here rather schematically, they preface the other aspects of natural priesthood discussed in this chapter.

---

1  Radu Bordeianu, "Maximus and Ecology: The Relevance of Maximus the Confessor's Theology of Creation for the Present Ecological Crisis," *The Downside Review* 127, no. 447 (2009): 103–26.

2  Miller affirms that natural priesthood was rendered ineffectual by the fall. (Charles Miller, "Presentation of the Gifts: Orthodox Insights for Western Liturgical Renewal," *Worship* 60, no. 1 [1986]: 94.) However, Miller's position stands in contrast with Staniloae's remarks in "Creation as Gift and the Sacraments," 19.

While God's presence in the world was evident before the fall, Adam's sin has corrupted our capacity to see this divine presence. Nature[3] ceased to be the transparent environment through which we could see the divine *logoi*—God's original ideas or intentions for creation. (Maximus defined the *logoi* as "the unifying, ordering, determinative, and defining principles in accordance with which God instituted created natures."[4])

While the entire universe is supposed to move from God, in God, and toward God, Adam regarded all material realities as meant to satisfy his passions and moving toward him. He wanted to be god without God, so he ate the forbidden fruit. This consumerist attitude disturbed the balance insured by nature's proper movement. It introduced an instability that has increased exponentially over time, resulting in the ecological crisis that we face so acutely today.

While the entire universe is interconnected with the human being as the center that unites the spiritual and material worlds, our fall has corrupted the rest of creation, which now groans in labor pains, having been "subjected to futility, not of its own will but by the will of the one who subjected it" (Rom. 8.20).

While Adam was called to look at creation sacramentally as mediating God and to lift it as a sacrifice to God, he viewed the cosmos simply as his possession. By looking at nature exclusively through the eyes of the senses, he deprived matter of its spiritual dimension and of its Godward movement.

While the fall attributed to the world a false sense of ultimacy, Christ restored to it the dimension of a gift that bears its Offerer. God and the world became united again when the Son assumed a body interrelated with the material world. In Jesus' humanity, matter became fully transparent to God's presence in it.[5]

---

3   I use the terms nature, universe, world, and creation interchangeably in the sense of nonhuman creation, even though humans are part of creation. Similarly, priesthood toward creation is synonymous with natural priesthood.

4   See Adam G. Cooper, *The Body in St Maximus the Confessor: Holy Flesh, Wholly Deified*, The Oxford Early Christian Studies (Oxford, NY: Oxford University Press, 2005), 93. Moreover, Staniloae explained that all elements of creation are symbols of the *logoi* through which God created them. As symbols, there is neither confusion, nor separation between the elements of creation and their *logoi*, since the *logoi* are also the means through which God exercises his providence in the world: "This constitutes the antinomy of the symbol: in order to know what is invisible, one must look at what is visible, but at the same time must pass beyond what is visible.... One must not stop at what is visible, because this would mean its transformation into an idol [as opposed to being an icon]. But the transcending does not leave behind the visible, because the prototype that is transparent through it, works in it, without being one [i.e., confused] with it." Dumitru Staniloae, "Simbolul ca anticipare si temei al posibilitatii icoanei [The Symbol as Anticipation and Foundation of the Possibility of the Icon]," *Studii Teologice* 7, no. 7–8 (1957): 450.

5   Staniloae, "Creation as Gift and the Sacraments," 11–16.

Moreover, Staniloae affirmed that Christ gathered in himself all human beings and all of creation, so when he brought himself as a sacrifice to the Father, he also offered creation in its totality. Christ is the ultimate High Priest of the cosmic Liturgy. And yet, it is a synergic celebration, where we also need to offer ourselves as willing sacrifices, empowered by Christ's offering.[6]

While the fall introduced a separation between creation and Creator, the hypostatic union of Christ's two natures reestablished the communion between created and uncreated.[7] By mediating between God and the world, Christ restored humankind's mediating aptitude. He activated fully the potentiality inherent in human nature to be priest of creation.[8] It is now up to each human being to assume and share in the work of Christ, the priest of creation *par excellence*.

## Sharing in Christ's Priesthood toward Creation

### Seeing God's Presence in the World

As opposed to other forms of spirituality that see only evil in the world and society, we ought to observe nature with pure eyes, to see God's eternal intentions within creation and an uncorrupted image of the universe. As Maximus writes, "All of God's beings . . . herald mysteriously the *logoi* according to which they were made and reveal through these *logoi* the purpose embedded by God in each creature."[9] Moreover, these *logoi* are compared to some words that, read dispassionately, reveal God.[10] The key here is to look at creation dispassionately.

Similarly, Staniloae affirmed that by living in a proper relationship with the world and with divine assistance, the purified human person sees more easily God in creation. God's presence in the world will be fully revealed only in the eschaton. Nonetheless, the contemplation of God in creation is an anticipation of God's full revelation at the end of time.[11] Both Maximus and Staniloae assumed

---

6   Staniloae, *Spirituality and Communion*, 22.
7   Maximus ascribed special importance to Christ's ascension, when "this world truly ascended to heaven together with God the Logos." *Ambigua* 149. Maximus the Confessor, *Ambigua (Romanian)*, 328.
8   Staniloae, *Dogmatics 3*, 10–11.
9   Maximus the Confessor, *Answers to Thalasius*, 65.
10  Maximus the Confessor, *Ambigua (Romanian)*, 218.
11  Staniloae, "The Symbol as Anticipation and Foundation of the Possibility of the Icon," 452.

here the dialectic of God's transcendence and immanence, together with many other Greek patristic writers who affirm that God is wholly other than creation, even while being present in it as its source and goal.[12] For Staniloae, the essence-energies distinction-in-unity allows for both God's transcendence and for his communicability in creation.

There is a second way in which we share in Christ's priesthood.

## Reestablishing Creation's Godward Movement

Through his sacrifice on the Cross, Christ restored both the dimension of the world as a gift and our natural priesthood as the capacity to offer creation back to God.[13] As Maximus wrote, all creation belongs to God and must be offered back to God as a gift. The one who offers creation is precisely the human person who, liberated from passions, contemplates creation spiritually and offers the divine *logoi* present in the world "as 'gifts' to the Lord."[14] This attitude is eucharistic: we lift up to God what already belongs to him, reestablishing creation's movement in God and toward God.

Staniloae, too, considered that the world was created as a gift in which humans receive divine grace and thus salvation. In turn, Adam and Eve were supposed to exercise their natural priesthood by offering the world back to God in a "dialogue of the gift."[15] The two elements of the dialogue are clearly emphasized: God descends to us through the gift of creation, while we lift the world up to God. "This," Staniloae added, "is the sacred, priestly ministry to which we were destined within cosmic creation. Partaking of these gifts while giving thanks to God is an image of the Eucharist. Through all things we partake of the 'body' of the Word."[16] This imagery implies Staniloae's appropriation of Maximus's idea that the Word is present or, indeed, incarnate, not only in Jesus, but also in creation, the Eucharist, and the words of Scripture, through which we are able to partake of Christ.

---

12  See an excellent analysis of several patristic authors, especially Gregory of Nyssa and Gregory of Nazianzen, in Williams, *The Divine Sense: The Intellect in Patristic Theology*, 115–18.

13  Staniloae, "Creation as Gift and the Sacraments," 11–16. Staniloae did not mean that all human beings are automatically acting fully as priests of creation in the sense outlined above, but that humans have the potential to be fully aware of God's presence in the world and reestablish the right relationship between God and creation.

14  Maximus the Confessor, *Answers to Thalasius*, 216, 20.

15  Staniloae, *The Experience of God 2*, 22.

16  Staniloae, *Spirituality and Communion*, 20.

Furthermore, we need to use the elements of creation as gifts among us, after we make them more beautiful through our work,[17] and this, too, is an exercise in our natural priesthood. Staniloae considered that through scientific discoveries, humankind organizes the forces of nature in conformity with their *logoi* for the benefit of society. We reveal the beauty of creation through arts and literature. Other forms of celebrating the cosmic Liturgy include the sacrifices of parents for their children, the transformation of the family home into a temple of God, and the work of those who contribute to a better society.[18] As Miller comments on these remarks, "Nature becomes the medium in which humanity grows spiritually when we comprehend, shape and bring to fruition its 'unlimited potentiality.'"[19]

A third way of continuing Christ's priesthood is ...

## The Spiritualization of Creation

Adam was created at the center of creation, with both spirit and body, or, in the words of both Gregory Nazianzen and Maximus, as a "mixed worshipper."[20] According to Staniloae, Adam's position as "mixed worshipper," gave him the ability to infuse material creation with his spirituality.[21] Just as the human soul imprints its spirituality onto the body, so the human being spiritualizes material creation, which in turn is connected with the human body, thus uniting the spiritual and material realms. To fulfill this role, it was necessary for the human person to be created at the intersection of spirit and matter.

This central position occupied by humans is the etymological meaning of anthropocentrism. Nevertheless, since our contemporary definition of anthropocentrism is a power-term and implies that humanity is at the center *without*

---

17 While also emphasizing the solidarity that work creates among humans and with God, Staniloae added in this sense: "Only the animal takes its place totally within the framework of what nature invariably provides for it. The human being proves himself the 'master' of nature in this respect as well, while nature shows itself as malleable, contingent reality, equated to the measure of the creative human imagination.... Humans must work and think in solidarity with regard to the transformation of the gifts of nature. Thus, it is through the mediation of nature that solidarity is created among humans, and work, guided by thought, is a principal virtue creative of communion among humans." Staniloae, *The Experience of God 2*, 4–5.

18 Staniloae, *Spirituality and Communion*, 19–20, 27.

19 Miller, *The Gift of the World*, 96.

20 This expression does not appear in the English version, but Staniloae used it in his Romanian translation. See Maximus the Confessor, *Ambigua (Romanian)*, 95–96.

21 Staniloae, *The Experience of God 2*, 51.

God, one cannot use it when nature is logocentric (or theocentric) and when humankind is regarded as priest of creation who sanctifies the world from the center.[22]

How do we sanctify creation? By fully realizing the sanctity of creation, not in the pantheistic sense that creation is holy, but that God is transparent through and present in it, as its creator and purpose. We further sanctify the world when we discover its value as gift and sacrifice due to God, as when we offer creation back to God in the Liturgy with the words, "Your own of your own, we offer to you in all and for all." These considerations lead to an analysis of the sacramentality of creation.

Our relationship with creation is a two-way street: on the one hand, our salvation depends on the world, and creation is the environment of our spiritual growth; in this sense, the world is already a sacrament. On the other hand, the vocation of humankind is to turn the universe fully into a sacrament, representing the fourth aspect of natural priesthood as a continuation of Christ's priesthood.

### The World as Sacrament

Staniloae affirmed that the cosmos is a sacrament created to make God transparent in it, or to manifest God's presence in it. Hence, the world has sacramental-liturgical and revelatory functions.[23]

To be precise, on this side of the eschaton, nature is not a sacrament proper. It is more correct to speak of the sacramentality of creation as visible sign and instrument through which grace is communicated.[24] Presently, the universe is

---

22  Lynn White accused the Judeo-Christian tradition in general, and Western Christianity in particular, of being intrinsically anthropocentric and dominant over nature in a sense that caused the ecological crisis (Lynn White, "The Historical Roots of Our Ecologic Crisis," *Science* 155, no. March 10 [1967]: 1203–07.) Given the above considerations, Staniloae would disagree. Furthermore, Moltmann rightly observes that this alleged anthropocentrism is more than 3000 years old, whereas the insistence of the Enlightenment on the idea that since God's pre-eminent characteristic is power, so the human being (created in the image of God) must strive for power, chronologically coincides better with the ecological crisis. Jürgen Moltmann, *God in Creation: A New Theology of Creation and the Spirit of God*, trans. Margaret Kohl (Minneapolis, MN: Fortress Press, 1993), 26.

23  Staniloae, *Dogmatics 3*, 10–13. Staniloae, *The Experience of God 1*, 67. Staniloae, *The Experience of God 2*, 45. Staniloae, *Jesus Christ, the Light of the World*, 31.

24  For Schmemann's account of the sacramentality inherent in all creation and the human responsibility to recognize it as such, see Schmemann, *The Eucharist*, 222.

not fully a Church; though redeemed, it is on its way to perfection. In the esch-aton, however, nature will be fully the medium of God's manifestation, when God will be "all in all" (1 Cor. 15.28). In other words, the universe that will have become a Church, will be God's all-encompassing sacrament.[25] Thus, the process of spiritualization will be fulfilled in the eschaton, when creation will become fully a sacrament or, in Staniloae's estimation, the only sacrament, the milieu in which God and humankind will be in communion.[26] To borrow an image from Rev. 5.13, humankind will praise the Lamb together with "every creature in heaven and on earth and under the earth and in the sea and all that is in them."

When creation and humankind praise God together, they both experience their integral state, as opposed to the "less than fully natural," separated state in which they are presently found.[27] We need to join in creation's praise of God, but also listen and learn from it. This pedagogical role of creation is another aspect of its sacramentality. According to Elizabeth Theokritoff, cre-ation teaches us faithfulness, since, as Athanasius wrote,[28] only human beings have strayed from God's purpose. The rest of creation has never ceased to recognize God the Word as their Maker and their King.[29] She continues: "We praise God *for* all creation, . . . but we equally praise him *with* all creation, animate or inanimate.[30] And in a certain sense we offer praise also *on behalf of* all creation."[31]

---

25  Staniloae, *Dogmatics 3*, 11.

26  Staniloae, "Creation as Gift and the Sacraments," 28. Miller comments on this Staniloaean passage that when the Church enlarges its boundaries to include the entire universe, "believers draw the Eucharist into the world and the world into the Eucharist. [This is] a eucharistic celebration no longer experienced by faith but by sight, no longer restricted to particular times and places but embracing all time, all space. The gifts of bread and wine, indeed the gift of ourselves, will, by the trans-figuring Spirit, include the whole of a transformed and transfigured humanity and creation." Miller, *The Gift of the World*, 103.

27  For more on this issue, see Stanley Harakas, "The Integrity of Creation: Ethical Issues," in *Justice, Peace and the Integrity of Creation: Insights from Orthodoxy*, ed. Gennadios Limouris (Geneva: WCC Publications, 1990), 70–82.

28  *On the Incarnation 43.*

29  Elizabeth Theokritoff, *Living in God's Creation: Orthodox Perspectives on Ecology* (Crestwood, NY: St Vladimir's Seminary Press, 2009), 167.

30  See, for example, the Song of the Three Youths who call on the heavens, angels, sun and moon, showers and dew, mountains and hills, whales and monsters, and all the elements of creation, to join them in praising the true God (Prayer of Azariah 1.29-68).

31  Theokritoff, *Living in God's Creation*, 157–58.

This imagery of humans offering praise on behalf of all creation leads to the second aspect of sacramentality, namely the role of the human person in the full transformation of the world into a sacrament.

## Fully a Sacrament

According to Maximus, the entire universe was created to celebrate a cosmic Liturgy and be transformed into a Church through the priestly mediation of the human being.[32] The cosmos praises and glorifies God, but "with silent voices," and that praise is not heard until we give it a voice, until we praise God in and with creation.[33] Staniloae explained that the material world praises God in silence because it does not have discursive reason. This is also the case in the spiritual realm: angels do not have discursive, but intuitive reason, which does not use words.[34]

How do we give creation a voice? By making explicit its sacramentality. As Staniloae put it, our natural priesthood "opens up the world for a more efficient work of God in it."[35] He affirmed that Orthodox sacramental theology is based on the ability of the human person as embodied spirit to become a vehicle through which the Holy Spirit infuses the material world. God's transfiguration and spiritualization of creation through human beings thus represents the "natural" basis of the Church's sacraments.[36] There are, of course, many examples that illustrate the infusion of the Spirit in creation through the liturgical life of the Church. Prominent among these is the church building. Staniloae affirmed that the church as temple,

> as liturgical space, is for the faithful another world, or a created world transfigured, or in the process of transfiguration. It is a world that surpasses

---

32 See especially Maximus the Confessor, "*Mystagogia*," Chapters 3 and 6. For example, in *Mystagogia* 3, p. 189, Maximus sees the church-building as a symbol of the visible world: "Likewise the world is a church since it possesses heaven corresponding to a sanctuary, and for a nave it has the adornment of the earth." Here Maximus is in continuation with a longstanding tradition that regards the universe as a temple. For example, see Origen, *Contra Celsum* 7.44. See also Hans Urs von Balthasar, *Cosmic Liturgy: The Universe According to Maximus the Confessor*, trans. Brian Daley, Communio Books (Ft. Collins, CO: Ignatius Press, 2003); Lars Thumberg, *Man and the Cosmos: The Vision of St. Maximus the Confessor* (New York: St. Vladimir's Seminary Press, 1985), 119–21, 26; Riou, *Le Monde et l'Église*, 153.

33 Maximus the Confessor, *Answers to Thalasius*, 221.

34 Staniloae, note 71 to Maximus the Confessor, *Ambigua (Romanian)*, 95–96.

35 Staniloae, *Spirituality and Communion*, 19.

36 Staniloae, *Dogmatics 3*, 7–9. Miller, *The Gift of the World*, 87.

the separation between past, present, and eschatological future, between earth and heaven, between created and uncreated. This experience of the temple is significantly enhanced by its icons.... Eastern iconography is an overflow of merciful eternity over earthly life, sweetening it with the quietness full of hope of eternity.[37]

At this point it is important to note that iconographers exercise their universal priesthood by sanctifying creation, by offering the matter of wood and paint back to God, transfigured in the icon. Iconographers also have a prophetic calling, since the icon is a Gospel in images, theology in color, book for the illiterate (and literate). It addresses people within their culture: Christ wears Byzantine imperial garbs, even though, historically speaking, he was a poor Jewish peasant. Russian architecture decorates the background, replacing the improvised tents and humble huts, characteristic of the biblical context. Demons are dressed as Persian or Turkish soldiers, to speak to Balkan people under constant attacks.

While the icon teaches in an inculturated language, it also presents the fully sacramental world that God intended and that God will restore in the eschaton. Even for nocturnal scenes, uncreated light comes from everywhere to show God's omnipresence. Chronologically and spatially consecutive events are presented simultaneously in a transcendence of time and space.[38] Mountains represented below knee-height suggest that humans have dominion over passions. John the Baptist with his elongated body and wings calls earthly human beings to live a heavenly life. In the icon, a transfigured cosmos finds its peace and harmony, singing a hymn of triumph. Realized eschatology is experienced in stylized, nonnaturalistic, inverse perspective, which is spiritually more real

---

37 Staniloae, *Spirituality and Communion*, 79, 81.
38 In the Nativity icon, for example, Jesus' humanity is suggested by his bathing after birth, while the animals keeping him warm indicate his divinity: they serve him as the Lord of creation, recognizing his majesty (cf. Isa. 1.3: "The ox knows its owner and the donkey its master's crib"). In the same icon, Joseph is tempted by the devil to doubt Mary's virginity, while Mary is already resting after birth. The magi arrive not at a house, days after the birth, but at the cave, near which the shepherds receive the news of Jesus' nativity and angels sing. This transcendence of space and time encompasses not only events that took place in close proximity to each other, but includes even angels who minister to Jesus, when in fact they are biblically mentioned only after Jesus' temptation in the desert (Mt. 4.11). Lastly, to illustrate that Jesus was born to die for our salvation, he is wrapped in swaddling clothes that intimate his burial and placed in a cave reminiscent of his tomb.

than normal perspective.[39] These brief elements of iconography show clearly the sacramentality of creation as experienced in the sacred, liturgical space.[40]

There are, of course, other instances in which the Church transfigures creation, as when it blesses the water, the oil, or the crops. The world thus becomes transparent to God's presence in it. God becomes all in all, even if not with the same sacramental fullness as in the Eucharist. As Maximus's *Mystagia* suggests, the eucharistic celebration represents the highest degree of reordering, transfiguration, and deification of the cosmos.

During the Divine Liturgy, the priest[41] lifts up the gifts of bread and wine saying, "we offer to you these gifts from your own gifts, in all and for all."[42] Then the *epiclesis* follows, when the bread and wine are changed into the Body and Blood of Christ. God's gifts of wheat and grapes are first transformed by our work into bread and wine; they are then changed through the Spirit into the Body and Blood of Christ and represent the spiritual sacrifice of the community to the Father. (As shown in the previous chapter, the community brings itself as a sacrifice in the pieces of bread that represent it on the paten.) This liturgical instance summarizes very well what our attitude should be toward creation: the entire universe belongs to God, who is the source of this gift, and we, as priests of creation, are called to identify with nature, transform it through our work, lift it up, and offer it back to God. In turn, the Father will send his Spirit to reshape the cosmos in conformity with Christ. The trinitarian understanding of the Church presented thus far in this book acquires here an ecological nuance.

Another way in which we offer creation to God is by uniting our purified and grateful thoughts about creation with the *logoi* present in the world. We thus unite these *logoi* with ourselves, we gather them in ourselves, and we return them to the Logos: "Your own of your own, we offer to you." Gathered in the Liturgy, the faithful advance explicitly and consciously toward God who can be found on the altar table.[43] And since they have gathered the *logoi* in their being, they also return creation back to the Logos.

---

39  See also John Chryssavgis, "The World of the Icon and Creation: An Orthodox Perspective on Ecology and Pneumatology," in *Christianity and Ecology*, ed. Rosemary Radford Ruether and Dieter Hessel (Cambridge, MA: Harvard University Press, 2000), 83–96.

40  For more, see Radu Bordeianu, "Icons," in *Dictionary of Christian Spirituality*, edited by Glen G. Scorgie (Grand Rapids, MI: Zondervan, 2011): 518–19.

41  It is actually not the priest alone who offers the sacrifice, but the entire community celebrates the Liturgy, as I will show in the next chapter.

42  John Chrysostom, *The Divine Liturgy*, 22.

43  Staniloae, *Spirituality and Communion*, 21–24.

Furthermore, the Eucharist represents an anticipation of the eschaton, pointing to the proper consumption of creation. The Eucharist is an anticipation of the heavenly banquet not in the sense of an unrelated image pointing to a remote reality, but as the presence here and now of an eschatological reality, that of the Kingdom of God portrayed as banquet. In this context, consumption of creation becomes a means to get closer to the Creator, rather than a selfish act. And this consumption happens only after the sanctification of creation in the Liturgy, as an anticipation of the end times, when all creation will be united with the Creator in the Church. As Staniloae wrote, "the Church is the union of all that exists, or is destined to encompass all that exists: God and creation. It is the fulfillment of the eternal plan of God: the union of all."[44]

If the discussion of natural priesthood began in reference to humankind in general, it has gradually shifted to a more specific analysis of the Church's priesthood toward creation. This distinction needs to be made more explicit.

### Natural, Universal, and Ordained Priesthood[45]

Even though natural priesthood is manifested in a general sense in all human beings who are called to discover the sanctity of creation and foster communion with the universe, it receives a new, special meaning in the Church. Natural priesthood is fulfilled through its baptismal consecration or, indeed, ordination into universal priesthood.[46] Through Baptism, those who are already priests of creation partake more fully of Christ's priesthood by virtue of their consecration into universal priesthood.[47]

Staniloae affirmed that creation is a Church that is not yet fully developed or actualized. Given the interpenetration among creation, humans, and the Church, the Church proper functions as a leaven, or ferment within the world, helping

---

44  Staniloae, *Dogmatics 2*, 137.
45  Staniloae referred in Romanian to "preotia generala," which literally means, "general priesthood," or, closer to common English usage, "universal priesthood." He also wrote about "preotia slujitoare" translated literally as "serving priesthood" or "ministerial priesthood" (ministerial as a derivation of the noun "ministry"), but I prefer to render it in English as "ordained priesthood." Miller prefers common and ministerial priesthood, respectively. Miller, *The Gift of the World*, 96.
46  Miller considers that the Romanian word for layperson, *mirean*, means anointed one, probably because the Romanian word *mir* means "myrrh," and indicates in part the priestly consecration of the baptized. Schmemann, however, affirmed that the Slavonic *miriane* means "worldly ones." Schmemann, *The Eucharist*, 232.
47  Staniloae, "Jesus Christ, Eternal High Priest," 229.

it develop fully into a Church.[48] The Church is the liturgical center of creation, from which the trinitarian unity is imprinted on creation, resulting in a more accentuated penetration of creation with the unifying power of the Trinity.[49] This work of the Trinity is done through the members of the Church who unveil and promote the ecclesial character of creation by exercising their sanctifying priesthood upon their own being, which is related to the rest of creation. Hence, Staniloae considered that universal priesthood includes natural priesthood.[50]

The same holds true when adding the discussion of ordained priesthood. Since natural, universal, and ordained priesthood share in the same unifying priesthood of Christ, Staniloae emphasized their interconnectedness and communion: "The sacraments of Chrismation and Ordination . . . strengthen natural priesthood with the divine power of . . . Christ's priesthood."[51] Far from ascribing the capacity to sanctify only to the ordained, Staniloae affirmed the role of all humankind in the sanctification of life through natural and universal priesthood, as well.[52] He saw a gradual passing from the natural order to the sacramental realm, denying a clear separation between them. Given these considerations, Miller refers to universal priesthood as mediating between natural and ordained priesthood, having the role of revealing the sacramentality of creation and the artificial character of the separation between the sacred and profane.[53] For Staniloae there is no profane. All creation is spiritual, or even mystical. In what is probably a reaction against the "scientific materialism" put forth by communist authorities, Staniloae referred to the "*mystical materialism*" and "*sacred matter*" (his emphases) that Christianity upholds.[54] Theokritoff

---

48   Staniloae, *Spirituality and Communion*, 14–15.

49   Ibid., 28.

50   Ibid., 17.

51   Staniloae, "Creation as Gift and the Sacraments," 27. In the exercise of their natural priesthood, the distinction (not separation) between the clergy and the people is maintained by the differentiated liturgical roles that they have when creation is sanctified in the blessing of the water or in the changing of bread and wine into the Body and Blood of Christ. Dumitru Staniloae, "Dumnezeu Cuvintul cel Intrupat sfinteste creatia prin cuvintul si fapta omeneasca a sa si a omului si in special a preotului [The Incarnate Word of God Sanctifies Creation through the Human Words and Actions of Himself and of the Human Being, especially the Priest]," *Mitropolia Olteniei* 43, no. 4 (1991): 14.

52   Staniloae wrote: "the fact that the faithful belong to Christ through Baptism and through previous receptions of Communion gives them too the power to bring their gifts . . . to Christ up to a certain point. This offering is perfected through the priest." Staniloae, "Creation as Gift and the Sacraments," 19.

53   Miller, *The Gift of the World*, 96–97.

54   Staniloae, *Dogmatics 3*, 278. See also Toma, *Tradition and Actuality*, 46.

observed in this sense that in the Eucharist we use the natural elements of grains and grapes and change them into bread and wine, but, in Baptism, we do not change the water. In this latter case, natural elements are used sacramentally without any human transformation. She adds,

> Matter used in a sacrament is not a separate category of matter, sacred as opposed to profane; it could better be described as matter unveiled, revealing to us the true Godwardness—the *sacramental quality*—of things we use and handle every day. The Orthodox understanding of the world as a whole may be described as a *sacramental cosmology*.[55]

Staniloae's presentation of the interdependence between natural, universal, and ordained priesthood is very significant ecumenically. It transcends the Protestant-Catholic polemics surrounding the relationship between the ordained and non-ordained. As a result of this polemic, Protestant churches concentrate on the unity of priesthood *within* the Church, shared among all believers. They rarely address natural priesthood and the sacramentality of the cosmos. Staniloae's considerations about a natural priesthood shared in common by all human beings could supplement Protestant theology with a dimension outside the Church. Catholic theologians, too, could benefit from Staniloae's understanding of priesthood outside the sacrament of Orders, as a supplement to the role of the ordained in blessing creation.[56]

---

55  Theokritoff, *Living in God's Creation*, 181. See also Alexander Schmemann, *For the Life of the World: Sacraments and Orthodoxy*, Second ed. (Crestwood, NY: St Vladimir's Seminary Press, 1973), 72–73, 132.

56  For Western perspectives on the sacramentality of the cosmos, though still largely lacking an explicit discussion of natural priesthood (Habgood and Moltmann address this topic briefly on p. 53 and 71, respectively), see John Habgood, "A Sacramental Approach to Environmental Issues," in *Liberating Life: Contemporary Approaches in Ecological Theology*, ed. Charles Birch, William Eakin, and Jay B. McDaniel (Maryknoll, NY: Orbis Books, 1990), 46–53. Kevin W. Irwin, "The Sacramentality of Creation and the Role of Creation in Liturgy and Sacraments," in *And God Saw that It Was Good: Catholic Theology and the Environment*, ed. Drew Christiansen and Walter Grazer (Washington: USCC, 1996), 105–47. Moltmann, *God in Creation*. See also a solid theological foundation that sustains an exquisite poetical edifice in Pierre Teilhard de Chardin, "La Messe sur le Monde," in *Hymne de l'Univers* (Paris: Seuil, 1961), especially 21, 29, 34, 52, 57. For other Orthodox perspectives on priesthood toward creation, see Kallistos Ware, "The Value of the Material Creation," *Sobornost*, no. 3 (1971): 154–65. John D. Zizioulas, "Ecological Asceticism: A Cultural Revolution," *Sourozh* 67, no. February (1997): 23. John D. Zizioulas, "Preserving God's Creation: Three Lectures on Theology and Ecology," *King's Theological Review* 12 (1989): 3.

Furthermore, natural priesthood and its intrinsic connection with the sacramentality of the cosmos represents a challenge to regard priesthood as directed toward all of creation, and not limit it to human society or, even more narrowly, to the community of the baptized. It is important to note that natural priesthood characterizes all human beings. And yet, Staniloae would say, Christians who share in the sacramental life of the Church partake fully of the sacramentality of creation, while non-Christians enjoy it to a lesser degree, since they cannot see the connection between the material world and its salvation in Christ. This distinction in degree, however, does not deny the natural priesthood of non-Christians.[57]

Thus, Staniloae's theology of natural priesthood is relevant for ecological concerns, ecumenism, and interreligious dialogue. It calls for a common, priestly, and eucharistic attitude toward creation, an attitude that can, and urgently needs to, be shared among all people, regardless of their religious affiliation. These principles lead to the last section of this chapter, dedicated to their practical implementation.

### The Liturgy after the Liturgy (Eco-Activism)

The expression, "Liturgy after Liturgy" designates the relationship between worship and social justice,[58] including ecological issues. "Liturgy after Liturgy" commands that Christians exercise their natural priesthood through a eucharistic and ascetic life:[59] give thanks for creation, sanctify it, consume it properly, respectfully, and in moderation through fasting. Such an attitude, of course, is informed and empowered by the Liturgy proper. Our attitude toward creation should be as toward the Eucharist, which we handle attentively so that no minuscule crumb would fall and be trampled upon or wasted. We should have the same care for all the fragments of creation and thus put a stop to our wasteful and careless attitudes, which have caused and perpetuate the present ecological crisis. Staniloae wrote about the impact of the Church

---

57   Staniloae, "Creation as Gift and the Sacraments," 28.

58   See, for example, Ion Bria, *The Liturgy after the Liturgy: Mission and Witness from an Orthodox Perspective* (Geneva: WCC Publications, 1996).

59   Theokritoff writes about the ascetic attitude toward creation as respect, forbiddance of waste, and the notion that everything we use is in a sense sacred and worthy of respect, similar to sacred altar vessels. Moreover, she replaces the dictum "Help save the earth: commit suicide" with "Help save the earth: die to the world," understood in the sense of asceticism. Theokritoff, *Living in God's Creation*, 93–116.

upon the world as Christians experience intratrinitarian communion in the Liturgy:

> The force of attraction of the Trinity is experienced perfectly in the Divine Liturgy and this experience extends in the life of the Christians as ecclesiastical community, meant to extend the attraction force of the Trinity to the entire human society, to perfect it as communion.[60]

This ecclesiastical communion realized in the Liturgy needs to be taken outside the Church, to the rest of humankind, so that the Church may transform human society into the image of the trinitarian communion. One could even say that the Church acts as a sacrament of the Trinity in the world, in the sense that the Trinity works through the Church to bring the world into trinitarian communion. Staniloae closed the circle this way: God manifested his love "outside" the Trinity by creating the world in order to bring the world into communion with him, and God does that through the Church and its Liturgy, which acts as an instrument of God's force of attraction toward him.[61] This is a first aspect of the expression, "Liturgy after Liturgy."

Furthermore, the belief that our salvation is related to the environment makes us more responsible toward creation.[62] It is not only an interdiction against abusing nature, to satisfy our selfish, utilitarian, consumerist, and fallen passions, but it is also a positive call to mold the world in conformity with God's eternal intentions, or the *logoi*. As Theokritoff observes, secular ecological activism requires us to leave no trace on the landscapes with which we interact. However, as restored human beings celebrating the cosmic Liturgy, we must change or spiritualize our surroundings. In the words of the Liturgy of St. Basil the Great, we leave "in place of things corruptible, things incorruptible."[63] This way, the Church becomes a community in which we have a foretaste of the new creation,

---

60  Staniloae, *Spirituality and Communion*, 379.

61  Cf. Ibid.

62  Humans must get closer to nature in an age when they are drifting further and further from it. Francis Bacon wrote, "God Almighty first planted a garden. And indeed, it is the purest of human pleasures" even if—I would add—nowadays this involves a mower and a leaf blower.

63  Theokritoff, *Living in God's Creation*, 149–50. Theokritoff's remarks are challenging for those who enjoy camping and hiking and whose rule is, "leave no trace." By preserving the environment, they allow others to enjoy the same unadulterated, unutilized natural beauty. Theologically, however, both are saying that pollution mutes the hymn of glory that creation sings to its Maker and both encourage the human observer to praise God in the beauty of nature or, as previously stated, to give creation a voice in its praise.

in which the divisions between humans and the rest of creation are healed.[64] A concrete example in this regard is Amphilochios of Patmos, the twentieth-century spiritual father who would be described today as a tree-hugger. He said, "Whoever does not love trees does not love Christ" and, if he ever gave a penance, it was to plant trees.[65] His care for the environment and its relationship with our spirituality revealed the Church as agent of a new creation.

The retrieval of an ascetic and eucharistic attitude to creation, characteristic of Staniloae and the Orthodox Tradition, is insufficient. The communal and systematic sin of ecocide calls for structural changes, going beyond changes in personal attitudes, even if informed by the public worship of the Church. These two aspects, however, cannot be separated, since the present economic and political structures reflect a consumerist mentality that runs counter to the theological principles outlined above.

### Conclusion

At the intersection of the theology of creation, Triadology, Soteriology, and ecclesiology, Staniloae's understanding of natural priesthood contributes significantly to ecclesiology. With its strong spiritual component as evidenced in sacraments, liturgy, and eco-activism, it also advances a practical way of experiencing communion with nature. Humans were created as priests of creation but, because of the fall, natural priesthood was greatly impoverished. Christ fulfilled this ministry and now humankind in general and the Church in particular share in Christ's priesthood toward creation by sanctifying and reestablishing the Godward movement of creation, regarding it as God's presence, gift, and sacrament. Such an understanding of the priestly vocation of humankind toward creation is particularly relevant in contemporary ecological, ecumenical, and interreligious discussions. It also shows concretely how the world and the Church are "filled with the Trinity," as discussed in the first two parts of this book.

---

64   For more on the Church's ecological calling and the biblical image of the church as the "first fruits" of the new creation, see Ernst Conradie et al., "Seeking Eco-Justice in the South African Context," in *Earth Habitat: Eco-Injustice and the Church's Response*, ed. Dieter T. Hessel and Larry L. Rasmussen (Minneapolis, MN: Augsburg Fortress, 2001), 135–57.

65   Ware, *The Orthodox Church*, 132.

## Chapter 7

## THE PRIESTHOOD OF THE CHURCH:
## COMMUNION BETWEEN CLERGY AND THE PEOPLE

Staniloae's understanding of natural priesthood in its general sense is inclusive of all humankind and is fulfilled in the Church. The baptized, in their exercise of universal and ordained priesthood, continue to act as priests of creation in a special sense. In the present chapter I continue the discussion of the Church's priesthood, emphasizing the communion between universal and ordained priesthood, as an application of the relationship between the Trinity and the Church presented thus far. I also examine Staniloae's contribution to an Orthodox understanding of the Church from an ecumenical perspective. If some of the questions addressed here originate in the West, Staniloae's answers are rooted primarily in the Eastern patristic tradition, supplemented by other Orthodox theologians exploring the same venues.

As in the case of natural priesthood, Staniloae wrote that Christ is the Priest *par excellence* and the Church shares in his priesthood through the Holy Spirit. He affirmed that "Christ is the universal High Priest and the source of priesthood because he sacrifices himself and because he is the source of everybody's power of sacrifice. We become priests by acquiring Christ's power of sacrifice, by personally acquiring his state of sacrifice."[1] The priesthood of the Church participates actively in Christ's prophetic, priestly, and kingly offices.[2] More specifically, Christ continues his priesthood through the entire Church, the clergy and the people who collaborate with him.[3]

Staniloae was critical of Orthodox manual theology that left the impression that the priesthood of the Church replaces that of an absent Christ. He responded that Christ acts sacramentally from within the Church, which is the "extension of the mystery of Christ" as an actualization of the potential for Christ's work in the Church that the incarnation has initiated.[4] Thus, in a sense,

---

1   Staniloae, *Spirituality and Communion*, 139.
2   Staniloae, *Dogmatics 2*, 152.
3   Staniloae, "Jesus Christ, Eternal High Priest," 229.
4   Staniloae, *Dogmatics 3*, 13. Staniloae, *Jesus Christ or the Restoration of Humankind*, 392–93.

there is only one priesthood in the Church, namely that of Christ. This, however, does not mean that other kinds of priesthood are obsolete; universal and ordained priesthoods are concrete manifestations of Christ's priesthood.

## Universal Priesthood

After some brief terminological remarks and a succinct description of the place of universal priesthood in Staniloae's theology, a multifaceted definition of universal priesthood will emerge: it is the fulfillment of natural priesthood, the mediator between natural and ordained priesthoods, and shares in the kingly, priestly, and prophetic offices of Christ.

The most frequently used term when referring to the universal priesthood of all the baptized is "laity." Alexander Schmemann, for example, considered that the Greek term *laïkos* denotes the belonging of all Christians to the People (*laos*) of God (cf. 1 Pt 2.9).[5] On the contrary, Hans Küng avoids the term "laity" because in the ancient Greek world it referred to the uneducated masses and in the Jewish tradition to somebody who was neither priest nor Levite.[6] The Lima Document on *Baptism, Eucharist and Ministry* uses terms such as "People of God," "ministry" (in the sense of universal priesthood), and "ordained ministry."[7] My preference is to use the term, "people" because in the Orthodox Liturgy the community prays "for the clergy and the people," *tou klerou kai tou laou*.[8] Additionally, Staniloae referred to those who are not ordained as "faithful" (Romanian *credinciosi*), a term that I use as well. Naturally, I presuppose that these terms do not exclude the clergy from the People of God or from those who have faith.

After these terminological considerations, it is important to look succinctly at the place of universal priesthood in Staniloae's theology. Unfortunately,

---

5   Schmemann, *The Eucharist*, 232. Schmemann's mentor, Afanassieff, avoided this term and invented a word that did not previously exist in Russian, namely "laics."

6   Küng, *The Church*, 492–94. Although I concur with Küng's reservations toward the term, "laity," I disagree with his avoidance of the word, "clergy." The latter term, Küng affirms, acquired a new meaning shortly after the apostolic era, similar to its contemporary sense. I do not see anything intrinsically negative about this linguistic evolution from "share" and "lot" in the biblical usage, to the ordained, later on. Moreover, the term "clergy" is used in Orthodox liturgies.

7   Lima, *Baptism, Eucharist and Ministry* (Geneva: WCC, 1982). See also Research Team CTSA, "A Global Evaluation of BEM," in *Catholic Perspectives on BAPTISM, EUCHARIST AND MINISTRY: A Study Commissioned by the Catholic Theological Society of America*, ed. Michael A. Fahey (New York: University Press of America, 1986).

8   *The Liturgikon*, trans. Leonidas Contos (Northridge, CA: Narthex Press, 1996), 68.

Orthodox theologians did not emphasize this subject enough because of its association with the Protestant Reformation. They might have feared accusations of Protestant influences, at a time when Orthodoxy was emancipating from its Western captivity (see Chapter 1). In his most representative work, *Dogmatics*, Staniloae dedicated no more than two paragraphs to this issue in the section on "Christ's priesthood in the Church through the universal priesthood," in which he affirmed that the human being is king, priest, and prophet.[9] The criticism that this important topic should have been treated much more thoroughly in *Dogmatics* is unavoidable, even for sympathetic readers of Staniloae such as Miller[10] and me. However, the Protestant theologian Danut Manastireanu goes too far when writing that, in Staniloae's theology, the universal priesthood "is left not only unexplained, but also void of any concrete content."[11] In other works by Staniloae, this is certainly not the case. There is, for instance, an abundance of references to the roles of the faithful in *Spirituality and Communion in the Orthodox Liturgy* (not yet translated into English), which I bring to the fore in the following pages.

Still, Manastireanu's Protestant sensitivity to the subject of nonordained priesthood is an indication that Orthodox theologians should dwell more on this important subject. I consider that an ecumenical analysis of universal priesthood would be mutually enriching for both the Orthodox, who would discover more fully the richness of this concept, and for Protestants, who would better connect the priesthood of all believers with ordained priesthood. Moreover, we are now at a crossroad. After a period when theology overemphasized the role of the clergy, we were inclined to focus exclusively on the role of the nonordained. We now need to reach a balance, a true theology of communion between the clergy and the faithful.

## Universal and Ordained Priesthoods

In the previous chapter I described the communion among natural, universal, and ordained priesthoods, all of which share in the priesthood of Christ. I already analyzed the relationship between natural and universal priesthoods, where universal priesthood is the fulfillment of natural priesthood and mediates between natural and ordained ministries. It is now time to stress the communion between clergy and the people. Within the universal priesthood of all the

---

9    Staniloae, *Dogmatics 2*, 155.
10   Miller, *The Gift of the World*, 96–97.
11   Manastireanu, "Dumitru Staniloae's Theology of Ministry," 135.

baptized, there are different charisms that function in communion with each other. Ordained priesthood is such a charism. Staniloae wrote that

> Episcopal communion or synodality is included as a specific difference within the larger communion of the Church. It is as a small circle within the larger circle.... It must contribute to the development of general communion. It is as a lung within the body of the Church, necessary to the body, but sustained by it.... The general communion of the Church, sustained by the Spirit of Christ, fills with its life-giving breath all the constitutive organs of the Church, including the hierarchy.... And the communion of the hierarchy extends its spirit in the entire communion of the Church.[12]

Hence, because the clergy are not above the Church but within it, hierarchy and communion do not stand in tension. Staniloae's analogy of the two circles suggests that ordained priesthood is part of the priesthood of the Church. Similar and distinct at the same time, the two priesthoods interact and enrich each other in communion. Later in the article, Staniloae stated explicitly: "the members of the hierarchy are a part of the general communion of the Church not only through this special complementarity with the nonordained people of the Church, but also through the fact that they are members of the Church in need of salvation, who make efforts for their sanctification and perfection."[13] Moreover, starting from the fact that the minor orders are not properly part of the clergy but are consecrated for specific liturgical tasks, Staniloae affirmed that the distinction between the clergy and the people is gradual and not abrupt, without separation between them.[14] For Staniloae, there is only one common work of the Church, since there is one Spirit present in it. But the Spirit imparts different charisms to different members, and ordained priesthood is one of these gifts or charisms—such a significant statement! In Staniloae's words:

> In this unity of the gifts and ministries in the Church, explained by the unity of the organism of the Church and by the unity of the Spirit in it, are included also the ministries and gifts of the hierarchy. But only in part. That is because, on the one hand, they do not remain exterior to the other

---

12  Staniloae, "The Theological Foundations of Hierarchy and Synodality," 171–72. Given these considerations, Staniloae would probably agree with *Lumen Gentium* 21, which defined the Church as "hierarchic communion." Vatican, *Vatican Council II: The Conciliar and Postconciliar Documents*, 373.

13  Staniloae, "The Theological Foundations of Hierarchy and Synodality," 177.

14  Dumitru Staniloae, "Slujirile bisericesti si atributiile lor [Ecclesial Ministries and their Attributions]," *Ortodoxia* 22, no. 3 (1970): 468.

ministries and cannot be exercised without their fulfillment through the activation of all the gifts in the Church. But, on the other hand, the ministries and gifts of the hierarchy are different from all other gifts and ministries, because they represent the basis of the transcendent origin of all the other gifts and ministries, generating and activating them.[15]

Although for Staniloae priesthood is one charism among the other gifts of the Spirit, the hierarchy represents the means through which the faithful are entrusted with different charisms. Ordained ministers baptize and chrismate people in the Church, which is a condition for the reception of the Spirit's unmediated gifts by all the faithful. The hierarchy unites charisms, orienting them toward the edification of the Body of Christ and enhancing the communitarian character of the Church. Simultaneously, all other charisms are a condition for the proper functioning of the gifts of the hierarchy. Thus, the inclusion of the ordained within the universal priesthood of the Church does not deprive Ordination of content, but rather insures its communion with the rest of the faithful. Staniloae's theology needs to be appropriated and developed adequately, providing a corrective to unilateral approaches to priesthood primarily from the perspective of Ordination: the clergy exercise their ministry only within the ministry of all the baptized.

Other Orthodox contributions concerning Baptism as the basis of universal priesthood should be mentioned here, especially by Nissiotis and Afanassieff.[16] Many interesting developments took place within Catholic circles, as well.[17] Due to space limitations, however, I am able to add only a simple remark about

---

15 Staniloae, "The Theological Foundations of Hierarchy and Synodality," 176–77. Along the same lines, in his commentary on Basil of Caesarea's *Moralia* 60, Rico Monge writes that clerical leadership is a charism among the many gifts in the Church. Monge continues: Basil's "idea that no individual member can possess all of the gifts is a reminder that although clergy possess the charism of leadership, the totality of spiritual gifts cannot be localized in the clergy. In addition, Basil's requirement that all members of the Church must work in harmony with each other regardless of their specific gifts implies that those granted the charism of leadership, the clergy, cannot dominate followers in an authoritarian way. At the same time, however, it also suggests that the laity cannot be fractious or stubbornly insubordinate." Rico Gabriel Monge, "Submission to One Head: Basil of Caesarea on Order and Authority in the Church." *St Vladimir's Theological Quarterly* 52, no. 2 (2010), 227.

16 Nissiotis, "The Charismatic Church and the Theology of the Laity," 31–35. Afanassieff, *The Church of the Holy Spirit*, 9–32.

17 See John Ford, "Ministries in the Church," in *The Gift of the Church: A Textbook on Ecclesiology in Honor of Patrick Granfield, O.S.B.*, ed. Peter C. Phan (Collegeville, MN: Liturgical Press, 2000), 293–314. Jon Nilson, "The Laity," in *The Gift of the Church*, 395–414.

Congar's departure from the pre-Vatican II hierarchology described in Chapter 5. Joseph Famerée contends that Congar's *Lay People in the Church*[18] had the merit of considerably revaluing the function of the faithful in the Church and of having a "communitarian" vision of the Church, where there is no opposition between the clergy and the people.[19] Rather, the Church has to re-become one People, a communion between the universal and ordained ministries, both having their roots in the same baptismal grace.[20] A few years later, Vatican II's *Lumen Gentium* (LG) 10 affirmed that the baptized, being anointed with the Spirit, are consecrated to be a spiritual house and a holy priesthood and thus offer spiritual sacrifices and proclaim the power of Christ (cf. 1 Pt 2.4-10).[21]

---

18    Yves Congar, *Jalons pour une théologie du laïcat* (Paris: Cerf, 1953). English translation: Yves Congar, *Lay People in the Church: A Study for a Theology of Laity* (London: Bloomsbury Pub. Co, 1957).

19    To better explain this development, I need to mention three instances of earlier Catholic theology. In the nineteenth century, J. A. Mohler had to oppose the view that "God created the hierarchy and thus has more than sufficiently provided for the needs of the Church until the end of the world." Moreover, on February 11, 1906, in his encyclical *Vehementer Nos*, Pius X affirmed: "In the hierarchy alone reside the right and authority needed to promote and direct all the members towards society's end. As for the multitude, they have no other right than that of letting themselves be led and submissively following their pastors." (Both quoted in Forte, *The Church: Icon of the Trinity*, 38–39.) Karl Rahner addressed a similar issue when he wrote against some pre-Vatican II Catholic theologians "who hold the view, tacitly and in the background, but all the more operative and dangerous on that account, that the hierarchy is the only vehicle of the Spirit or the only portal through which the Spirit enters the Church." As a response, Rahner stressed the idea that "there are charismata, that is, the impulsion and guidance of God's Spirit for the Church, in addition to and outside her official ministry." Karl Rahner, *The Dynamic Element in the Church, Quaestiones disputatae 12* (New York: Herder and Herder, 1964), 47–49.

20    Joseph Famerée, *L'Ecclésiologie d'Yves Congar avant Vatican II: Histoire et Église: Analyse et Reprise Critique* (Leuven: Leuven University Press, 1992), 215–16.

21    Vatican, *Vatican Council II: The Conciliar and Postconciliar Documents*, 361. At the same time, while establishing a close relationship between the ordained and the nonordained, LG 10 affirmed that the distinction between them is ontological and not simply in degree: *licet essentia et non gradu tantum differant*. It would be interesting at this point to discuss the tension (in unity) that arises when Baptism and Ordination are considered together, on which neither Catholic nor Orthodox theologians agree unanimously among themselves. But this important subject will have to be treated in another context. For now, see Donald C. Maldari, "A Reconsideration of the Ministries of the Sacrament of Holy Orders," *Horizons* 34, no. 2 (2007): 238–64. Nissiotis, "The Charismatic Church and the Theology of the Laity," 33–34. John D. Zizioulas, "Ordination-A Sacrament? An Orthodox Reply," in *The Plurality of Ministries*, ed. Hans Küng and Walter Kasper, *Concilium 74* (New York: Herder and Herder, 1974), 33–40.

The contributions of the three theologians mentioned only briefly here deserve a separate study.

### Sharing in Christ's Three Offices

Another important aspect of Staniloae's theology of universal priesthood is that the faithful manifest their universal ministry by sharing in Christ's offices of king, priest, and prophet. I described in the first chapter Staniloae's appropriation of Calvin's systematization of the three offices of Christ as open sobornicity. I argued that he avoided the dangers of scholastic oversystematization by presenting the spirituality of our participation in Christ's threefold ministry. Here, again, an Orthodox-Protestant encounter proves beneficial for systematizing Eastern thought on priesthood.

Commenting on Rev. 5.9-10,[22] Staniloae affirmed that, through his sacrifice, Christ became king and priest in his humanity. In Christ, we also become kings and priests, liberated from the dominion of death and corruption, so we manifest our kingship through dominion over passions, thus sharing in Christ's priesthood.[23] Moreover, Staniloae noted that the elders in the book of Revelation manifest their priesthood through the use of incense, which symbolizes the prayers of all the faithful, meaning that

> all the faithful are priests and pray, but their prayers are gathered in unity by the ordained priest, to be lifted up as a unitary wave, pure and well-pleasing to God.... Saint Apostle Peter unites the believers' quality of priests and that of kings into one: "royal priesthood" [cf. 1 Pt 2.5-9]. The faithful have this double quality as a result of Christ's sacrifice, their spiritual sacrifices representing the fruits of Christ's power of sacrifice. Through [their spiritual sacrifices, the faithful] on the one hand serve God as priests, and on the other hand, liberate themselves from passions and death, as kings. Thus, those who liberate themselves from passions through sacrifices, make up a royal

---

22  The twenty-four elders sing the following hymn, dedicated to the Lamb: "You are worthy to take the scroll and to open its seals, for you were slaughtered and by your blood you ransomed for God saints from every tribe and language and people and nation; you have made them to be a kingdom and priests serving our God, and they will reign on earth" (Rev. 5.9-10).

23  Staniloae, *Dogmatics 2*, 153. Similarly, the desert father Joseph of Panepho exclaimed: "I am a king today because I rule over the passions" (10/PG 65.251).

priesthood, or a tightly knit community that advances in the bosom of the Holy Trinity.[24]

Implied here is Staniloae's understanding (described in Chapter 4) that Christ brings as a sacrifice not only his personal body, but also his Body understood as Church, which is sacrificed in the Liturgy, so all the faithful are sacrificed and purified, and are united with Christ in the Eucharist. Similar to Christ who is both the sacrifice and the priest who brings the sacrifice, the faithful become sacrifices and priests of their own sacrifice, thus exercising their universal priesthood by sharing in Christ's priesthood.[25] Staniloae captured our identification with Christ's sacrificed state and the contents of our sacrifice when he affirmed that

> On the one hand, Christ the High Priest brings us as sacrifices together with his sacrifice. On the other hand, we surrender ourselves to him as sacrifice, so that Christ would bring us as sacrifices to God the Father.... Our sacrifice consists in a pure life, in prayer, and in other gifts for our neighbors in need, as well as for the support of the Church's work for salvation. Our sacrifice consists essentially in our self-renunciation, in order to enter in a loving relationship with God.[26]

It is important to note in this passage that the priestly office has, besides its obvious liturgical connotation, a charitable dimension directed toward those in need and an ecclesial aspect that includes the missionary nature of the Church (Staniloae put it generally as "the Church's work for salvation"). In other words, the priestly calling of the faithful embraces *leitourgia, diaconia,* and *martyria*, categories that encompass all aspects of spirituality. The same principle will apply to ordained priesthood. Thus, spiritual growth represents the necessary condition for the full manifestation of priesthood. Moreover, in both quotes presented here, our sharing in Christ's offices strengthens the communion of the Church and lifts it up into the bosom of the Trinity. Staniloae's ecclesiology remains trinitarian throughout, having a spiritual motivation. His

---

24  Staniloae, *Spirituality and Communion*, 140–41.

25  Staniloae, *Dogmatics 2*, 153–54.

26  Ibid. Schmemann wrote along the same lines: "The 'priesthood' of the laity does not consist in their being some sort of priests of a second order in the Church—for the ministries are distinct and must never be confused—but in that being the faithful, i.e., the members of the Church, they are ordained into the ministry of Christ to the world, and they realize this, above all, through participation in the offering of Christ's sacrifice on behalf of the world." Schmemann, *The Eucharist*, 93.

departure from scholastic oversystematization and lack of spiritual concern is plainly evident.

In summary, universal priesthood consists in the fulfillment of natural priesthood through Baptism and in sharing in the three offices of Christ: ruling over passions as kings, offering spiritual sacrifices as priests, and as teachers in the reception of doctrine, which I discuss shortly.

### Ordained Priesthood

Since the topic of ordained priesthood encompasses more facets than can be treated here, I concentrate on the following question: Does the priest or the bishop[27] act *in persona Christi* and/or *in nomine Christi* and/or *in persona ecclesiae*? I use *in persona* to mean that Christ/the Church acts through the priest and *in nomine* to indicate that it is the priest who acts, although being commissioned by Christ/the Church to do so through Ordination.

Even though the understanding that the clergy and the people share together in Christ's priesthood has been a longstanding Eastern tradition, Orthodox theologians at the beginning of the twentieth century did not write extensively on this subject. It was only in the middle of the twentieth century that they displayed a more sustained interest in this topic. The shift was due to two reasons: internally, Orthodox theologians engaged with Afanassieff, whose thought on the relationship between the ordained and the people (sadly, less popular than his eucharistic ecclesiology) sparked an important discussion;[28] externally, Orthodox theologians conversed with Catholic thinkers such as Congar who had already brought this subject into the spotlight. From that point onward, Orthodox and Catholic theologies have continued to inform each other, growing together in their understanding of the communion between the clergy and the people. Thus, a brief analysis of Congar's position on the relationship between Christ, the Church, and the priest is necessary at this point.

---

27   For the purpose of this discussion I use texts that refer to either priest or bishop, and I simply refer in both cases to the role of the priest.

28   This influence can be seen especially in the works of Evdokimov. Moreover, Afanassieff was quoted at Vatican II and the participating bishops were asked to read some of his works. His influence can be seen especially in *Lumen Gentium*'s sections on the local church and the laity. ("Preface" by Olivier Rousseau, in Nicolas Afanassieff, *L'Église du Saint-Esprit*, trans. Marianne Drobot (Paris: Cerf, 1975), 8–9.) Rousseau's affirmation, of course, is not meant to diminish Congar's influence on the council in these respects.

As shown in Chapter 5, early on in his career Congar's perspective was more christological than pneumatological. As a result, he considered that the priest acts *in persona Christi* to the detriment of the understanding of the minister- ial work *in persona ecclesiae* and affirmed the ontological and temporal pre- cedence of ordained ministers over the faithful.[29] However, as a result of his increased interest in Pneumatology due to his encounter with Orthodox theo- logians, from 1969 onward Congar began to argue that "the Church is built up by a multitude of ministries, some ordained and some lay."[30] If Congar's interest in Pneumatology was encouraged by his encounter with the East, it was now Orthodoxy's turn to benefit from him. Given its constant dialogue with Catholic theologians such as Congar, Eastern theology became preoccupied with a question of Western origin, namely whether the priest acts *in persona Christi* and/or *in nomine Christi* and/or *in persona ecclesiae*, a question that was hitherto marginal at best. Asking a Western question has its inherent dangers, such as the instances when Orthodox theology did not find a proper balance between the clergy and the people in the communion of the Church. (See the discussion of institution and charisms in Chapter 5). At the same time, engaging in this dialogue also proved a fortuitous opportunity for mutual growth and open sobornicity.

Evdokimov considered that the priest acts *in persona ecclesiae* and *in nom- ine Christi*, but not *in persona Christi*. He deemphasized the role of the priest based on the prayer during the Cherubic Hymn ("For you, Christ our God, are the Offerer and the Offered, the One who receives and is distributed") and the fact that the priest does not say for himself during the anamnesis "this is my body." Moreover, Christ's priesthood is manifested through the entire Church, since at the epiclesis the Holy Spirit comes upon the entire community, not only upon the priest.[31] I consider that Evdokimov's negation that the priest acts *in persona Christi* is inconsistent with his claim that Christ manifests his priesthood through the entire Church, which includes the priest. Furthermore, Staniloae's liturgical interpretation presented previously sug- gests that the entire Church, including the clergy, shares in Christ's priest- hood and brings itself as a sacrifice to the Father, united with Christ in the Spirit.

Most other contemporary Orthodox theologians agree with Evdokimov's assertion that the priest acts *in persona ecclesiae et in nomine Christi*, adding

---

29   Groppe, "The Contribution of Yves Congar's Theology of the Holy Spirit," 461, 68–73.

30   Yves Congar, "My Path-Findings in the Theology of Laity and Ministries," *The Jurist* 32, no. 2 (1972): 176.

31   Evdokimov, *Présence de l'Esprit-Saint dans la tradition orthodoxe*, 104–08.

that the priest also acts *in persona Christi*. To show that the bishop acts *in persona ecclesiae*, they quote frequently Tertullian's principle that "The bishop is in the Church and the Church is in the bishop"[32] and Ignatius of Antioch who considered that the bishop is an image of Christ at the Last Supper.[33] Moreover, the priest acts *in nomine Christi* by virtue of his ordination and *in persona Christi* because, as John Chrysostom wrote, "the priest merely lends his tongue and provides his hand"[34] to Christ, the ultimate celebrant of all sacraments. Based on these patristic writings, Afanassieff and Schmemann affirmed that the priest acts *in nomine Christi*, *in persona Christi* and *in persona ecclesiae*. A closer look at these theologians, followed by Florovsky and Zizioulas is necessary.

At times, Afanassieff gave the impression that he minimized the role of the bishop in the eucharistic assembly. Zizioulas criticizes him rather harshly in this regard, while Staniloae was satisfied with Afanassieff's portrayal of the relationship between the bishop and the Church (see the next chapter). Afanassieff defined the limits of the Church according to the eucharistic assembly that includes the bishop, and not exclusively according to the bishop as, allegedly, Cyprian of Carthage did. [35]

In line with the inseparability of the bishop from the eucharistic assembly, Afanassieff developed a topological understanding of the role of the presider and of apostolic succession: the place of Christ at the Last Supper was taken by the apostles at the Liturgy and they transmitted this ministry to the bishops whom they ordained. Afanassieff wrote: "receiving from the apostles their ministry of presidency, bishops were not the successors of their apostolic ministry but rather merely of their place in the eucharistic assembly."[36] Given these considerations, Afanassieff would have probably agreed that the bishop acts *in persona Christi*. He balanced these statements with the understanding that all sacraments are celebrated by the entire Church, "without separation or

---

32   Tertullian, *Letter* xvi, 8.

33   In his *Epistle to the Ephesians*, 6 (PG 5, 649-650A), Ignatius wrote that "we should look upon the bishop even as we would look upon the Lord himself, standing, as he does, before the Lord," i.e., in the Liturgy.

34   John Chrysostom, *Homilies on John*, lxxxvi, 4, translated in Ware, *The Orthodox Church*, 277. Here Ware leaves the impression that the priest acts *in persona Christi*. Surprisingly, elsewhere he explicitly denies it, based on the priest's westward position and on the fulfilling of Christ's words by the "Amen" of the community. Ware, *The Holy Spirit in the Liturgy of St John Chrysostom*, 18–19.

35   Nicolas Afanassieff, "Una Sancta," in *Tradition Alive: On the Church and the Christian Life in Our Time: Readings from the Eastern Church*, ed. Michael Plekon (Lanham, MD: Rowan & Littlefield, 2003), 452–53.

36   Afanassieff, *The Church of the Holy Spirit*, 248.

division" between clergy and the people. The entire people of God is priestly by virtue of Baptism, while the bishop represents the image (*typos*) of Christ at the eucharistic assembly.[37]

Afanassieff's student at St. Serge Institute in Paris, Schmemann, followed and further developed these arguments. All the baptized are ordained into the universal priesthood of the Church, which is the priesthood of Christ.[38] The entire assembly has a priestly function in the Liturgy (i.e., "the work of the people"), while the bishop is the main celebrant at the assembly. Writing on the "indissoluble bond of bishop, eucharist and the Church," Schmemann portrayed the bishop as both "one of the gathered but also as the image of the Lord, vested in his power and authority."[39] His iconic understanding of priesthood supports the affirmation that the priest acts *in persona ecclesiae* (being one of the gathered), *in persona* and *in nomine Christi*, vested with Christ's power and authority, respectively.

Though Florovsky contended that ministers act primarily *in persona Christi* as "representatives" of Christ, he added immediately that the priest also acts *in persona ecclesiae*, which results in several practices such as the forbiddance of abstract Ordinations (bishops ordained for no specific diocese) and of a retired bishop to ordain other bishops because he does not represent a community.[40]

Zizioulas follows Florovsky—his *Doktorväter*—by affirming the intrinsic relationship between the bishop and the Church in the context of the Eucharist and thus, implicitly, that the celebrant acts *in persona Christi et ecclesiae*. At the heart of his early account of communion ecclesiology (in *Eucharist, Bishop, Church*), he identifies the bishop with both Christ and the entire local Church. In response to Afanassieff's eucharistic ecclesiology, Zizioulas concludes that the unity of the Church is not simply eucharistic, but also hierarchical:

> The Divine Eucharist is closely bound up *with the Bishop* as he is in turn with "the whole Church." These elements are so deeply bound up with one another that they are not clearly distinguished in Ignatius's thought.... *The Bishop is identified with the entire local Church*. Thus, we reach the classic passage "where the Bishop is, there is the multitude." The Bishop forms a

37   Ibid., 57, 233.
38   Alexander Schmemann, *Of Water and the Spirit: A Liturgical Study of Baptism* (Crestwood, NY: St Vladimir's Seminary Press, 1974), 94–95.
39   Schmemann, *The Eucharist*, 63–99.
40   Florovsky, "The Historical Problem of a Definition of the Church," 32.

"type" and icon of Christ or of the Father Himself, an icon and type not in a symbolic but in a real sense.[41]

Zizioulas's communion ecclesiology will later focus on the relationship between person and nature, especially as manifested in the context of the Eucharist. In his most recent book, *Communion and Otherness*, he affirms that "the Eucharist is *communion*, and this means that otherness is experienced as *relational.*"[42] Thus, Zizioulas affirms the intrinsic relationship between the celebrant and the community in the Eucharist, both in his earlier historical analysis and in his later theology of personhood. Indeed, the celebrant acts *in persona Christi et ecclesiae*.

Most contemporary Orthodox theologians analyzed here consider that the priest acts *in nomine Christi, in persona Christi et in persona ecclesiae*. Despite significant variations that some of their ecclesiologies have suffered over time, they are consistent concerning the relationship between Christ, the Church, and the priest.

Staniloae did not insist on the priest's commission to serve *in nomine Christi* but argued that the priest acts both *in persona Christi* and *in persona ecclesiae*: the priest represents (being an image of) both Christ and the community.[43] The priest is simultaneously a mediator of Christ and part of the community without being above it. The mediation of the priest should be understood as providing the occasion for Christ to act, and not as if this power[44] would belong to the priest, separate from the community. The power of Christ manifested in the actions of the priest belongs to the whole Church, which means that Ordination is a ministry within the priesthood of the Church. Still, the responsibility to exercise it has been entrusted to the ordained minister, hence Staniloae agreed with Gregory Nazianzen that the priest is concelebrant (*suniereusonta*) with Christ.[45] At the

---

41  Zizioulas, *Eucharist, Bishop, Church*, 114–16. In his recent *Communion and Otherness*, Zizioulas adds a new eschatological dimension to the understanding of the bishop as an image of Christ. Seated on the throne, the bishop represents Christ, thus manifesting the eschaton in the Liturgy. Zizioulas, *Communion and Otherness*, 296, 300.

42  Zizioulas, *Communion and Otherness*, 91–92.

43  Staniloae, "Theology of the Eucharist," 358. French translation: Dumitru Staniloae, "Théologie de l'Eucharistie," *Contacts* 71 (1970): 184–211.

44  The term "power" runs of risk of bearing clericalist connotations. However, I chose to keep Staniloae's terminology that implies the energy, grace, and spiritual strength that Christ imparts through the Church, which is different from Aquinas's use of the term "power" (*potestas*) given at Ordination once and for all, as indelible character irrespective of the priest's relationship with the community.

45  (*Or.* 2.73, PG 35, 481A) Staniloae, *Dogmatics 2*, 159–60.

same time, the faithful are not merely passive at the celebration of the sacraments, but they contribute actively in the liturgy.[46] Considering that Christ works simultaneously through the priest and the entire Church, Staniloae avoided the tension between *in persona Christi* and *in persona ecclesiae* found in Evdokimov.

To support the view that the priest acts *in persona ecclesiae*, Staniloae affirmed that ordained priesthood completes the universal priestly offering of the baptized by explicit invocation of the Spirit in the services of the Church.[47] Christ changes the gifts of bread and wine into his Body and Blood by working through the community,[48] so the epiclectic prayer recited by the priest takes place *in persona ecclesiae*. Significantly, Staniloae did not regard the priest's consecration of the Eucharist exclusively as an act *in persona Christi* as in magisterial Catholic pronouncements, but also *in persona ecclesiae*.

LG 10 affirmed that, acting *"in the person of Christ*, [the priest] effects the eucharistic sacrifice and offers it to God *in the name* of all the people [*sacrificium eucharisticum* in persona Christi *conficit illudque* nomine *totius populi Deo offert*]. The faithful indeed, by virtue of their royal priesthood, *participate in the offering* of the Eucharist" (emphases mine).[49] Neither LG 10 nor Staniloae separates the action of the priest from that of the people; rather they put them in a complementary relationship. Yet, the two accounts are different. In Vatican II's document, the priest, acting *in the person* of Christ, presents the sacrifice *in the name* of the people, which is different from *in persona ecclesiae*. This understanding is based on Thomas Aquinas who wrote:

> The priest, in reciting the prayers of the mass, speaks instead of the Church [*in persona Ecclesiae*], in whose unity he remains; but in consecrating the sacrament he speaks as in the person of Christ [*in persona Christi*], whose place he holds by the power of his Orders. Consequently, if a priest severed from the unity of the Church celebrates mass, not having lost the power of the Order, he consecrates Christ's true body and blood; but because he is severed from the unity of the Church, his prayers have no efficacy.[50]

---

46   Staniloae, "Ecclesial Ministries and their Attributions," 467.

47   Miller, *The Gift of the World*, 97–98.

48   Staniloae, "Creation as Gift and the Sacraments," 20.

49   Vatican, *Vatican Council II: The Conciliar and Postconciliar Documents*, 361.

50   *Summa Theologica* IIIa, q. 82, art. 7, ad 3 Aquinas, *Summa Theologiae, Complete English Edition in Five Volumes*, vol. 5, 2503. For a further analysis, see Mary M. Schaefer, "'In Persona Christi': Cult of the Priest's Person or Active Presence of Christ?" in *In God's Hands: Essays on the Church and Ecumenism in Honour of Michael A. Fahey, S.J.*, ed. Jaroslav Z. Skira and Michael S. Attridge (Leuven: Leuven University Press, 2006), 192.

Staniloae would have also disagreed with the Catholic practice that the priest can celebrate the Liturgy when the faithful are not present,[51] since the act *in persona ecclesiae* is essential to his priestly ministry, including when he consecrates the gifts.[52] This is the theological explanation for the Orthodox interdiction of the priest to celebrate the Liturgy alone. When the consecration takes place in the Orthodox Liturgy, both the priest and the congregation face Eastwards, a liturgical gesture that implies their communion, which is confirmed by the prayer of invocation (*epiclesis*): "send down your Holy Spirit upon us [i.e., the priest and the people seen as one] and upon these gifts here presented." Joseph Cardinal Ratzinger (now Pope Benedict XVI) makes a very convincing argument for the necessity to face *versus orientem* (the place of the rising sun, symbol of Jesus Christ) as an expression of the communion between clergy and the people, including at the moment of consecration. That is not to say that when the celebrant faces the people their communion suffers.[53] Concurring with Ratzinger's last point, Schmemann affirms that, when the bishop turns toward the congregation to bless it, he is both "one of the gathered but also as the image of the Lord, vested in his power and authority."[54]

Concerning the priest's ministry *in persona Christi*, Staniloae added that the ordained priest is the visible instrument that makes visible the invisible ministry of Christ, the High Priest. Because we are not merely souls, but also bodies, we need visible signs of God's presence in the Church. Consequently, as Christ made himself visible in his body before his ascension and mediated his divine power through his body, so now he makes himself visible through the priests as mediating visible instruments.[55] But the ordained do not have this power in themselves; they receive it from the Son of God.[56] Ultimately, it is Christ who

---

51  Vatican II's *Decree on the Ministry and Life of Priests—Presbyterorum Ordinis* 13 makes reference to the priest acting in the person of Christ even when he celebrates daily Mass without the presence of the faithful.

52  Staniloae, "Ecclesial Ministries and their Attributions," 467.

53  Joseph Ratzinger, *The Spirit of the Liturgy*, trans. John Saward (San Francisco: Ignatius Press, 2000), 75–80.

54  Schmemann, *The Eucharist*, 63.

55  Starting from Heb. 9.12, 14; 10.19, Staniloae affirmed that "the priest represents Christ.... If God communicates his powers through the humanity of Christ, ... why would this mediating role of the humanity of Christ not extend through the humanity of the priest, chosen to be a visible center of the gathering of the faithful? ... If we are recapitulated invisibly in Christ, we are recapitulated visibly in the priest." Staniloae, *Spirituality and Communion*, 147.

56  Staniloae, *Dogmatics 2*, 165.

offers himself in the gifts of bread and wine.[57] The priest acknowledges this principle in the prayer during the Cherubic Hymn: "make me, Your sinful and unworthy servant, worthy to offer to You these gifts. For You, Christ our God, are the Offerer (the one who offers Yourself) and the Offered, the One who receives and is distributed."[58]

Furthermore, Staniloae considered that Ordination does not come from the community or from individuals (here I interpret Staniloae to mean bishops in themselves, without reference to Christ), but it belongs to the deepest subject of the Church, who is Christ. It is Christ who chooses and ordains a certain group—the clergy—to preach the Gospel and manifest his work visibly. This is why the clergy

> do not take from themselves this power of subjects fully awakened to the responsibility of preaching the Revelation, and neither do the other members of the Church give it to them, because they do not have it themselves. [This power] can only come from [the subject] of the Church, that is, from Christ.... This is why it cannot be said that the grace of the sacraments, including Ordination, comes from Christ as if he were somewhere separated from the Church; rather, by coming from Christ, it comes from the deep of the Church.[59]

Staniloae did not accept a separation between *in persona Christi* and *in persona ecclesiae*, even though he distinguished between the two expressions, thus avoiding the tension that Evdokimov put between them. That is because ordained priesthood is a ministry within the priesthood of the Church, through which Christ manifests his priesthood. The priest acts *in nomine Christi, in persona Christi et in persona ecclesiae* because the priesthood of Christ can be separated

---

57  "Christ himself prays in the priest for the faithful, addresses them, gathers the prayers and the gifts of the people, uniting them with his gifts. Through the priest, Christ teaches in the Gospel, changes the gifts of the faithful into his Body and Blood, unites the faithful with himself in Holy Communion to present them to the Father as children filled of the Holy Spirit." Staniloae, *Spirituality and Communion*, 7. See also Dumitru Staniloae, "Biserica in sensul de lacas si de larga comuniune in Hristos [The Church as Place of Worship and All-embracing Communion in Christ]," *Ortodoxia* 34, no. 3 (1982): 340. Staniloae, "Jesus Christ, Eternal High Priest," 223–24.

58  Staniloae, *Spirituality and Communion*, 227. Staniloae made the clarification between parentheses inserted into the text of the Liturgy to show more clearly that the priest acknowledges that Christ offers himself in the Eucharist.

59  Staniloae, *Jesus Christ or the Restoration of Humankind*, 391–93.

neither from the universal priesthood of the Church, nor from the priesthood of the ordained. In a sense, actually, these three coincide.

## Communion between the Clergy and the People

All members of the Church, ordained or not, exercise their priestly, kingly, and prophetic vocation in communion.

### Priestly Office

Christ imparts his blessings upon the people through the liturgical blessing of the priest, initiating a prayerful dialogue between the celebrant who blesses the community with the words, "Peace be with you" or similar variations, and the faithful who respond, "And with your spirit."[60] Moreover, to show how ordained priesthood contributes to the prayers of the people, Staniloae affirmed repeatedly that the priest gathers the prayers of the liturgical assembly offering them to God together with his own prayers. This is why the people need the priest to be—as Nicholas Cabasilas wrote—their herald and leader without however being separated from the people.[61] Simultaneously, universal priesthood contributes to the prayers of the ordained. The work of the ordained needs the "active contribution of the people" who "fulfill with their offices" the work of the hierarchy in the celebration of the sacraments.[62] The two key expressions that Staniloae used here—"active contribution" and "fulfill" in the sense of making whole—reflect the important role that he ascribes to universal priesthood in relationship to ordained priesthood.

Other Orthodox theologians support the idea that the Liturgy expresses the communion and complementarity between the clergy and the people. Afanassieff made a thorough analysis of the similarities between the rites of Baptism-Chrismation as performed in the early Church and that of Ordination in his book, *The Church of the Holy Spirit*. Here, he offered what I consider to be the best treatise of Orthodox ecclesiology in general, and of universal priesthood in particular. It is by no means a faultless ecclesiology, and it has attracted vehement criticism especially from Zizioulas and Staniloae concerning the relationship between the local and universal aspects

---

60    Staniloae, *Spirituality and Communion*, 406, 10.
61    Ibid., 166, 259.
62    Staniloae, "Ecclesial Ministries and their Attributions," 467.

of the Church. Yet, its portrayal of universal priesthood and Ordination, as well as the eucharistic nature of the Church (with the limitations inherent in such a pioneering work) give Afanassieff a prominent place among Orthodox ecclesiologists.[63]

Afanassieff wrote that in the early Church the catechumen was received into the Church through the imposition of the hands, anointing (as in the case of kings and prophets in the Jewish tradition), received vestments (the white robe of Baptism), a miter, was tonsured, was taken three times around the altar table, and the word "to serve" was mentioned. All these liturgical elements demonstrate that the early Church regarded the rite of initiation as ordination into the royal priesthood. Moreover, since sacerdotal acts are accomplished by the entire people of God—clergy and laics together—the people have a sacerdotal function. Afanassieff concluded that priesthood belongs to all because it belongs to the Church.[64]

Some of these liturgical elements gradually disappeared from the rite of initiation and Afanassieff noted a growing separation between clergy and people, until the latter was considered profane. This separation was even more accentuated when certain liturgical practices were introduced: the iconostasis separating the altar from the nave, the forbiddance of the faithful to enter inside the altar, and the different ways in which the clergy and the people receive Communion. He attributed this decline to later Byzantine theology that regarded Ordination, and not Baptism, as the sacrament of consecration, as well as manual theology that separated the ordained and the laity, where only the former were regarded as consecrated. These influences were manifested in the decisions of the 1917–18 Council of Moscow, which did not ascribe a priestly role to the laics, but entrusted them exclusively with administrative duties, thus turning them into "lay people" deprived of charisms and with a diminished liturgical role. However, Afanassieff continued, the core of the Liturgy could not be changed by these historical factors, so the priestly function of the people is still reflected in elements such as the plural used in eucharistic prayers, or the "Amen" of the faithful during the *epiclesis*.[65]

---

63  Bordeianu, "The Church of the Holy Spirit [Review Article]," 245.
64  Afanassieff, *The Church of the Holy Spirit*, 24–30, 38. Staniloae wrote in similar terms about Baptism as consecration into universal priesthood, which is why the people can baptize in case of emergency. Moreover, Staniloae referred to Nicholas Cabasilas who related the anointing of the altar during the consecration of a church with the sacrament of Chrismation, when those who are anointed become altars at which they serve God as priests. Staniloae, "Ecclesial Ministries and their Attributions," 468.
65  Afanassieff, *The Church of the Holy Spirit*, 38–50.

Schmemann is probably the only Orthodox theologian who went further and wrote about the "clericalization" of the Orthodox Church in the sense of the "great distancing of the clergy and laity from each other," adding that

> Entry to the altar, approach to the sanctuary came to be forbidden to the laity, and their presence at the Eucharist became passive. It is accomplished on behalf of them, for them, but they do not take part in its accomplishment. If earlier the line separating the Church from "this world" embraced the laity, it now excluded them.[66]

In Schmemann's estimation, this distancing between clergy and the people is based on the "pre-Christian, clergy-versus-laity dichotomy, whose main emphasis is precisely on the nonpriestly nature of those called laity."[67] It results in "a false dilemma: either the institutional priesthood excludes from the Church any idea of the 'priestly' character of all Christians as such, or then the priestly character of the laity and indeed of the entire Church (defined by the Apostle [1 Pt 2.9] as 'royal priesthood') ought to exclude the institutional priesthood."[68] Such a view is an impoverishment of the early Church's understanding of the entire people of God as celebrating the Eucharist in communion, as they all share in the priesthood of Christ.

Based on the theologians analyzed in this chapter, I disagree with Schmemann and Afanassieff in regard to the existence in Orthodoxy of a mentality according to which the clergy alone pertain to the holy and can sanctify, while the people are profane spectators passively observing the sanctification accomplished by the priest. I actually see a distinction between the Church (clergy and faithful alike) and the world, but not between clergy and the world, the latter including the people. Moreover, the presence of the people at the Eucharist is not as passive as Schmemann suggested, although he was right that it is considerably less active than in the first centuries. I also dispute Schmemann's charge of clericalism, given that this term is understood in the West as the cloistered attitude of the clergy who are responsible only to themselves and exercise their power (as opposed to spiritual authority) in matters that do not pertain to the Church; in virtue of their Ordination, they claim to be first-class citizens in their religious community, above the people who have the duty to follow them. The situation in the East is significantly different, especially in Staniloae's context in which, under communist persecution, both clergy and the people suffered at the hands

---

66    Schmemann, *The Eucharist*, 232.
67    Schmemann, *Of Water and the Spirit*, 94–95.
68    Ibid., 94.

of a common oppressor. Staniloae experienced the communion between the clergy and the people not only in the Liturgy (that Christians attended at great risk), but also in his five years of communist incarceration, where both clergy and the people suffered together and, if they were treated differently, the clergy certainly did not enjoy first-class status. Quite the opposite.

In general, Schmemann tends toward the extreme of being overly critical of the present "separation" between the clergy and the people, idealizing the past, when all the baptized had the consciousness of belonging to the universal priesthood of the Church. At the other extreme, Staniloae tends to be insufficiently critical of the present state of Orthodox liturgical life, concentrating exclusively on the unchanged core of the Liturgy, still marked by communion between clergy and the people. I believe that, despite Afanassieff's association between the people and the world described above, he presented a more balanced position than Staniloae and Schmemann. And yet they all share the idea that the core of the Liturgy expresses the communion between the clergy and the people, both sharing in Christ's priestly office.

### Kingly Office

As stated above, Staniloae considered that all the members of the Church manifest communally their kingly office by striving to have dominion over their passions. Next, one would expect a thorough treatment of the clergy and people's shared role in the leadership and administration of the Church. However, such considerations are not prominent in Staniloae. I argue that this omission was determined by the communist persecution of the Orthodox Church during his time. To substantiate this claim, it is important to remember that the role of the people in the Church was drastically limited compared to the precommunist era because the official ideology of the time claimed that Orthodoxy (and religion in general) should have no place in the public sphere.[69] Religiosity was considered a superstition, inferior to the "scientific socialism" that was imposed on Romanian citizens, so religiosity was limited as much as possible, primarily to the clergy and (grudgingly) to the elderly who were considered "indoctrinated" during the precommunist era.[70] In this situation, the faithful did not play a

---

69    Mihail Neamtu, "Between the Gospel and the Nation: Dumitru Staniloae's Ethno-Theology," *Archaeus* 10, no. 3 (2006): 27.
70    During the publication process of Staniloae's *Dogmatics*, the communist censure forced him to replace all references to the religiosity of human beings with the faithfulness of Christians, thus limiting religiosity to a specific group rather than considering it something intrinsic to human nature, which Staniloae initially did.

prominent role in the administration of the Romanian Orthodox Church during Communism, and this is probably why Staniloae was not able to develop satisfactorily this aspect of the kingly office of the people.

However, there are some notable exceptions that suggest that, had he lived in a different context, Staniloae would have emphasized this subject further. He wrote that while the clergy are responsible for Church administration and social-charitable projects, they need to fulfill these tasks together with the representatives of the people who thus acquire an important role in parish councils or other aspects of ecclesial life.[71] Furthermore, he affirmed that "in many Orthodox churches . . . the priests are chosen by the people and then ordained by the bishop, and the bishops are elected before being ordained by an electoral committee, in which the bishops are not the only members, but also the representatives of the priests and of the people."[72] He also noted the involvement of the faithful in the leadership of the Church at national levels in several Orthodox Churches, especially in Romania and Serbia.[73]

These affirmations, unfortunately, are sporadic in Staniloae's work because their application was significantly limited by Communism. The reality was that parish councils were functionally nonexistent, parishes did not formally elect their priests, and the nonordained representatives serving on electoral committees were not as free as they should have been. Thus, the involvement of the faithful in the leadership of the Church at local and national levels was rather nominal.

These principles were actually applied in the Romanian Orthodox Church before Communism and especially after its fall in 1989. The National Ecclesiastical Assembly—the central representative body responsible for all

---

71  Staniloae, "Ecclesial Ministries and their Attributions," 468–69. It is also important to mention here the words of Cyprian of Carthage (*Epistle* 5/Oxford14:4): "I made this a rule, from the beginning of my episcopate, not to decide anything without your [presbyters] council and without the approval of the people."

72  Staniloae, "The Theological Foundations of Hierarchy and Synodality," 174. Similarly, Ware mentions that "in the early Church the bishop was often elected by the people of the diocese, clergy and laity together. In Orthodoxy today it is usually the Governing Synod in each autocephalous Church which appoints bishops to vacant sees; but in some Churches—Antioch, for example, and Cyprus—a modified system of popular election still exists. The Moscow Council of 1917–1918 laid down that henceforward bishops in the Russian Church should be elected by the clergy and laity of the diocese; this ruling is followed by the Paris group of Russians and by the Orthodox Church in America, but in the Soviet Union under Communism such election was for obvious reasons impossible." Ware, *The Orthodox Church*, 292.

73  Staniloae, "Unity and diversity in Orthodox tradition," 33–34.

economic and administrative matters—is currently composed of three representatives of each diocese, *one ordained and two nonordained*. The National
Ecclesiastical Council—the supreme administrative body for the affairs of the
entire Romanian Orthodox Church and the executive body of the Holy Synod
and of the National Ecclesiastical Assembly—is composed of nine members,
*three ordained and six nonordained*, one of its attributions being the *election* of
new hierarchs.[74] Moreover, many of the faithful today are involved in charities,
youth organizations, or professional associations. If one adds the prominent
role of the people in the administration of Orthodox churches in America, there
are certainly many ways in which the clergy and the people share together in the
kingly office of Christ.[75]

   In conclusion, the content of the kingly office as shared by the ordained and
nonordained is twofold. On the one hand, they strive together to have dominion over their passions and overcome social injustice, manifested for example in
communist persecution or in poverty. On the other hand, they participate in the
administrative life of the Church and elect hierarchs communally. Again, given
the limitations of his context, Staniloae did not emphasize adequately this latter
aspect, concentrating on the kingly office as mastery over passions. He provided
more insights into the relationship between the clergy and the people in regard
to the prophetic function of the Church.

### Prophetic Office

History shows that ordained ministers of the highest rank can sometimes
uphold heretical positions. For example, Nestorius of Constantinople (428–31)
was condemned at the third ecumenical council (Ephesus 431) for his diopro-
sopist views, and Pope Honorius I (624–38) was anathematized at the sixth

---

74   www.patriarhia.ro/ro/structura_bor, official website of the Romanian Orthodox
     Church.
75   Even though Orthodox churches in the U.S. are making significant efforts to express
     the communion between the clergy and the people, in some communities there is
     an overemphasis on the administrative role of the faithful, which sometimes results
     in business-like attitudes toward Church life. A more liturgical and catechetical
     approach would compensate for this shortcoming, pointing to the spiritual charac-
     ter of all the ministries in the Church. At the same time, there is a need for a correct
     understanding of the role of the clergy and the significance of Ordination in the
     context of a communitarian Church-life. Such theology would encourage clergy
     and the people to work together in an even more meaningful way. Emphasizing the
     concept of communion, ecclesiology escapes the danger of opposing institution and
     charisms, or of giving priority to either clergy or the people.

ecumenical council (Constantinople 680–81) for his monothelist position; these anathemas were ratified by subsequent councils and popes. Moreover, the councils of Ephesus II (449), Lyons II (1274), and Ferarra-Florence (1438–45) had the approval of most participating bishops, but they are not considered ecumenical in the East because the Orthodox faithful did not accept their decisions. This is why not only the hierarchy but the entire Church has to agree on a specific doctrine in order for it to be accepted as normative.[76] Under the guidance of the Holy Spirit, the Church recognizes a certain teaching as its own, as being in communion with the way in which the Christian community has lived its faith (especially in its liturgical life), and as having the consensus of all the faithful, through reception.

Staniloae addressed the subject of reception on several occasions. He affirmed that the councils are extensions of Christ. It is Christ who works infallibly through the communion between the bishops who bring to the council the faith of their communities, and the communities that receive the decisions of the bishops after the council:

> The Church *in its totality*, as the Body of Christ, is infallible because Christ is infallible and he exercises his threefold office in it as one whole.

---

76  In the famous *Encyclical Letter of the One, Holy, Catholic and Apostolic Church to the Orthodox Christians of All Lands*, the authors state that hierarchy and the people collaborate in the preservation of the truth, which is "entrusted to the whole people of the Church." Quoted in Schmemann, *The Eucharist*, 79. This encyclical represents the response of the Patriarchs of Constantinople, Alexandria, Antioch, and Jerusalem, and the Synods of Constantinople, Antioch, and Jerusalem to Pope Pius IX's Encyclical of January 6, 1848 to the Christians of the East. Similarly, Basil of Caesarea assumes that the faithful are well instructed in the Scriptures and in their faith, able to discern the proclamation of the clergy. He writes that the minister of the word "must be judged and borne witness to by the very people who are entrusted to him" (*Moralia* 70.37) and that the faithful, or the "hearers as have been instructed in the Scriptures should test what their teachers say, and receive what agrees with the Scriptures but reject what disagrees; and sternly decline dealings with those who persist in such teachings" (*Moralia* 72.1). Basil states these principles based on several biblical passages, chief among which are the following: "anyone who does not enter the sheepfold by the gate but climbs in by another way is a bandit and a bandit . . . They will not follow a stranger, but they will run from him because they do not know the voice of strangers" (Jn 10.1, 5); Paul instructed the Galatians: "even if we or another angel from heaven should proclaim to you a gospel contrary to what we proclaimed to you, let that one be accursed!" (Gal. 1.8); and finally, Basil quotes the instruction to "not despise the words of prophets, but test everything; hold fast to what is good; abstain from every form of evil" (1 Thess. 5.20-22). See Monge, "Submission to One Head," 238–39.

The Church partakes of his infallibility because it partakes of his three offices. *The episcopacy takes doctrinal decisions infallibly because it takes them in the name of the Church, in inner connection with it and by taking into account the mind of the Church related to its life in Christ* [emphases mine]. The episcopacy can do this because it decides in communion. Their communion insures not only every bishop, but also all of them together, against dictatorial tendencies in the Church. Each one and all of them together are limited in exercising the right to decide in matters of faith by their mutual inter-relatedness and because they seek together the accord among themselves and with the tradition of the Church.[77]

Several elements stand out in this quote. First, infallibility is an attribute of the Church because Christ extends his infallibility to his Body, the Church. Second, infallibility is not expressed through the bishops gathered in a council separate from the faithful. On the contrary, the bishops decide infallibly because they base their affirmations on the faith and the sacramental life of their communities. The bishops then bring the decisions of the council back to their churches. Only those decisions which are accepted and incorporated in the liturgical life of the Church ("its life in Christ") are considered infallible and, as Staniloae would add later, confirmed as coming from the Holy Spirit[78] because they reflect "the faith and the sacramental life of the Church inherited through tradition."[79] Third, Staniloae implied (and shortly thereafter stated clearly) that, gathered in ecumenical councils, the bishops extend their authority beyond their local church to the entire Church.[80] Thus, infallibility belongs to the whole Church, as the Body of Christ partaking of the infallibility of its Head, manifested concretely through councils and their reception as

---

77  Staniloae, *Dogmatics* 2, 164.
78  Staniloae, "The Authority of the Church," 209.
79  Staniloae, *Dogmatics* 2, 164, 249–50. Since earlier I brought up the councils of Lyons and Ferarra-Florence as evidence for the necessity of reception, it is important to nuance the affirmation that only those teachings that reflect the life of the Church are received. By considering these councils as general rather than ecumenical, more recent Catholic theology upholds the validity of their decisions for the West, while acknowledging the lack of their reception in the East. (Frans Bouwen, "Ecumenical Councils," in *Dictionary of the Ecumenical Movement*, ed. Nicholas Lossky, et al. [Grand Rapids, MI: Eerdmans, 1991], 338.) Orthodox theologians, on their part, have a more irenic approach toward the issues discussed at these councils, primarily the Filioque.
80  Staniloae, *Dogmatics* 2, 165.

ecumenical and inspired by the Holy Spirit.[81] Staniloae reiterated these principles when he observed that, in the ancient Church, the bishops were not the only participants at the councils, but also

> the representatives of the clergy, of the monastics, and of the people, their opinion being asked before the adoption of conciliar definitions. Moreover, each bishop signed these definitions only after being convinced that they correspond to the faith of his Church, which included its clergy and people and was in line with its apostolic Tradition. The definitive adoption of conciliar decisions by the entire Church was made through the so-called reception.[82]

Guided by the Holy Spirit, the episcopacy has the role of formulating the faith of the Church, but the verification of these formulas is done, under the inspiration of the Spirit, by the entire Church through reception. In line with other Orthodox theologians such as Afanassieff, Lossky, Evdokimov, Florovsky, and Ware,[83] Staniloae affirmed that, even though the entire Church is entrusted with the transmission of the faith, the differences between ministries is not erased, since the bishop is still the articulator of the faith of his community. As Stefan Lupu commented on Staniloae's theology,

> the common responsibility to preserve the faith does not erase the difference between ministries in the Church: the ordained ministries have the

---

81  These affirmations should be read in light of Staniloae's balanced understanding of the presence of Christ and the Spirit in the Church: "The Church infallibly understands the meaning of revelation, because she herself is the work of revelation, of the Holy Spirit, and because she moves within revelation as one who is organically united with it. The Holy Spirit who, together with Christ, is the author of revelation, the one who brought the Church into existence and the one who inspires Scriptures—this same Spirit is at work within the Church, helping her to understand and to appropriate, in an authentic and practical way, the content of revelation, that is, Christ in the fullness of his gifts." Staniloae, *The Experience of God 1*, 58. See also Staniloae, *Theology and the Church*, 50. The understanding of the Spirit's role to maintain the truth through the consensus of the faithful (*consensus fidelium*), both clergy and the people, became more prevalent in Catholic theology after Congar. See Ormond Rush, *The Reception of Doctrine: An Appropriation of Hans Robert Jauss' Reception Aesthetics and Literary Hermeneutics* (Rome: Pontificia Università Gregoriana, 1997), 156.

82  Staniloae, "The Theological Foundations of Hierarchy and Synodality," 172.

83  Afanassieff, *The Church of the Holy Spirit*, 69–75. Lossky, *Mystical Theology*, 16. Evdokimov, *L'Orthodoxie*, 162–63. Georges Florovsky, "The Catholicity of the Church," in *Bible, Church, Tradition, Collected Works 1*, 53. Ware, *The Orthodox Church*, 251–52.

mission to observe, prepare, and propose the faith to the faithful, especially when celebrating the sacraments. The faithful have the role to guard the faith of the Church and to contribute, together with the ordained ministers, to the understanding of the discovery of the most fitted formulas for the expression of the truth of faith.[84]

These considerations refer to two categories involved in reception: bishops and the people. Included in these categories are professional theologians and parish priests who, besides participating in the Church's sense of the faith, have several gifts and opportunities that allow them to contribute to the process of reception. First, because of their education and their vocation to teach, professional theologians have an important role in the discernment and dissemination of the faith, provided that they are in touch with the reality of the Church by being active in their faith communities.[85] Second, parish priests have the advantage of being theologically educated, so they are able to analyze the teachings that are proposed to their attention in the process of reception. They are also close to the people and have a realistic sense of the way people react to a certain teaching. Common exercise of the prophetic office shared by the clergy and the people is most visible at this level.

There are, however, several difficulties concerning reception. First, it does not happen immediately after the proclamation of a certain teaching; reception can actually take many centuries. Second, and related to the first difficulty, it is not always clear when reception can be considered as completed. For example, most theologians thought that the reception of the third and fourth ecumenical councils was over, only to realize in the twentieth century that Eastern and Oriental Orthodox churches profess the same faith, despite their contradictory theological terminology.[86] Now they are faced with the task of completing the reception of the latter ecumenical councils in an irenic spirit. Third, reception is complicated by the divided state of Christianity. Staniloae considered that reception is the task of the Church in its broadest understanding, not only of the Orthodox Church. The Church gathered in ecumenical councils, the Church

---

84   Stefan Lupu, "Sinodalitatea si/sau conciliaritatea: Expresie a unitatii si catolicitatii Bisericii [Synodality and/or Conciliarity: Expression of the Unity and Catholicity of the Church]," *Dialog Teologic* 4, no. 7 (2001): 69.

85   Theologians who are not active in faith communities can still have an impact on the faith of the Church, although indirectly.

86   See for example the "Agreed Statement, Third Unofficial Conversation between Eastern and Oriental Orthodox Church, 1970," in Michael Kinnamon and Brian E. Cope, *The Ecumenical Movement: An Anthology of Key Texts and Voices* (Grand Rapids, MI: Eerdmans, 1997), 147–49.

that cannot err, is the Church that represents the entire Christian world.[87] Fourth, reception is sometimes vague, resulting in the need to reactualize the list of canons by discerning which ones were never received or have become outdated, so that they will not be indiscriminately enforced today.[88] These four difficulties do not diminish the importance of reception but rather represent obstacles that can be overcome by strengthening the communion between the clergy and the people through the common exercise of their calling as prophets, kings, and priests.

### Conclusion

Whether knowingly or not, intentionally or by accident, Staniloae has engaged with other Eastern and Western theologies of priesthood. He has contributed to a better understanding of the underdeveloped topics of universal priesthood of all the baptized and the three offices of Christ, generally associated with Protestant theology. He has also discussed themes that were of interest to Orthodox theologians because of their dialogue with Catholic theology, especially Congar and Vatican II. Such is the case of the relationship between the clergy and the people in a Church regarded as communion in the image of the Trinity, the relationship between the priesthood of Christ and that of the Church, and the reception of doctrine. Eastern theologians are indebted to the West for inspiring their interest in rearticulating and actualizing the Orthodox position on these themes.

At the same time, Staniloae's considerations about the mutual interdependence between the ordained and the people, or the hierarchical and communal characters of priesthood are a most-needed perspective both ecumenically and in Orthodox theology. The East continues the struggle to integrate the Christological and pneumatological aspects of its trinitarian ecclesiology in a theology of communion between institution and charism. Protestant theologians

---

87 Staniloae quoted Nissiotis who wrote that Vatican II was not ecumenical because it did not convoke the whole Christian world and because non-Catholic observers did not enjoy a position equal to that of the representatives of the Catholic Church. (Staniloae, *Theology and the Church*, 46.) Moreover, Zizioulas writes that today reception is more complicated because of the divided state of Christianity, where we need first to receive one another, and then to receive one from the other. John D. Zizioulas, "The Theological Problem of 'Reception'," *One in Christ* 21, no. 3 (1985): 188.

88 This is even more necessary when, in some monastic circles, such canons are being imposed to the detriment of people's spiritual lives. Roberson, "Contemporary Romanian Orthodox Ecclesiology," 167. Manastireanu, "Dumitru Staniloae's Theology of Ministry," 143.

could find valuable insights in Staniloae's considerations about the mutual interdependence between the ordained and the people, and the hierarchical and
communal characters of priesthood. Catholic theologians could benefit from
Staniloae's approach to the liturgical role of the priest in communion with the
people, as well as his view of conciliarity and the reception of doctrine as an
exercise of the entire church. Thus, all three major Christian families have the
opportunity to grow together in their theological understanding of priesthood,
and Staniloae has a major contribution in this regard.

Some elements presented here show the local Church as communion in the
image of the Trinity. This is the case of the communion between the clergy and
the people as celebrants of their liturgical sacrifice to the Father, united with the
Son, in the Spirit, to give just one example. Other aspects, such as the reception of ecumenical councils by the entire priestly People of God, Body of Christ
under the inspiration of the Spirit, point to the communion of the Church at
the universal level. The relationship between the local and universal aspects of
ecclesiology represents the focus of the next chapter.

# Chapter 8

## LOCALITY AND UNIVERSALITY: EUCHARISTIC ECCLESIOLOGY

One way in which Orthodox and Catholic ecclesiologies converge today is in understanding the Church as communion. Contemporary Orthodox theology owes this approach mainly to Zizioulas who criticized Afanassieff's eucharistic ecclesiology,[1] although, in a recent book, *Communion and Otherness*, Zizioulas has come closer to Afanassieff than in the past. To better serve the cause of Christian unity, the positions of Zizioulas and Afanassieff need to be complemented or at times even corrected by Staniloae's ecclesiology. After an analysis of Afanassieff's ecclesiology, I present the similarities and differences between the communion ecclesiologies of Zizioulas and Staniloae, as they both respond to Afanassieff. Next, I identify the strengths of these three Orthodox theologians, which introduce two models of ecclesial unity based on their emphasis on either the local or universal church and on the Eucharist as either a means or sign of unity. Finally, I submit a constructive proposal for approaching ecclesial unity from the perspective of a communion ecclesiology that advances the dialogue between the Orthodox and Catholic churches.

### *Afanassieff's Eucharistic Ecclesiology*

The eucharistic ecclesiology of Afanassieff represents a milestone in the development of Orthodox ecclesiology, with its emphasis on unity of faith, eucharistic communion, and the relationship between the local and universal aspects of the Church.[2]

---

1   For another excellent treatment of eucharistic ecclesiology from a Catholic perspective with ecumenical sensitivity, see Paul McPartlan, *Sacrament of Salvation: An Introduction to Eucharistic Ecclesiology* (Edinburgh: T&T Clark, 1995).

2   Afanassieff first proposed eucharistic ecclesiology in the winter of 1932–33. Marianne Afanassieff, "La genèse de 'L'Église du Saint-Esprit' [The Genesis of 'The Church of the Holy Spirit']," in *L'Église du Saint-Esprit* (Paris: Cerf, 1975), 17.

Afanassieff claimed that the early Church had a eucharistic ecclesiology in which the eucharistic assembly of the local church contained the fullness of the Church. Local churches were autonomous and independent, but at the same time they related to other local churches through bishops, through the acceptance of other local churches' ecclesial life, and—most importantly—through mutual identity, as they each represented the fullness of Christ's presence in the local eucharistic assembly. It was Cyprian of Carthage, Afanassieff argued, who later replaced eucharistic ecclesiology with universal ecclesiology, wherein only the universal church possesses fullness and is made up of parts; local churches do not possess fullness[3] because all the parts of the universal church are united through their bishops.[4] Consequently, the limits of the Church are drawn by the episcopate, and outside these limits there is no Church, according to Cyprian's formula: "The bishop is in the Church and the Church in the bishop, and if anyone is not with the bishop, he is not in the Church" (*Epist.* LXVI, VIII, 3).[5]

In Afanassieff's estimation, the basic principles of Cyprian's doctrine still perpetuate the schism between the Orthodox and Catholic churches.[6] Afanassieff proposed the application of eucharistic ecclesiology to twentieth-century Orthodox-Catholic relations in order to manifest the (forgotten) unity that still exists between them and thus end their schism. Several aspects of Afanassieff's eucharistic ecclesiology are relevant today:

First, because Christ is fully present in the Eucharist, the eucharistic assembly of the local church (including the bishop) fully manifests the Church *Una Sancta*, which is the Body of Christ. Consequently, Afanassieff submitted the fundamental thesis of eucharistic ecclesiology:

> The Church is where the eucharistic assembly is. It is also possible to formulate this in another way. Where the Eucharist is, there is the Church of God, and where the Church of God is, there is the Eucharist. It follows that the eucharistic assembly is the distinctive, empirical sign of the

---

3   According to Cyprian, "Just as we can distinguish members in the Church, the Body of Christ, so the one and only Church, physically speaking, is made up of different local churches, which are her limbs or members: *ecclesia per totum mundum in multa membra divisa*" (*Epist.* LV, XXIV, 2; cf. *Epist.* XXXVI, IV, 1). Nicolas Afanassieff, "The Church Which Presides in Love," in *The Primacy of Peter: Essays in Ecclesiology and the Early Church*, ed. John Meyendorff (Crestwood, NY: St Vladimir's Seminary Press, 1992), 95. See the same idea in Nicolas Afanassieff, "Una Sancta," *Irénikon* 36, no. 4 (1963): 440.

4   Cyprian, *De unitate ecclesiae*, V.

5   Afanassieff, "Una Sancta," 12–13.

6   Afanassieff, "Una Sancta," French original, 440. This passage is missing from the English translation.

Church.... The actual limits of the Church are determined by the limits of the eucharistic assembly. In affirming that the eucharistic assembly is the principle of the unity of the Church, the thesis that the bishop is the distinctive empirical sign of the local church is not excluded, because the bishop is included in the very concept of the Eucharist.[7]

If Cyprian's universal ecclesiology regarded the bishop as the principle of unity and the point of reference for the limits of the Church, Afanassieff attributed these roles to the eucharistic assembly that includes the bishop as its president.

Second, Afanassieff affirmed the autonomy and independence of the local church based on the fullness of the local eucharistic assembly. Containing in itself everything necessary to its life, the local church "did not depend on any other local church or any bishop whatever outside itself . . . because any power, of any kind, exercised over it would be exercised over Christ and His Body."[8]

Third, he emphasized a unity by "mutual identity"[9] among diverse local manifestations of the same ecclesial reality, in contrast with Cyprian's thesis that local churches are parts of a whole: "Each local church would unite in herself [all] the local churches, for she possessed all the fullness of the Church of God and all the local churches together were united because the same Church of God dwelt in them all."[10] This kind of unity preserves the universal character of the Church since, as Afanassieff continued, "What was celebrated in one church was also celebrated in the others, because everything was celebrated in

---

7 Afanassieff, "Una Sancta," 14.

8 Afanassieff, "The Church Which Presides in Love," 107–09.

9 Ware observes that, for Ignatius, "various local churches are related to each other, not as part of a whole, but on the principle of *mutual identity*, because in each local Church there is celebrated the one, unique and indivisible Eucharist." Timothy (Kallistos) Ware, "Church and Eucharist, Communion and Intercommunion," *Sobornost* 7, no. 7 (1978): 554.

10 Afanassieff, "Una Sancta," 15. Most contemporary Orthodox and Catholic theologians would agree with Afanassieff's affirmation based on the principle of catholicity, according to which the whole is present in the part and the part is in the whole ("catholicity" derives from *cath'olon*). This principle is valid both for the Eucharist, where every communicant receives the entire Body and Blood of Christ, and for the Church, as a description of the relationship between its local and universal aspects. A further reason for Orthodox theologians to agree with this statement is that here Afanassieff seems to come close to the model of autocephalous Orthodox churches, where they are administratively autonomous and independent, but united in faith and Eucharist. This comparison with contemporary autocephalous Orthodox churches, however, needs even further qualification: Afanassieff criticized this model because it ascribes autonomy only to the autocephalous church and not to the dioceses (as eucharistic centers) that form it.

the Church of God in Christ. Because of their universal nature, local churches were neither locked in themselves, nor 'provincial.'"[11] By maintaining that nothing can stand above the local eucharistic assembly and that the *Una Sancta* is not subordinate to the local church, Afanassieff intended to keep a proper balance between the universal and local aspects of the Church.

Fourth, he contended that both Catholic and Orthodox churches celebrate the same Eucharist, which unites all those who receive it, whether they be Catholic or Orthodox, in spite of their canonical and dogmatic divergences. He consequently criticized Cyprian's affirmation that separated churches place themselves outside of the Church (*Una Sancta*), so that their sacraments are not valid.[12] Paradoxically, however, both Catholic and Orthodox churches have adopted Cyprian's position, each considering itself to be the true Church. They have altered Cyprian's position and affirmed that the other Church contains a "diminished existence of the Church, or certain 'vestiges' of the Church, which allow the separated parts of the Church to continue their ecclesiastical life and for the sacraments to be administered."[13] Afanassieff considered that such a position cannot be defended theologically, since "the nature of the Church presupposes that either she exists in her fullness or she does not exist at all, but there can be no partial existence nor can there be vestiges existing here and there."[14] Interestingly, Afanassieff did not accept differing degrees of belonging to the Church, so he implicitly upheld Cyprian's position that there is no ecclesial life outside the canonical boundaries of the Church.[15]

---

11 Afanassieff, *L'Église du Saint-Esprit*, 29.
12 Afanassieff, "Una Sancta," French original, 442.
13 Ibid.: 443–44.
14 Afanassieff, "Una Sancta," 8.
15 Florovsky made the distinction between canonical and charismatic boundaries of the Church. He identified the first boundary with the Orthodox Church, and the second one with the rest of Christendom. Florovsky did not accept Cyprian's idea that the charismatic and canonical boundaries coincide. He preferred Augustine's position, which recognized the validity of sacraments outside the canonical boundaries of the Church. He pointed out that some heretics were received into the Church without the administration of Baptism or their orders were recognized without performing another Ordination. These sacraments are validly performed "by virtue of the Holy Spirit." Moreover, according to Florovsky, "the unity of the Church is based on a twofold bond—the 'unity of the Spirit' and the 'union of peace' (cf. Eph. 4.3). In sects and divisions the 'union of peace' is broken and torn apart, but in the sacraments the 'unity of the Spirit' is not terminated. This is the unique paradox of sectarian existence." Thus, Florovsky considered that the canonical and charismatic boundaries of the Church do not coincide because of the presence of the Holy Spirit "outside" the Church. Georges Florovsky, "The

Fifth, based on the creedal affirmation that the Church is "one, holy, catholic, and apostolic," Afanassieff reinforced his contention that the Church is one, even in the present context of dogmatic disunity. Consequently, "if one recognized the quality of church in [either] part of the divided church, one would be minimizing the importance of dogmatic differences, leaving them integral as they are. If one or the other parts are both the church, then the sacraments are celebrated and salvation is possible in both, for this is the purpose of the church."[16] Afanassieff was subtle here; applied to the present Orthodox-Catholic situation, this statement means that the two churches recognize each other's sacraments and character of Church (each being a local church of the same *Una Sancta*),[17] so, in practice, they actually deemphasize the importance of the dogmatic differences between them, even though they might be reluctant to admit it officially. I return to this aspect shortly.

Sixth, Afanassieff considered the possibility of ecclesial unity without episcopal communion. He criticized universal ecclesiology for its position that the principle of Church unity is the episcopate. According to eucharistic ecclesiology, however, unity finds concrete expression in the fullest manifestation of the Church in the Eucharist, which includes the episcopate.[18] This is an essential argument, since it implicitly poses the following question: Does disunion in episcopacy preclude union in the Eucharist? The answer to this question will determine whether the Orthodox and Catholic churches are still united or not.

Seventh, Afanassieff contended that the lack of eucharistic communion between the Orthodox and Catholic churches has never affected the essence of their unity because it is based merely on canonical grounds (surprisingly for a professor of canon law). And yet, he added, these canonical reasons

---

Boundaries of the Church," in *Ecumenism I: A Doctrinal Approach, Collected Works 13* (Belmont, MA: Nordland Publishing Company, 1989), 37, 42. See also Georges Florovsky, "St. Cyprian and St. Augustine on Schism," in *Ecumenism II: A Historical Approach, Collected Works 14* (Belmont, MA: Nordland Publishing Company, 1989), 49.

16   Afanassieff, "Una Sancta," 5–6.

17   Afanassieff wrote: "For eucharistic ecclesiology, the orthodox church and the catholic church are both Churches, or to be more exact, each local church of both groups remains a Church—as it was before so it is after the 'separation.' I put 'separation' in quotation marks for it did not take place and there is no separation. The Church of God is forever and remains one and unique. The break in communion was not able to produce the division of the Church which, by her very nature, cannot be divided into parts." Ibid., 22.

18   Ibid., 14–15.

impede us from expressing our unity by sharing in the same Eucharist.[19] For Afanassieff, exclusion from the Eucharist is the expected result of any schism, and it certainly does not imply the impoverishment or even cessation of ecclesial status:

> The nature of the break in communion indicated that the local church deprived of communion with the other churches ceased to exist for the latter, for there were no longer links by which this communion could be realized. But such a church did not cease to remain in itself the Church of God despite its isolated situation. If we think that such a local church is no longer the Church, we reject the only distinctive sign by which we can judge the existence of a Church: where there is the eucharistic assembly, there is Church, and there is the Church of God in Christ. This sign applies not only to churches that are part of the multitude-of-churches-linked-by-Love-and-peace but also to those that are separated.[20]

Afanassieff seems inconsistent here by allowing a church to exist in isolation from other local churches, an assertion he has previously denied. Moreover, I disagree with Afanassieff that lack of love is not a church-dividing issue, since two local communities cannot share in the same eucharistic celebration without love. For him, the unity of the Church depends primarily (almost exclusively) on the same Eucharist's being celebrated in different local churches, not on the interdependence of local communities, dogmatic union, episcopal communion, or bond of love.

Afanassieff called for a return to the eucharistic ecclesiology of the early Church, meaning that, today, those who receive the Eucharist "are united with all those who at that moment also participate in eucharistic assemblies—not only those of the orthodox church but also those of the catholic church—for

---

19   Nicolas Afanassieff, "The Eucharist: Principal Link Between the Catholics and the Orthodox," in *Tradition Alive: On the Church and the Christian Life in Our Time: Readings from the Eastern Church*, ed. Michael Plekon (Lanham, MD: Rowan & Littlefield, 2003), 49. Original French: Nicolas Afanassieff, "L'Eucharistie, principal lien entre les Catholiques et les Orthodoxes," *Irénikon* 38, no. 3 (1965): 339. (The English translation of this article is incomplete and does not reflect all these ideas. For a complete account, see the French original.) History supports Afanassieff's affirmation, since the events that led to the schism in 1054 were not so much doctrinal differences but canonical (although not completely separate from dogma), and the schism was sealed only in 1204, with the fourth crusade. Even in the earlier Photian schism (867–70), unity was restored after agreement was reached in canonical issues, without solving the theological issue of the Filioque.

20   Afanassieff, "Una Sancta," 18.

everywhere there is only the one and the same Eucharist being celebrated."[21] Because of this unity manifested in the Eucharist, "the links between the Catholic Church and the Orthodox Church were never entirely broken and continue to exist until the present. The essential link between us is the Eucharist."[22] Thus, Afanassieff arrived at the heart of eucharistic ecclesiology: Since Orthodox and Catholic churches celebrate the same Eucharist, they are united through their mutual identity in the Eucharist. As a practical consequence of his theology, he recommended that the Orthodox and Catholic churches work toward manifesting their already existing unity by renewing their communion and postponing the solution of dogmatic divergences for the time when they would be able to address them in the spirit of love. In the meantime, the doctrinal divergences (including papal primacy) between the two churches would remain dogmas that are not recognized by the other.[23]

As if knowing that his daring affirmation would be met with strong criticism, Afanassieff defended his proposal by contending that, even though different local churches ideally should enjoy absolute dogmatic harmony, this has never been the case in history and is certainly unattainable in the present state of animosity. The Orthodox and Catholic churches have a better chance of solving their dogmatic differences in the context of unity. Afanassieff claimed that he did not minimize the importance of dogmatic formulations and he did not advocate doctrinal relativism or indifferentism, but he hoped that differences could be solved in the spirit of love.[24] Thus, dogmatic differences should not stand in the way of communion.

What does renewing the communion between the Orthodox and Catholic churches mean? Ware contends that Afanassieff regarded intercommunion (that is, sharing in the Eucharist among separate churches) as a practical consequence of his theology. He believed that Christians need to share in the Eucharist, so that they discover the unity that already exists in Christ and in the Eucharist. This union would be built from the inside, rather than from the outside.[25]

The reception of Afanassieff's theology varied from enthusiastic embrace (Evdokimov[26]) to vehement rejection (Ware,[27] Zizioulas, and Staniloae). The

---

21 Ibid., 24.
22 Afanassieff, "The Eucharist: Principal Link," 48–49.
23 Afanassieff, "Una Sancta," 25–26.
24 See Ibid., 27–28.
25 Summarized in Ware, "Church and Eucharist," 557–58.
26 In *L'Orthodoxie*, Evdokimov dedicated an entire chapter to "eucharistic ecclesiology" and expressed his unreserved agreement with Afanassieff. See pages 128–31, 56.
27 Ware affirms that the Eucharist alone does not create the Church, but that two other ingredients are necessary: "dogmatic unity (unity in faith) . . . [and] ecclesial unity (unity in the bishop)" in the local bishop. Moreover, Ware disagrees with Afanassieff's view on intercommunion. See Ware, "Church and Eucharist," 558.

next two sections will concentrate on Zizioulas's and Staniloae's criticisms of eucharistic ecclesiology.

## Zizioulas's Response to Afanassieff: Episcopal Communion

Zizioulas's main criticism of Afanassieff is that churches cannot have eucharistic communion without sharing the same teaching and without communion among bishops. Alternatively, Zizioulas proposes communion ecclesiology, which emphasizes the relationships among bishops gathered in synods and in communion with one another.[28] Zizioulas first challenges Afanassieff's historical analysis of the contrast between the eucharistic ecclesiology of Ignatius and the universal ecclesiology of Cyprian.[29] Second, appealing to the authority of Irenaeus who affirmed that "our doctrine [that is, the orthodox faith] is agreed on the Eucharist, and the Eucharist confirms our doctrine,"[30] Zizioulas contends that "*orthodoxy is unthinkable without the Eucharist*" and "*the Eucharist without orthodoxy is an impossibility.*"[31] Hence, he writes:

> In addition to the Eucharist other essential elements are required, such as right faith without which "even the Eucharist is an impossibility." It is consequently a negative element in the extreme positions of eucharistic ecclesiology that through them dogmatic differences tend to become unimportant in the unity of the Church.[32]

Third, Zizioulas criticizes the term "intercommunion" as inept, considering that eucharistic communion can take place only in a fully united Church. In the meantime, "the avoidance of communion with the heterodox, far from having any sense of self-satisfaction or arrogance, expresses a continuing experience of the tragedy of schism as expressed in the most existential way through the refusal of eucharistic communion."[33]

Zizioulas's fourth criticism of Afanassieff, which coincides with the heart of his early account of communion ecclesiology, stresses that episcopal communion

---

28   See also Turcescu, "Eucharistic Ecclesiology or Open Sobornicity?," 92–94.
29   Zizioulas, *Eucharist, Bishop, Church*, 126. See also Ware's similar criticism in "Church and Eucharist," 556, n. 20.
30   *Against Heresies* 4:18:3; PG 7:1028A.
31   Zizioulas, *Eucharist, Bishop, Church*, 133.
32   Ibid., 257–58.
33   Ibid.

is the necessary condition for Christian unity. Zizioulas identifies the bishop with the entire local eucharistic assembly and therefore concludes that the unity of the Church is not simply eucharistic but also hierarchical: "*the community cannot even be called a church without the clergy*, i.e., the Bishop, presbyters and deacons.[34]

Fifth, Zizioulas criticizes Afanassieff for giving priority to the local over the universal aspects of the Church. Zizioulas claims that, because the Eucharist is celebrated at the local level but is offered in the name of the entire Church, "the Eucharist points not in the direction of the priority of the local Church but in that of the *simultaneity* of both local and universal.... The dilemma 'local or universal' is transcended in the Eucharist."[35] Moreover, for a local church fully to exist, it must exist in communion with different local churches. This principle is a major contribution to ecclesiology and stems from Zizioulas's understanding of the person as "being in communion," where a person (applied to God, humanity, and the Church) exists fully only in communion with other persons.[36] Over time, Zizioulas's communion ecclesiology became more and more centered on his theology of personhood.

In *Communion and Otherness*, he continues to reject the practice of intercommunion. Defending this position is difficult since Zizioulas's major premise is that communion—which embraces and presupposes otherness—is a matter of ontology, inherent in existence in general, but especially in the triune God, in the human person, and in the Church. Although communion with "the other" is constitutive for the being of the Church and the Eucharist, Zizioulas justifies the exclusion from eucharistic communion of "other" Christians:

> There is only one kind of exclusion that eucharistic communion permits, and that is the exclusion of exclusion itself, that is, of those things

---

34  Ibid., 116.
35  Zizioulas, *Being as Communion*, 133.
36  Zizioulas accuses Afanassieff of regarding Christ first as an individual who *then* becomes corporate personality, which would mean Afanassieff affirmed that the faithful are *identically* Christ rather than *differentiatedly* Christ and that local churches are united through their mutual identity. Instead, Zizioulas (in McPartlan's summary) suggests that the unity of the local churches "derives not from their sameness but from their existence in this differentiated configuration." (McPartlan, *The Eucharist Makes the Church*, 229, 33–35.) In my estimation, Afanassieff did not work within the framework of Christ as individual/corporate personality or of the local churches united identically/differentiatedly, but Zizioulas "forces" Afanassieff to fit into this scheme.

that involve rejection and division. Such are the things that *in principle* and by *an act of faith*—not by way of failure to apply the true faith[37]— lead to a kind of communion that disturbs Trinitarian, Christological, Pneumatological and ecclesiological faith.[38]

Zizioulas thus considers that the life of the Church is impoverished by heresies and schisms as acts of exclusion. His position stands in opposition to Afanassieff's contention that dogmatic differences resulting in schism do not affect essentially the Church unity still manifested in the Eucharist.

Another issue resurfacing in *Communion and Otherness* is that of the relationship between the local and the universal church. Zizioulas reads Catholic ecclesiology as represented by Karl Rahner and Joseph Ratzinger "to justify the ontological priority of the universal Church over against the local: it is, in effect, nothing other than the argument that the 'one' precedes the 'many' and that substance has priority over existence."[39] Zizioulas argues that "Roman Catholic ecclesiology, as represented in the above authors, would say that the one Church precedes and 'subsists' in each local church.[40] Protestant ecclesiology would tend to be more 'congregationalist' and to give priority to the local community, sometimes not even bothering about the one Church, at least in its visible form." Zizioulas then formulates the synthesis between thesis and antithesis and affirms, "The one cannot precede the many, and otherness cannot be secondary to unity. The 'many' must have a constitutive and not a derivative role in the Church's being; local and universal must somehow coincide."[41]

Zizioulas's objective to give equal importance to the local and the universal is commendable, but many times it appears to be merely an unfulfilled desiderate,

---

37  Zizioulas subtly refers here to the Orthodox in the Diaspora where, even though there is communion among different ethnic churches *in principle*, their communion *as an act of faith* is greatly impoverished by the existence of overlapping jurisdictions separated ethnically or politically. Zizioulas, *Communion and Otherness*, 8–9.

38  Ibid., 7–8.

39  Ibid., 38.

40  Surprisingly, at this point Zizioulas mentions in a footnote the debate between Kasper and Ratzinger but does not take into consideration Kasper's position, which is certainly in disagreement with Ratzinger's. For instance, see Walter Kasper, "On the Church: A Friendly Reply to Cardinal Ratzinger," *America* 184, no. 14 (2001): 8–14 and Joseph Ratzinger, "The Local Church and the Universal Church: A Response to Walter Kasper," *America* 185, no. 16 (2001): 7–11.

41  Zizioulas, *Communion and Otherness*, 38.

as several scholars have contended.[42] Despite his announced intention to find a balance between "one" and "many," "nature" and "person," "universal" and "local," Zizioulas repeatedly gives priority to "many," "person," and "local."[43] This brings him closer to Afanassieff than he would probably want to be, since Afanassieff also gave priority to the local church, despite his claim to balance it with the universality of the Church.

Overall, Zizioulas provides important responses to Afanassieff's eucharistic ecclesiology, especially in regard to the interdependence of the Eucharist, local church, and the bishop, as well as regarding Afanassieff's rejection of intercommunion. However, Zizioulas's departure from Afanassieff is not entirely satisfactory concerning the relationship between the local and the universal church, because both theologians give priority to the local. Staniloae's response to Afanassieff's ecclesiology is more complete, especially regarding the relationship between the Eucharist and the common confession of faith.

### Staniloae's Response to Afanassieff: Doctrinal Communion

Staniloae reacted rather strongly against eucharistic ecclesiology,[44] especially in his essay on "The Universal and Catholic Church" and in his book on *Spirituality and Communion in the Orthodox Liturgy*, neither of which is available in English. While supporting Afanassieff's positive intention to ease the path toward Christian unity, Staniloae considered that eucharistic ecclesiology does a disservice to the ecumenical cause by being relativistic and by creating an illegitimate compromise;[45] he later referred to it as a "theory

---

42  See, e.g., André de Halleux, "Personnalisme ou essentialisme trinitaire chez les pères Cappadociens?," in *Patrologie et oecuménisme: Recueil d'études*, ed. André de Halleux, *Bibliotheca Ephemeridum theologicarum Lovaniensium 93* (Leuven: Leuven University Press, 1990), 215–68; Lucian Turcescu, "'Person' versus 'Individual', and Other Modern Misreadings of Gregory of Nyssa," *Modern Theology* 18, no. 4 (2002); and Turcescu, "Eucharistic Ecclesiology or Open Sobornicity?" In *Communion and Otherness* Zizioulas engages with Turcescu, but, in my estimation, Zizioulas's arguments are not convincing.

43  E.g., Zizioulas, *Communion and Otherness*, 142.

44  Staniloae concentrated especially on Afanassieff, "Una Sancta," 470–72. and Afanassieff, "L'Eucharistie, principal lien," 366–69. For another analysis of some of these criticisms, see Turcescu, "Eucharistic Ecclesiology or Open Sobornicity?" 96ff.

45  Dumitru Staniloae, "Biserica universala si soborniceasca [The Universal and Catholic Church]," *Ortodoxia* 18, no. 2 (1966): 167.

invented by the theologian Afanassieff."[46] Staniloae criticized several aspects of eucharistic ecclesiology, but interestingly, the relationship between the Eucharist and the bishop—so prominent in Zizioulas—did not receive any attention because Staniloae thought that Afanassieff actually did emphasize this relationship.[47]

First, Staniloae considered that eucharistic ecclesiology does not adequately stress the importance of the right faith as a condition for the changing of the bread and the wine into the Body and Blood of Christ within the local eucharistic community.[48] Staniloae contended that orthodoxy does not result from the Eucharist, but that the true Eucharist results from orthodoxy, so that eucharistic communion can only take place within the context of sharing in the same faith.[49] This conclusion stems from the order of the Divine Liturgy, where the community first affirms the same faith, and then the *epiclesis* takes place. He continued:

> The confession of the unity in faith before the Sacrament of the changing [of the bread and wine into the Body and Blood of Christ] under the guidance of the priest, who maintains the connection with the entire Church through the bishop, reaches its climax when the priest says, "Let us love one another, that with one mind we may confess." The community responds, "Father, Son, and Holy Spirit, Trinity one in essence and inseparable," and then . . . recites the Nicene-Constantinopolitan Creed, which contains in a concentrated way the entire right faith.... What is required from the members of the community is not only the assurance of mutual love, so that they would then proceed with the Sacrament, the divergences of faith remaining to be appeased in a common Creed, after the Sacrament and receiving Communion. This is what eucharistic ecclesiology and other appeals for intercommunion among those of different faiths (commonly receiving the Eucharist) propose, in the hope that the love they promise to each other and the common sharing in the Eucharist would later on bring them to the unity of the faith. Mutual love, if it is true and total, must be made manifest immediately in the confession "with one mind" of the common faith.[50]

---

46   Staniloae, *Spirituality and Communion*, 397–98.
47   Staniloae, "The Universal and Catholic Church," 168–69.
48   Staniloae, *Spirituality and Communion*, 397. See also Staniloae, "The Universal and Catholic Church," 169, 72.
49   Staniloae, *Spirituality and Communion*, 398–99.
50   Ibid., 399.

Thus, Staniloae rejected intercommunion,[51] affirming that eucharistic communion is based on unity of faith, the role of the faithful to profess a common faith, the love among members of different communities, the unity between the priest and the bishop who appoints him to preside over the eucharistic assembly, and the communion between the bishop and the rest of the Church. According to Staniloae, all these elements are interrelated and condition one another.[52]

Second, Staniloae disagreed with Afanassieff's assertion that the division between the Orthodox and Catholic churches has affected only the surface of their ecclesiastical lives and has only a canonical character.[53] For Staniloae, doctrinal disunity creates an essential separation between churches, which can be healed only within the context of a common confession of faith. Presently, Christians do not share in the fullness of the faith, even though they agree on the fundamental truths of Revelation. They all belong to the same *Una Sancta*, but not fully, so they all need to come together and arrive at the fullness of

---

51 Besides the passage quoted previously and many other similar instances, Ware recollects Staniloae saying, "I cannot understand how communion in the Holy Eucharist can somehow compensate for non-communion in faith." Ware, "Church and Eucharist," 558.

    Along the same lines, Florovsky did not embrace the possibility of "charitable union," or union based exclusively on love, disregarding the doctrinal differences, because "charity should never be set against the truth." (Georges Florovsky, "The Quest for Christian Unity and the Orthodox Church," in *Ecumenism I: A Doctrinal Approach*, 144. Georges Florovsky, "The Tragedy of Christian Divisions," in *Ecumenism I: A Doctrinal Approach*, 29–31.) Moreover, Florovsky wrote: "The isolation of the most 'important' points is a highly controversial premise. It is proposed to consider the controversial point nonessential, thereby avoiding dissent. In this way, 'moralism' [i.e., unity based on purely moral grounds, such as peace or tolerance] is always a kind of dogmatic minimalism, if not outright 'adogmatism.' . . . 'Moralism' is a call to unite in poverty, in impoverishment, in need—not accord, but agreement in silence and preterition. This is equalization in indigence, in accordance with the weakest common denominator. . . . Unification and communion must be sought in richness and fullness, not in poverty." Georges Florovsky, "The Problematic of Christian Reunification: The Dangerous Path of Dogmatic Minimalism," in *Ecumenism I: A Doctrinal Approach*, 16–17.

52 For similar considerations, see Staniloae, "Theology of the Eucharist," 357, 61.

53 Staniloae, "The Universal and Catholic Church," 195. Staniloae, *Spirituality and Communion*, 397–98. In the latter reference, after describing Afanassieff's position that the separation between the Catholic and Orthodox churches, "even though it was provoked by dogmatic differences, still has a canonical character (?)" Staniloae inserted a question mark in parentheses, indicating that this contention can be dismissed without any further comment.

truth.[54] Staniloae regarded the Orthodox Church as the fullness of the Church, but he did not exclude other denominations from the *Una Sancta*, although they have different degrees of closeness to the fullness of the Church.[55] His remarks contrast Afanassieff's refusal to acknowledge vestiges of the Church outside the fullness of the Church. On this issue, Evdokimov agreed with Staniloae and added the memorable words, "We know where the Church is, but we cannot judge where the Church is not."[56]

Third, Staniloae considered this theory to be a backdoor means of including Orthodoxy in a universal church under papal primacy. He criticized Afanassieff's affirmation that, in a spirit of love (which takes precedence over unity of faith), the Orthodox and Catholic churches could establish communion between them despite their doctrinal differences regarding papal primacy. But, Afanassieff continued, this would only be a temporary solution, since within this reestablished communion, the Church of Rome would receive the first place that it had in the early Church: "Because of the reestablishment of the unity joined by Love and without imposing primacy by constraint, Rome would have certainly acquired it better by Love than by law."[57] According to Staniloae, this makes the Orthodox Church part of the universal Roman Catholic Church without regard to the theological and practical differences between the two.[58] To interpret Staniloae correctly, one needs to understand that he did not deny the inclusion of the Orthodox Church in a future united Church, not even a universal church in which the pope would be *primus inter pares*. Staniloae rejected union "without regard to the theological and practical differences" between churches, especially on the role of the bishop of Rome.

---

54  Staniloae, "The Authority of the Church," 214. Quoted in and translated by Roberson, "Dumitru Staniloae on Christian Unity," 119. Staniloae added that for these reasons Orthodoxy cannot hold an ecumenical council without the participation of other churches.

55  Staniloae, *Dogmatics 2*, 176. Catholic theologians would qualify this affirmation, since Vatican II made the distinction between *ecclesiae* and *communitates ecclesiales* (LG 15,8; OE 4,12; UR 3,26; 3,29; 3,35; 4,12; OT 16,36; AG 15,33; GS 40,33). The determinant criterion for making this distinction is the episcopal structure or apostolic succession, which is the foundation of episcopal structure, and this in turn affects the validity of the Eucharist. Ecclesial communities do not have episcopal structure, but they preserve the fundamental, constitutive elements of the Church. Lupu, "Synodality and/or Conciliarity," 73.

56  Evdokimov, *L'Orthodoxie*, 343. See the same idea adopted in Ware, *The Orthodox Church*, 308.

57  Afanassieff, "Una Sancta," 27.

58  Staniloae, *Spirituality and Communion*, 398.

Fourth, according to Staniloae, the local church possesses ecclesial pleni-tude precisely because it does not break from the ensemble formed by all local churches, having at work in it the same Spirit that is present in other local churches.[59] He accepted the idea of a local church's ecclesial plenitude, but only qualified by the existence of the local church within the framework of the uni-versal church, conditioned by its communion in the Spirit and in the same faith with all the other local churches. Staniloae arrived at this conclusion starting from a text by Irenaeus: "Where the Church is, there is the Spirit of God; and where the Spirit of God is, there is the Church and all grace; and the Spirit is the truth. Those, therefore, who do not participate in the Spirit neither feed at their mother's breasts nor drink the bright fountain issuing from Christ's body."[60] Staniloae considered that in Irenaeus's definition, the Eucharist is included in the truth. In other words, to say only that the Church is where the Eucharist is, as Afanassieff did, represents a narrower definition than to say that the Church is where the Eucharist and the truth are.

Essentially, both Afanassieff and Staniloae affirmed that local churches are united because of their mutual identity, yet they arrived at this conclusion in two different ways: Afanassieff emphasized that local churches are united in the same Christ who is present in the same Eucharist, while Staniloae stressed their unity in the Spirit, who is the Spirit of truth present in Christ's Body—the Church. These two different ways are complementary in Staniloae's estimation, since local churches are united by sharing in the same Spirit, faith, Eucharist,[61] and episcopal communion. Thus, Staniloae affirmed the fullness of the local church, but not its absolute independence. In certain writings, Afanassieff's con-clusions appear to agree with Staniloae's considerations, yet in other writings disagreement is apparent. Staniloae attributed this disagreement to inconsisten-cies in Afanassieff's theology of the interdependence and self-sufficiency of the local church.[62] At this point, a few more remarks on the relationship between the local and universal aspects of the Church are in order.

---

59  Staniloae, "The Universal and Catholic Church," 171. See also Staniloae, *Dogmatics* 2, 187.

60  *Adversus Haereseos* 3, 24, 1, PG 7:966A–C. Quoted in Staniloae, *Spirituality and Communion*, 402.

61  See, e.g., Ibid., 81–82.

62  Staniloae, "The Universal and Catholic Church," 170–77. Turcescu also pointed out an internal contradiction in Afanassieff, who, on the one hand, affirmed that local churches are "independent by not depending on any other local Church or any bishop whatsoever outside itself," while, on the other hand, wrote that a local church depends on the recognition of other local churches and that its bishop is ordained by other bishops. Turcescu, "Eucharistic Ecclesiology or Open Sobornicity?" 88.

According to Staniloae, there is communion of teaching, sacraments, and structure among local churches. Based on the introductory litanies from the Divine Liturgy, in which the priest and the community pray for all the Orthodox Christians affirming the solidarity of those who share in the same faith, as well as for the unity of the faith, Staniloae concluded that each community prays for other communities. Then, they pray for the local bishop who is in communion with the other bishops, as well as for the clergy and the people from everywhere. Staniloae added that each local church maintains "the unity in the same faith of the community throughout space and among generations, by celebrating the same sacraments and by teaching the same faith."[63]

Thus, communion involves the bishops living in a certain period, but also their predecessors. It is a communion in space and time because the same Christ works in the Ordination of the bishops in the past and in the present, and the same Christ works in their actions as bishops.[64] Moreover, each bishop is ordained by more than one bishop, in the name of all the bishops, receiving the same teaching that the Apostles handed down to us, and the capacity to impart the divine grace to the people of God.[65] The communion among bishops then extends to the people and the local churches they represent, which led Staniloae to conclude that not only the bishops, but also each faithful is "part of a greater spiritual communion, present, past, and future. This is the Church."[66]

Staniloae ended his discussion of eucharistic ecclesiology on a more reconciliatory tone. He probably realized that his insistence on the relationship between the Eucharist and orthodoxy should not be interpreted to mean that the Catholic Church has fallen so much from the true faith that its Eucharist is not valid. Staniloae certainly wanted to dissipate such suspicions. Thus, he recognized that the Catholic Church admits the presence of the Body and Blood of Christ in the Eucharist, through its teaching on transubstantiation "or through something similar to the changing of the bread and the wine, just as the Orthodox Church."[67] (So even though Staniloae had reservations about the theory of transubstantiation, he considered this teaching an attempt to explain what both Catholic and Orthodox churches hold in common, namely, that the Eucharist is the Body and Blood of Christ.) Moreover, he affirmed that the Catholic Church, just like the Orthodox Church, has preserved the faith in the Trinity and Christ, even if it has also added to the Church's ancient faith the dogma of papal primacy, papal infallibility, the Filioque, and purgatory.

---

63  Staniloae, *Spirituality and Communion*, 164.
64  Staniloae, *Dogmatics 2*, 158.
65  Ibid., 157, note 65.
66  Staniloae, *Jesus Christ or the Restoration of Humankind*, 380.
67  Staniloae, *Spirituality and Communion*, 81–82.

Among these, the dogma of papal primacy and infallibility are obstacles for communion[68] or church-dividing. (Again, Staniloae's openness towards an ecumenical solution to the issue of the Filioque is undeniable here.)

Thus, Staniloae's central criticism of Afanassieff's eucharistic ecclesiology is that the Orthodox and Catholic churches, although both having a valid Eucharist, cannot be in full eucharistic communion because they do not share in the same faith, especially concerning papal primacy and infallibility.[69] I agree. However, I also recognize with Emmanuel Lanne that there is a tendency in the Eastern Orthodox Churches today to apply a more "liberal" practice toward members of the Oriental Orthodox Churches, who are allowed to receive communion in Orthodox parishes. Lanne asks rhetorically whether there is not greater unity of faith between the Eastern Orthodox and the Roman Catholics—identical Christology, the seven ecumenical councils, and so on—than with the Oriental Orthodox. It seems that papacy is the only issue that divides Catholicism and Orthodoxy.[70] Still, I do not advocate seeing the papacy as a nondividing local tradition, as Afanassieff did. I believe there are possible grounds for both churches to overcome this impasse.

### Retrieving Eucharistic Ecclesiology

I have presented the preceding critiques of Afanassieff's eucharistic ecclesiology, not to completely discard it but to correct its deficiencies. After Zizioulas and Staniloae, eucharistic ecclesiology was regarded with suspicion and replaced by communion ecclesiology. It is now time to retrieve the aspects of eucharistic ecclesiology that have been unjustly dismissed[71] and to outline a communion ecclesiology that incorporates the strengths of Afanassieff, Zizioulas, and Staniloae. I do not attempt to propose a totally new understanding of the

---

68 Ibid., 401–02.
69 Karl Felmy considers that neither Afanassieff nor Zizioulas emphasized enough the importance of doctrinal unity, as Staniloae did. Felmy, *The Dogmatics of Ecclesial Experience*, 224.
70 Emmanuel Lanne, "Quelques questions posées à l'Église orthodoxe concernant la 'communicatio in sacris' dans l'eucharistie," *Irénikon* 72, no. 3–4 (1999).
71 For important elements of Afanassieff's theology that respond to some of Zizioulas's and Staniloae's criticisms, see Radu Bordeianu, "Orthodox-Catholic Dialogue: Retrieving Afanassieff's Eucharistic Ecclesiology after Zizioulas and Staniloae," *Journal of Ecumenical Studies* 44, no. 2 (2009): 259–60. Shorter version: Radu Bordeianu, "Retrieving Eucharistic Ecclesiology," in *Ecumenical Ecclesiology: Unity, Diversity and Otherness in a Fragmented World*, ed. Gesa E. Thiessen, *Ecclesiological Investigations* (New York: T&T Clark/Continuum, 2009), 136.

Church as communion but to continue the theological journey that these three theologians have already begun. While continuing this journey, I certainly do not claim to have reached its end.

At the present time, Orthodox theology needs to retrieve the ecumenical dimension of communion ecclesiology by refocusing on the cause of Christian unity. Afanassieff wrote in a context of ecumenical hope and optimism, when the Orthodox and Catholic churches entered into an earnest dialogue and expressed a real desire to make important steps toward unity.[72] He was a pioneer; this means that, on the one hand, the reactions against him have sometimes been too strong, since his proposals were challenging for those times and theologians were not yet ready to embrace them. On the other hand, his pioneering role resulted in a theological system that is not always consistent, so some of the criticisms are, in fact, justified. Today's Orthodox theological context is more prone to finding a balance between ecumenical openness and theological thoroughness in one's affirmation of faith. The same is true for the Catholic Church.

The analyses presented in this chapter show that ecumenical theology is faced today with two models for Christian unity, based on their emphasis on either the local or the universal church. If the local church has priority over the universal, then union represents the communion of these local churches; this is not necessarily a union based on sharing in the same faith, nor is it fully visible through communion among local bishops. If, however, the universal church has priority over the local, then union is accomplished through sharing in the same faith and through visible communion among the bishops heading the local churches. Moreover, in modern ecumenical terms, the first model emphasizes the Eucharist as a means toward unity, while the second sees it more as a sign of unity (or lack thereof).

## First Model

According to the first model, whose representative is Afanassieff,[73] the local church gathered as a eucharistic assembly has priority over the universal

---

72    Unfortunately, Afanassieff was overly optimistic when he wrote: "We believe that the hour is near when the Catholic Church, after having transcended human passions, would extend a fraternal hand to the Orthodox Church, and that this hand would not remain suspended in the air" Afanassieff, "Una Sancta," 27.

73    Similarly to Afanassieff, Forte reads LG 63 to affirm that the priority and fullness of the local eucharistic community is "grounded in the trinitarian and pneumatological origin of the Church and its eucharistic nature." He has even quoted Afanassieff's view on universality, catholicity, and the communitarian character of the Church concluding that, as a consequence of the local church's priority, the local church is by full right the "ecclesial subject," which implies its autonomy. See

church, so unity is accomplished through the mutual identity of different local churches' celebration of the same Eucharist. The merit of this model is that it earnestly seeks to explore the ecclesiological consequences of the recipro- cal recognition of the validity of the Eucharist in the Orthodox and Catholic churches. Theologians representing both of these traditions unanimously agree that the Eucharist has a constitutive role for the Church, even though some also emphasize other elements as constitutive of the Church, such as other sacra- ments (see Staniloae's position described in Chapter 4), teachings, and episcopal structure. Afanassieff is the only theologian analyzed here who concluded that both the Catholic and Orthodox churches are truly and fully manifestations of the Church *Una Sancta*, or, to be more precise, are the *Una Sancta* as mani- fested in various contexts.[74] Consequently, he affirmed that the Orthodox and Catholic churches are actually one and the same reality, so their disunion is only relative, or, in Afanassieff's terms, it has only a canonical character, which does not warrant the lack of eucharistic communion between the two churches. Contemporary theologians ought to continue to delineate the ecclesiological significance of mutual eucharistic recognition.

Another merit of this first model is that it calls for a reevaluation of the issues that were historically considered church-dividing. Newer bilateral dialogues prove that it is possible to affirm that some issues that were deemed church- dividing in the past need not be regarded as such any longer. (As mentioned already, this is the case of the Christological controversy between Eastern and Oriental Orthodox churches or of the Filioque.) I hope for a similar outcome on the issue of primacy from other official dialogues, for example, the Joint International Orthodox-Catholic Theological Commission, whose cochairs are Kasper (who tends to balance the local and universal church) and Zizioulas, who represents the second model that I evaluate momentarily. The advantage of the contemporary approach to church-dividing issues over Afanassieff's meth- odology is that it does not propose simply to ignore the theological differences between the two churches but to overcome them through earnest dialogue. Soon might be the time when, in the spirit of love, these issues will be overcome, as Afanassieff and Congar had hoped.

Afanassieff's suggestion for eucharistic communion, however, cannot be implemented yet, since both the Orthodox and the Catholic churches see today's understanding of the papacy as church-dividing. Moreover, Orthodox and

---

Forte, *The Church: Icon of the Trinity*, 71–74, 78. I think that Forte's concluding affirmation constitutes a departure from Vatican II's description of the relationship between local and universal. See also Evdokimov's acceptance of eucharistic ecclesi- ology mentioned above.

74   In similar terms, Paul greets "the Church of God that is in Corinth" (1 Cor. 1.2).

Catholics do not share in episcopal communion. From the perspective of their hierarchical structure, the two churches live totally separated lives, even though they coexist in the same place. If they do not share in doctrinal and episcopal communion, then the Eucharist cannot be the sign of their unity. Paradoxically, Afanassieff insisted that the Eucharist *is* the sign of their unity (he called it "link"), but he ended up deemphasizing the significance of the lack of eucharistic communion between the Orthodox and Catholic churches. Thus, he overemphasized the Eucharist as a means toward unity, hoping that the theological and canonical issues would eventually be solved through intercommunion.

### Second Model

According to the second model for Christian unity, whose representatives are Zizioulas and Staniloae, union is accomplished through sharing in the same faith and through visible communion among bishops. Cyprian could be placed in this category based on the priority that he gives to the universal over the local aspects of the Church, although this priority is not found in Zizioulas and Staniloae. However, all three representatives of the second model stress (in different degrees) doctrinal and episcopal communion as a condition for eucharistic sharing among different church communities.

A first merit of this model is its emphasis on doctrinal unity. The positions of Zizioulas and especially Staniloae are preferable to that of Afanassieff because they seek a type of union that stems from thorough theological dialogue and not from ignoring the points of divergence, even if only for a while. True, overemphasizing the intrinsic connection between unity of faith and eucharistic communion runs the risk of placing undue emphasis on theological issues that are not church-dividing. Yet, this risk can be avoided by a constant focus on the ultimate purpose of ecumenical dialogues, namely doctrinal unity manifested in common eucharistic celebrations.

Another positive aspect of the second model is that Staniloae and especially Zizioulas underline the need for communion among the bishops of the two churches. Zizioulas has convincingly demonstrated the essential role of the bishop within the local eucharistic assembly and the importance of the relationships among bishops, especially when gathered in synods as representatives of their local communities. Since the union we seek ought to preserve the richness of the ecclesial life of the first Christian centuries, episcopal communion cannot be ignored. At the same time, the second model runs the risk of transforming canonical issues into church-dividing elements, which was never the case in the early Church, where canonical disputes existed abundantly but, as Afanassieff has shown, were not reasons for division. Again, it is important to discern what elements need to be discussed before achieving eucharistic communion and what aspects can be postponed.

The main disadvantage of the second model is that neither Zizioulas nor Staniloae explores the consequences of the reciprocal recognition of the validity of the Eucharist in the Orthodox and Catholic churches, especially that they both recognize that, essentially though not exhaustively, the Eucharist makes the Church. The result is that a crucially important element in a discussion of Christian unity is missing from their theologies.

Moreover, there is the risk—sometimes present in Zizioulas—to overemphasize the hierarchical character of the Church and not to address sufficiently the role of the people in the quest for unity. Afanassieff and Staniloae, however, presented a more balanced view of the Church, where the faithful who are not ordained play a crucial role in the Church and toward unity. The bishop is a representative of the community, so episcopal communion would be meaningless without communion among the faithful of the two churches; this highlights the need for the faithful to work toward unity. At the same time, where the faithful are in communion, the bishops need to fully represent their flocks and express this unity at the episcopal level. Furthermore, through the process of the reception of doctrine, the faithful could influence the hierarchs on the level of dogmatic unity necessary for eucharistic communion between the two churches. Simultaneously, the hierarchs and the theologians need to educate their flocks and enable them to assess this level of unity. Afanassieff and Staniloae avoid the danger of overemphasizing the hierarchical character of the Church by consciously not separating the charism of teaching from reception by the faithful.[75]

### Continuing the Journey toward Communion Ecclesiology

In order to advance the Orthodox-Catholic dialogue, I now propose implementing elements of eucharistic ecclesiology into a communion ecclesiology that would balance the local and universal aspects of the Church. Staniloae has achieved this balance theoretically, but its practical consequences still need to be elucidated. I hope to present a way in which the Eucharist is simultaneously a sign of, and an instrument for, unity by analyzing four elements: doctrinal unity, episcopal communion, love, and eucharistic communion.

First, the unity we seek needs to be based on doctrinal consensus. It appears that the only church-dividing issues between Orthodoxy and Catholicism are

---

75  While certainly present in Zizioulas's work, the notion of reception is not as prominent. See Zizioulas, "The Theological Problem of 'Reception'," 187–93.

papal primacy and infallibility. Zizioulas began the exploration of this topic[76] and Staniloae affirmed its church-dividing character, but did not provide significant solutions. Afanassieff proposed that it would temporarily remain a dogma in the Catholic Church, unaccepted by the Orthodox, hoping that a lasting solution would eventually emerge.[77] Afanassieff's proposal is unacceptable for either church at the present time. However, it might suggest the way toward doctrinal unity in the future, if the Catholic Church changes its understanding of jurisdictional primacy to refer only to the West (even though the pope has recently renounced his title of "Patriarch of the West," which many Orthodox have regarded as a move in the opposite direction) and its view of infallibility to be in harmony with the concepts of conciliarity and reception of doctrine. The East, on its part, would have to reanalyze its understanding of the bishop of Rome as *primus inter pares*; if in the past the emphasis fell on "*inter pares*," now Orthodoxy must state positively what "*primus*" means. Most Orthodox theology has concentrated exclusively on refuting the Catholic position but now needs to propose concrete ways in which the papacy should be exercised in a united Christendom. It will not be a primacy of jurisdiction over the entire Christian world, but only in the West. At the same time, it cannot be merely a primacy of honor. The Orthodox should ascribe to the pope at least the same level of authority that they ascribe to the primates of their autocephalous churches—a primacy that would however be universal. This issue must urgently be explored, and my suggestions do not claim to be anything other than signposts along the way towards unity.

---

76   See for example the following works by Zizioulas: "The Development of Conciliar Structures to the Time of the First Ecumenical Council." In *Councils and the Ecumenical Movement*, edited by Faith and Order Secretariat (Geneva: WCC, 1968), 34–51. "The Institution of Episcopal Conferences: An Orthodox Reflection." *The Jurist* 48 (1988): 376–83. "Primacy in the Church: An Orthodox Approach." In *Petrine Ministry and the Unity of the Church: "Toward a Patient and Fraternal Dialogue": A Symposium Celebrating the 100th Anniversary of the Foundation of the Society of the Atonement, Rome, December 4-6, 1997*, edited by James F. Puglisi (Collegeville, MN: Liturgical Press, 1999), 115–25.

77   Staniloae raised three important questions that should be discussed in future ecumenical dialogues on this issue. First, eucharistic ecclesiology proposes the temporary acceptance of the idea of papal primacy; does this mean that the Catholic Church would accept union in sacraments without the recognition of papal primacy after this temporary period? Second, if the Church is eucharistic, does it necessarily mean that it is universal? Third, does the idea of a universal church necessarily imply that of primacy, or, on the contrary, do local churches have ecclesiastical plenitude by virtue of their belonging to the universal church, from which results the catholicity of the Church and the symphonic equality of all the local churches? Staniloae, "The Universal and Catholic Church," 182.

These remarks point to the need for episcopal communion, the second aspect of communion ecclesiology. Ideally from an Orthodox perspective, in a united Church, the pope would be *primus inter pares* within a unified synod of bishops, without overlapping jurisdictions. Bilateral dialogues are currently attempting to outline the concrete details of this proposal. However, I do not think that eucharistic communion must be postponed until the time of this perfect union. In line with Afanassieff's eucharistic ecclesiology, the Orthodox and Catholic churches could have eucharistic communion when their bishops would be gathered in a common synod (while temporarily still maintaining their separate structures), according to the model of the Orthodox churches in America.

Presently, Orthodox churches in America have eucharistic communion, even though they are separated by ethnicity (for example, Greek, Romanian, Serbian) or canonical affiliation (for example, Romanian under the Romanian Patriarchate and under the Orthodox Church in America [O.C.A.]). These Orthodox churches have the same geographical territory, so their jurisdictions overlap. Most of them have their own synod that decides on administrative issues pertaining to internal matters. All the hierarchs, however, gather periodically in the Episcopal Assembly of the Canonical Orthodox Hierarchs of North and Central America, which succeeded the Standing Conference of the Canonical Orthodox Bishops in the Americas (SCOBA).[78] This institution does not have any administrative authority over its members. (In this regard, the Episcopal Assembly is similar to U.S.C.C.B.—United States Conference of Catholic Bishops—whose decisions are authoritative to the extent to which individual bishops, as heads of their dioceses, support them.[79]) Besides individual synods and the Episcopal Assembly, there is a third model of church structure in America, namely, the O.C.A., which is comprised of several ethnic churches with overlapping jurisdictions, yet the synod and other authoritative structures of the O.C.A. have authority over all its members.

Despite many imperfections of Orthodoxy in America,[80] the separation here is only relative: The bishops do come together in the Episcopal Assembly, and

---

78  As an implementation of the decisions of the of the Fourth Pre-Conciliar Pan-Orthodox Conference held at Chambésy, Switzerland, from June 6–12, 2009, Orthodox churches in America are in a period of transition from SCOBA to the Episcopal Assembly of the Canonical Orthodox Hierarchs of North and Central America.

79  The similarity ends when considering that the decisions of the U.S.C.C.B. could also become authoritative if the Pope mandated them.

80  I fully agree with Zizioulas when he deplores the existence of overlapping jurisdictions within Orthodoxy, distinct from each other based on their ethnic or political character. He writes in a very categorical, though justified, tone: "The present-day situation of the Orthodox diaspora is such an *unfortunate, dangerous and totally unacceptable* phenomenon. It allows ethnic and cultural differences to become

the O.C.A. is one synod with administrative authority even though it is comprised of overlapping jurisdictions. Most importantly, the churches share one common Tradition (capital T) while maintaining a certain diversity that pertains to traditions (small t), such as calendar, discipline, or liturgical practices.

The situation of Orthodoxy in America shows that, along the path toward full unity with the Roman Catholic Church, eucharistic communion is possible even before solving all the juridical issues, by regarding the Orthodox and Catholic churches as two local churches of the same universal church, albeit with overlapping jurisdictions. Thus, a united Church might have overlapping jurisdictions as long as these member churches get together in an institution after the model of the Episcopal Assembly (no administrative authority), then the O.C.A. (full authority), and then one synod without overlapping jurisdictions, a situation that neither the Orthodox nor the Catholic families have yet accomplished internally.

Such a temporary situation should be acceptable to all Orthodox Churches in the world, which now tacitly but actively support the situation in the United States by having their representatives here, and to the Catholic Church, since Roman Catholic dioceses overlap with Byzantine Catholic dioceses, not to mention the multitude of ethnic dioceses overlapping within the Byzantine Catholic family. At that point, the role of the pope in a united Church with a common synod would have to be defined, and Afanassieff might again offer a viable solution: "the bishop possessing primacy acts with the agreement of the whole body of bishops: this agreement is made manifest in the council in which the primate bishop participates as its president."[81]

I do not support intercommunion in the current Catholic-Orthodox situation, but neither should eucharistic communion be postponed until all the canonical issues are solved. Theologians need to state clearly what they mean by doctrinal and episcopal communion, even though this will be a "theology of the abnormal," as Florovsky would say,[82] since it would describe a temporary, imperfect solution.

---

grounds of ecclesial communion centred on different bishops. A bishop who does not in himself transcend ethnic and cultural differences becomes a minister of division and not of unity. This is something that the Orthodox should consider very seriously indeed, if *distortion of the very nature of the Church* is to be avoided." Zizioulas, *Communion and Otherness*, 8–9.

81　Afanassieff, "The Church Which Presides in Love," 102–03.

82　Florovsky used the expression "theology of the abnormal" to describe any ecclesiology written in the context of the paradoxical, antinomical, and abnormal situation in which Christianity is divided among "separate brethren" while also being one Church. He wrote: "There is a 'disproportion' between the two dimensions of the same Church. There is a disproportion between the 'historical' and 'eschatological' dimensions. And there is a disproportion between the canonical and sacramental dimensions. And yet there is but one Church. This theory earnestly wrestles with the

The third aspect of communion ecclesiology refers to love. Eucharistic communion cannot be justified where there is only a fragile bond of love between the members of the Orthodox and Catholic churches. Such a contention might appear inadequate to an audience in the West, where there is relative harmony between the two churches. However, in other places, such as the former Yugoslavia or Russia, there are considerable tensions resulting in mutual accusations and even violence. This affirmation is not intended to create an unfairly hostile picture of Orthodox-Catholic relations in general, especially given the positive aspects of this relationship all over the world, such as the successful bilateral dialogues, the exchange of students and professors, or common charitable projects. However, Orthodox and Catholics need to strengthen the bond of love between them, and only then will they be able to solve their theological differences and reestablish eucharistic communion. Here, again, the situation in the U.S. might point toward a solution.

In the U.S., there is a rather strong bond of love between the Orthodox and Catholic churches, which are discovering more and more aspects of their unity and are finding significant ways to move beyond their differences in all aspects of church life, including love, episcopal collaboration, and doctrinal unity. These results are not enough to warrant eucharistic communion. However, one should not forget that local churches are interdependent, a fact that has two significant consequences. First, the Orthodox and Catholics in the U.S. cannot ignore the insufficient love in Eastern Europe. Second, Eastern Europeans cannot ignore the U.S., but need to strengthen their bond of love, thus receiving as their own the positive aspects of other local churches, as Afanassieff would say; in so doing, they would take an important step toward eucharistic communion.

A fourth aspect of communion ecclesiology is that the unity between the Orthodox and Catholic churches will be a full reality only when they reestablish eucharistic communion between them. At that point, the Eucharist would be both a sign of, and a means toward, greater unity: a sign, because there would be no more church-dividing theological issues between them, there would be a considerable degree of episcopal communion, and, most importantly, there would be a strong bond of love between the two families of the united Church. The Eucharist would also be a means toward greater unity because important differences would still require a solution, but their resolution can only emerge within the context of harmony and love of a united Church, in which members approach the same cup, continually strengthening their communion. In this phase, the Eucharist will be both a sign and an instrument of unity.

---

antinomy of schism and attempts to interpret it on a theological level. It is an essay in the 'theology of the abnormal.' It is by no means successful in resolving the paradox. Instead, it emphasized it." Florovsky, "St. Cyprian and St. Augustine on Schism," 50.

If this objective seems quite distant today, there is another element that could be solved much sooner, namely, communion in all the other sacraments except the Eucharist. The two churches have progressed considerably toward union by recognizing each other's Baptisms,[83] Ordinations,[84] and Marriages.[85] However, these bilateral agreements are not applied consistently in practice, as I mentioned in Chapter 1.

## Conclusion

These four elements of communion ecclesiology—doctrinal unity, episcopal communion, love, and eucharistic/sacramental communion—are simply signposts along the way, inspired by my analysis of Afanassieff, Zizioulas, and Staniloae. There is much more work to be done, especially in regard to the unity with the Protestant churches, which was not discussed here at all, because this is not the subject of eucharistic ecclesiology. In the meantime, I suggest that Afanassieff's eucharistic ecclesiology can be retrieved and improved in light of the theologies of Zizioulas and Staniloae to provide a valuable tool for the long journey toward communion ecclesiology and, ultimately, toward Christian unity, so that the Church will manifest visibly the unity of the Trinity.

---

83  With few exceptions, Orthodox and Catholics recognize each other's baptisms.

84  The Joint Committee of Orthodox and Catholic Bishops affirmed in 1988 that "'reordination' is impossible.... For both Orthodox Christians and Roman Catholics, when a member of the clergy who has been ordained in a church that shares with them an understanding of the priesthood and by a bishop in an unquestionable apostolic succession is received into either the Orthodox or the Roman Catholic Church, his ordination should be recognized. It should be noted, however, that until such time when the practice of the Orthodox Church will be unified, these cases will be decided by each autocephalous Orthodox Church." This statement could be seen as a practical application of an earlier statement of the Joint International Commission (Valamo #30, 1988), which affirmed that ordination is unrepeatable and that "on all the essential points concerning ordination our churches have a common doctrine and practice, even if on certain canonical and disciplinary requirements, such as celibacy, customs can be different because of pastoral and spiritual reasons." Both passages are included in Borelli and Erickson, eds., *The Quest for Unity* 136, 51.

85  As I mentioned in Chapter 1, I can only hope that all Orthodox Churches would soon implement the "Pastoral Statement on Orthodox-Roman Catholic Marriages" formulated by the Joint Committee of Orthodox and Catholic Bishops, 1990, which affirms that "our present differences of practice and theology concerning the required ecclesial context for marriage pertain to the level of secondary theological reflection rather than to the level of dogma." Consequently, the bishops recommended that mixed marriages between Orthodox and Catholics should be performed only once, in the presence of either one or both priests, and be recorded in the registries of both churches. Ibid. 239–43.

# Conclusion

Communion ecclesiology has the potential to bridge the divide between the Orthodox and Catholic churches. Staniloae contributed to the discussion of the relationship between the universal and local aspects of the Church, and various local churches among themselves, as an application of his trinitarian approach to ecclesiology. The unity of the trinitarian persons is reflected in, and imprinted upon, the unity of the local churches that make up the *Una Sancta*. Each of these local eucharistic assemblies possesses the fullness of the Church as long as it remains in communion with the other local churches. They are all united through mutual identity, since the same Christ is present in each one of them, through the Spirit, in a new filial and sacrificial relationship with the Father. This unity presupposes other elements related to, but also distinct from, the Eucharist. Local churches find themselves in relationship with other churches through their bishops, who are in communion of love and teaching with each other, and thus all the members of the local church are in communion with the baptized faithful in other local churches.

Sharing in the same faith and being united by the bond of love, local churches also manifest the communion between the clergy and the people, all sharing in the three offices of Christ: Prophet, Priest, and King. Thus, the bishops gathered in a council do not stand above the Church, but their teaching ministry is complemented by the prophetic office of all baptized Christians: the bishops represent the faith of their communities at the council and their decisions are then subject to reception by the faithful. The communion between the clergy and the people is also manifested as they both exercise their kingly office by having dominion over their passions and by participating in the administration of the Church communally, while maintaining the distinctions between their specific gifts. The same holds true as the entire community celebrates the Eucharist. In the Liturgy, heaven and earth praise God in unison, and the entire Church is gathered in worship: Virgin Mary, the saints, the angels, the living and the dead, clergy and the people—all surround the Lamb of God, all join in his sacrifice to the Father, and all are united in the same Spirit.

The liturgical life of the Church encompasses all creation, which was made to praise God in a cosmic Liturgy. The Church fulfills the natural priesthood of all human beings, who were created to manifest the sacramentality of the world and give voice to the praises of the entire universe.

In a general sense, all human beings are adoptive children of the Father, all share in Christ's restored humanity, and all are filled with the Spirit. In a special sense, however, the Church is fully united with the Father, the Son, and the Holy Spirit, acting as the sacrament of the Trinity in the world. The baptized are the People of God, manifesting the Kingdom of God as much as possible on this side of the eschaton, while knowing that at the end of time the Kingdom will extend to the rest of the universe. Christians also form the Body of Christ, extension of the incarnation, an organism endowed with various charisms—some ordained and some not. These charisms are empowered by the Holy Spirit for the building up of the Church, for missions *ad extra*, while simultaneously the Spirit empowers creation to become fully Church. Staniloae's theology becomes fully ecumenical (understood etymologically as household) to include not only the universe of the Church, but the entire cosmos.

These relationships among the trinitarian persons as they are manifested in the economy of salvation (the world and the Church) are the same as immanent, intratrinitarian relationships. At the basis of the example described above stands the eternal procession of the Holy Spirit from the Father to the Son, resting in the Son as the love of the Father, and also shining forth from the Son back toward the Father as the Son's response of love. To arrive at the conclusion that the same relationships are manifested both in the Trinity and the Church, I have systematized Staniloae's trinitarian ecclesiology into four models: the Church is a reflection of the Trinity, establishing an analogical relationship between them; icon of the Trinity, where the Church is a presence of the Trinity by grace, pointing toward the Trinity; the "third sacrament," as instrument and revelation of the Trinity; and the ecclesiological consequences of Staniloae's understanding of *theosis*. As an ecumenical application of these models, I addressed the ecclesiological consequences of the Filioque (or lack thereof), especially concerning the papacy. This is just one among many instances in which I presented Staniloae's ecumenical relevance.

Throughout the book, I attempted to show how the theology that he generally presented positively, as an intra-Orthodox matter, is relevant to the dialogue between the Orthodox and Catholic churches, with occasional remarks addressing Protestantism, interreligious dialogue, and social issues. I concentrated on the ecumenical aspect of Staniloae's theology in order to portray him as a neo-patristic theologian, deeply rooted in the patristic tradition of the Church, in the Liturgy, in spirituality, and engaged with contemporary society, philosophical thought, and, most importantly, with other Christians. He described open sobornicity as acceptance of concepts originating in other churches, which are in accordance with Scripture and Tradition and contribute to a united Christian proclamation. Staniloae adopted various ideas from Calvinism, scholasticism, and ultimately the manual tradition. Among these Western concepts I mentioned the systematization of the three offices of Christ, the seven sacraments, and the priest acting *in nomine Christi, in persona Christi et in persona ecclesiae*. In turn, I have presented Staniloae's contribution to an ecumenical understanding of the themes discussed in this book, so that the circle of open sobornicity would be complete and other churches would benefit from his insights.

The work of this great Romanian Orthodox theologian still awaits reception, and I hope that it will have a lasting contribution toward Christian unity. This book represents a humble gift toward the goal "that they all may be one" (Jn 17.22). I also hope that putting Staniloae in dialogue with Catholic, Protestant, and other Orthodox positions (including my own) will facilitate this ecumenical exercise. The book could also prove a valuable resource for the study of the Trinity, anthropology, ecology, cosmology, and history of theology. It is intended for an academic audience, but not merely as an academic exercise. Rather, theologians should exercise their prophetic charism and make a difference in the life of the Church. Thus, Church leaders and others involved in ecumenism might find this book useful.

Each Christian is a member of the Body of Christ, an adopted child of the Father, filled with the Holy Spirit. I hope this book helps my readers discern and enrich their ecumenical charisms. Inspired by Staniloae and emulating his example, each and every one of us is called to contribute with our gifts so that the unity of the Church will become fully visible, manifesting the unity of the Trinity.

# BIBLIOGRAPHY

## Primary Sources

Staniloae, Dumitru. "Autoritatea Bisericii [The Authority of the Church]." *Studii Teologice* 16, no. 3–4 (1964): 183–215.

——. "Biserica in sensul de lacas si de larga comuniune in Hristos [The Church as Place of Worship and All-embracing Communion in Christ]." *Ortodoxia* 34, no. 3 (1982): 336–46.

——. "Biserica universala si soborniceasca [The Universal and Catholic Church]." *Ortodoxia* 18, no. 2 (1966): 167–98.

——. *Chipul evanghelic al lui Iisus Hristos* [*The Evangelical Image of Jesus Christ*]. Sibiu: Editura Centrului Mitropolitan Sibiu, 1991.

——. "Coordonatele ecumenismului din punct de vedere Ortodox [The Coordinates of Ecumenism from the Orthodox Perspective]." *Ortodoxia* 19, no. 4 (1967): 494–540.

——. "Creatia ca dar si Tainele Bisericii [Creation as Gift and the Sacraments of the Church]." *Ortodoxia* 28, no. 1 (1976): 10–29.

——. "Din aspectul Sacramental al Bisericii [Of the Sacramental Aspect of the Church]." *Studii Teologice* 18, no. 9–10 (1966): 531–62.

——. "Dumnezeu Cuvintul cel Intrupat sfinteste creatia prin cuvintul si fapta omeneas-ca a sa si a omului si in special a preotului [The Incarnate Word of God Sanctifies Creation through the Human Words and Actions of Himself and of the Human Being, especially the Priest]." *Mitropolia Olteniei* 43, no. 4 (1991): 12–21.

——. *The Experience of God: Revelation and Knowledge of the Triune God*. Translated by Ioan Ionita and Robert Barringer. Second ed. Vol. 1. Brookline, MA: Holy Cross Orthodox Press, 1998.

——. *The Experience of God: The World – Creation and Deification*. Translated by Ioan Ionita and Robert Barringer. Vol. 2. Brookline, MA: Holy Cross Orthodox Press, 2000.

——. *Filocalia sau Culegere din scrierile Sfintilor Parinti care arata cum se poate omul curati, lumina si desavirsi* [*The Philokalia or Collection from the Writings of the Holy Fathers that Shows How One Can Be Purified, Illumined and Perfected*]. Fourth ed. 12 vols. Bucuresti: Harisma-Humanitas, 1993–.

——. *Iisus Hristos sau restaurarea omului* [*Jesus Christ or the Restoration of Humankind*]. Second ed. Craiova: Editura Omniscop, 1993.

——. "Iisus Hristos, Arhiereu in veac [Jesus Christ, Eternal High Priest]." *Ortodoxia* 31, no. 2 (1979): 217–31.

——. *Iisus Hristos, lumina lumii si indumnezeitorul omului* [*Jesus Christ, the Light of the World and the One Who Deifies Humankind*], Colectia Dogmatica. Bucuresti: Editura Anastasia, 1993.

——. "In problema intercomuniunii [On the Issue of Intercommunion]." *Ortodoxia* 23, no. 4 (1971): 561–84.

——. "Introducere [Introduction]." In *Sfantul Dionisie Areopagitul: Opere complete si Scoliile Sfantului Maxim Marturisitorul [Saint Dionysius the Areopagite: Complete Works and the Scholias of Saint Maximus the Confessor].* Bucuresti: Paideia, 1996.

——. "Le Saint Esprit dans la théologie Byzantine et dans la réflexion Orthodoxe contemporaine." In *Credo in Spiritum Sanctum – Pisteuo eis to Pneuma to Agion: Atti del Congresso Teologico Internazionale di Pneumatologia in occasione del 1600o anniversario del I Concilio di Constantinopoli e del 1550o anniversario del Concilio di Efeso, Roma 22–26 marzo 1982,* 661–79. Vatican: Libreria Editrice Vaticana, 1983.

——. "Locasul Bisericesc Propriu-Zis, Cerul pe Pamant sau Centrul Liturgic al Creatiei [The Church Temple: Heaven on Earth or the Liturgical Centre of Creation]." In *Sfantul Maxim Marturisitorul: Mystagogia: Cosmosul si Sufletul, Chipuri ale Bisericii.* Bucuresti: EIBMBOR, 2000.

——. *Natiune si Crestinism [Nation and Christianity].* Edited by Constantin Schifirnet. Bucuresti: Elion, 2003.

——. "Numarul Tainelor, raporturile intre ele si problema Tainelor din afara Bisericii [The Number of the Sacraments, Their Relationships, and the Problem of the Sacraments Outside the Church]." *Ortodoxia* 8, no. 2 (1956): 191–215.

——. *Orthodox Spirituality: A Practical Guide for the Faithful and a Definitive Manual for the Scholar.* Translated by Archimandrite Jerome (Newville) and Otilia Kloos. South Canaan, PA: St. Tikhon's Seminary Press, 2002.

——. *Orthodoxe Dogmatik.* Translated by Hermann Pitters. 3 vols, *Ökumenische Theologie 12, 15, 16.* Zürich, Gütersloh: Benziger Verlag, Gütersloher Verlagshaus Gerd Mohn, 1984–1995.

——. *Prière de Jesus et expérience de Saint Esprit, Théophanie.* Paris: Desclée de Brouwer, 1981.

——. "The Procession of the Holy Spirit from the Father and His Relation to the Son, as the Basis of our Deification and Adoption." In *Spirit of God, Spirit of Christ: Ecumenical Reflections on the Filioque Controversy. Faith and Order Paper No. 103,* edited by Lukas Vischer, 174–86. Geneva: World Council of Churches, 1981.

——. "Sfanta Treime, structura supremei iubiri [The Holy Trinity: Structure of Supreme Love]." *Studii Teologice* 22 (1970): 333–55.

——. "Simbolul ca anticipare si temei al posibilitatii icoanei [The Symbol as Anticipation and Foundation of the Possibility of the Icon]." *Studii Teologice* 7, no. 7–8 (1957): 427–52.

——. "Sinteza ecclesiologica [Ecclesiological Synthesis]." *Studii Teologice* 7, no. 5–6 (1955): 262–84.

——. "Slujirile bisericesti si atributiile lor [Ecclesial Ministries and their Attributions]." *Ortodoxia* 22, no. 3 (1970): 462–69.

——. "Sobornicitate deschisa [Open Sobornicity]." *Ortodoxia* 23, no. 2 (1971): 165–80.

——. *Spiritualitate si comuniune in Liturghia Ortodoxa [Spirituality and Communion in the Orthodox Liturgy].* Craiova: Editura Mitropoliei Olteniei, 1986.

——. "Temeiurile teologice ale ierarhiei si ale sinodalitatii [The Theological Foundations of Hierarchy and Synodality]." *Studii Teologice* 22, no. 3–4 (1970): 165–78.

——. *Teologia Dogmatica Ortodoxa [Orthodox Dogmatic Theology].* Second ed. Vols. 1–3. Bucharest: EIBMBOR, 1996–97.

——. "Teologia Euharistiei [The Theology of the Eucharist]." *Ortodoxia* 21, no. 3 (1969): 343–64.

——. "Théologie de l'Eucharistie." *Contacts* 71 (1970): 184–211.

——. *Theology and the Church*. Translated by Robert Barringer. Crestwood, NY: St Vladimir's Seminary Press, 1980.

——. "Transparenta Bisericii in viata Sacramentala [The Transparence of the Church in Sacramental Life]." *Ortodoxia* 22, no. 4 (1970): 501–16.

——. "Unity and Diversity in Orthodox Tradition." *Greek Orthodox Theological Review* 17, no. 1 (1972): 19–36.

Staniloae, Dumitru, and M. A. Costa de Beauregard. *Mica dogmatica vorbita: dialoguri la Cernica [Brief Spoken Dogmatics: Dialogues at Cernica]*. Translated by Maria-Cornelia Oros. Sibiu: Deisis, 1995.

——. *Ose comprendre que je t'aime*. Paris: Cerf, 1983.

## Secondary Sources

*Bibliografia Parintelui Academician Profesor Dr. Dumitru Staniloae [The Bibliography of Father Academician Professor Dr. Dumitru Staniloae]*. Bucuresti: EIBMBOR, 1993.

*Parintele Dumitru Staniloae in constiinta contemporanilor: marturii, evocari, amintiri [Father Dumitru Staniloae in Contemporary Conscience: Witnesses, Accounts, Memories]*. Iasi: Trinitas, 2003.

Anghelescu, Gheorghe F., and Ioan I. Ica jr. "Parintele Prof. Acad. Dumitru Staniloae: Bibliografie Sistematica [Father Professor Academician Dumitru Staniloae: Systematic Bibliography]." In *Persoana si Comuniune: Prinos de Cinstire Parintelui Profesor Academician Dumitru Staniloae la implinirea varstei de 90 de ani [Person and Communion: Offering to Honor Professor Academician Dumitru Staniloae on His Ninetieth Birthday]*, edited by Ioan I. Ica jr. and Mircea Pacurariu, 20–67. Sibiu: Editura Arhiepiscopiei Ortodoxe Sibiu, 1993.

Balan, Ioanichie, ed. *Convorbiri Duhovnicesti [Spiritual Conversations]*. Vol. 2. Roman: Editura Episcopiei Romanului si Husilor, 1988.

Bartos, Emil. "The Dynamics of Deification in the Theology of Dumitru Staniloae." In *Dumitru Staniloae: Tradition and Modernity in Theology*, edited by Lucian Turcescu, 207–48. Iasi, Romania; Palm Beach, FL: Center for Romanian Studies, 2002.

Berger, Calinic (Kevin M.). "Does the Eucharist Make the Church? An Ecclesiological Comparison of Staniloae and Zizioulas." *St Vladimir's Theological Quarterly* 51, no. 1 (2007): 23–70.

Bielawski, Maciej. *Parintele Dumitru Staniloae, o viziune filocalica despre lume [Father Dumitru Staniloae: A Philokalic Vision of the World]*. Translated by Ioan I. Ica jr., Dogmatica. Sibiu: Deisis, 1998.

Bordeianu, Radu. "Filled with the Trinity: The Contribution of Dumitru Staniloae's Ecclesiology to Ecumenism and Society." *Journal of Eastern Christian Studies* 62, no. 1–2 (2010): 71–101.

——. Interview with V. Rev. Fr. Roman Braga, November 30, 2002. Transfiguration Monastery, MI: unpublished audio material, 2002.

——. "Natural, Universal, and Ordained Priesthood: The Contribution of Dumitru Staniloae's Communion Ecclesiology." In *Pro Ecclesia* 19, no. 4 (2010): 405–33.

——. "Orthodox Spirituality: A Practical Guide for the Faithful and a Definitive Manual for the Scholar. By Dumitru Staniloae. Translated from the Romanian by Archimandrite Jerome (Newville) and Otilia Kloos. South Canaan, Pennsylvania:

St. Tikhon's Seminary Press, 2002. ISBN 1–878997–66–1. Pp. 397 [Book Review]."
*Archaeus* 12–13 (2007–2008): 414–16.

——. "Orthodox-Catholic Dialogue: Retrieving Afanassieff's Eucharistic Ecclesiology after
Zizioulas and Staniloae." *Journal of Ecumenical Studies* 44, no. 2 (2009): 239–65.

——. "Retrieving Eucharistic Ecclesiology." In *Ecumenical Ecclesiology: Unity, Diversity
and Otherness in a Fragmented World*, edited by Gesa E. Thiessen, 128–42. New York:
T&T Clark/Continuum, 2009.

Bria, Ion. "The Creative Vision of Dumitru Staniloae: An Introduction to His Theological
Thought." *Ecumenical Review* 33, no. 1 (1981): 53–59.

Ciobotea, Dan I. "Une dogmatique pour l'homme d'aujourd'hui [Review of *Teologia
Dogmatica Ortodoxa*]." *Irénikon* 54, no. 4 (1981): 472–84.

Clément, Olivier. "Le Père Dumitru Staniloae et le génie de l'Orthodoxie Roumaine." In
*Persoana si Comuniune. Prinos de Cinstire Parintelui Profesor Academician Dumitru
Staniloae la implinirea varstei de 90 de ani*, edited by Mircea Pacurariu and Ioan I. Ica
jr., 82–89. Sibiu: Ed. Arhiepiscopiei Ortodoxe Sibiu, 1993.

de Beauregard, Marc-Antoine Costa. "Le Cosmos et la Croix." In *Dumitru Staniloae:
Tradition and Modernity in Theology*, edited by Lucian Turcescu, 147–66. Iasi,
Romania; Palm Beach, FL: Center for Romanian Studies, 2002.

Dragulin, Gheorge. "Pseudo-Dionysios the Areopagite in Dumitru Staniloae's Theology."
In *Dumitru Staniloae: Tradition and Modernity in Theology*, edited by Lucian Turcescu,
71–80. Iasi, Romania; Palm Beach, FL: Center for Romanian Studies, 2002.

Louth, Andrew. "The Orthodox Dogmatic Theology of Dumitru Staniloae." In *Dumitru
Staniloae: Tradition and Modernity in Theology*, edited by Lucian Turcescu, 53–70.
Iasi, Romania; Palm Beach, FL: Center for Romanian Studies, 2002.

——. "The Orthodox Dogmatic Theology of Dumitru Staniloae." *Modern Theology* 13,
no. 2 (1997): 253–67.

Lupu, Stefan. "Sinodalitatea si/sau conciliaritatea: Expresie a unitatii si catolicitatii
Bisericii [Synodality and/or Conciliarity: Expression of the Unity and Catholicity of
the Church]." *Dialog Teologic* 4, no. 7 (2001): 59–84.

Manastireanu, Danut. "Dumitru Staniloae's Theology of Ministry." In *Dumitru Staniloae:
Tradition and Modernity in Theology*, edited by Lucian Turcescu, 126–44. Iasi,
Romania; Palm Beach, FL: Center for Romanian Studies, 2002.

Miller, Charles. *The Gift of the World: An Introduction to the Theology of Dumitru
Staniloae*. Edinburgh: T&T Clark, 2000.

——. "Presentation of the Gifts: Orthodox Insights for Western Liturgical Renewal."
*Worship* 60, no. 1 (1986): 22–38.

Neamtu, Mihail. "Between the Gospel and the Nation: Dumitru Staniloae's Ethno-
Theology." *Archaeus* 10, no. 3 (2006): 7–44.

Popa, Virginia. *Parintele Dumitru Staniloae: Bio-bibliografie [Father Dumitru Staniloae:
Bio-Bibliography]*. Iasi: Trinitas, 2004.

Roberson, Ronald G. "Contemporary Romanian Orthodox Ecclesiology: The
Contribution of Dumitru Staniloae and Younger Colleagues." Doctoral dissertation,
The Pontifical Oriental Institute in Rome, 1988.

——. "Dumitru Staniloae on Christian Unity." In *Dumitru Staniloae: Tradition
and Modernity in Theology*, edited by Lucian Turcescu, 104–25. Iasi, Romania;
Palm Beach, FL: Center for Romanian Studies, 2002.

Rogobete, Silviu Eugen. "Mystical Existentialism or Communitarian Participation?:
Vladimir Lossky and Dumitru Staniloae." In *Dumitru Staniloae: Tradition and*

*Modernity in Theology*, edited by Lucian Turcescu, 167–206. Iasi, Romania; Palm Beach, FL: Center for Romanian Studies, 2002.

Staniloae, Lidia. *Lumina faptei din lumina cuvantului: impreuna cu tatal meu, Dumitru Staniloae* [*The Light of the Deed from the Light of the Word: Together with My Father, Dumitru Staniloae*]. Bucuresti: Humanitas, 2000.

——. "Remembering My Father." In *Dumitru Staniloae: Tradition and Modernity in Theology*, edited by Lucian Turcescu, 15–21. Iasi, Oxford, Palm Beach, Portland: The Center for Romanian Studies, 2002.

Toma, Stefan L. *Traditie si actualitate la pr. Dumitru Staniloae* [*Tradition and Actuality in Fr. Dumitru Staniloae*]. Sibiu: Agnos, 2008.

Turcescu, Lucian. "Eucharistic Ecclesiology or Open Sobornicity?" In *Dumitru Staniloae: Tradition and Modernity in Theology*, edited by Lucian Turcescu, 83–103. Iasi, Romania; Palm Beach, FL: Center for Romanian Studies, 2002.

——. "Introduction." In *Dumitru Staniloae: Tradition and Modernity in Theology*, edited by Lucian Turcescu, 7–14. Iasi, Romania; Palm Beach, FL: Center for Romanian Studies, 2002.

Ware, Kallistos. "Foreword." In *The Experience of God: Revelation and Knowledge of the Triune God*, edited by Dumitru Staniloae, ix–xxvii. Brookline, MA: Holy Cross Orthodox Press, 1998.

## Other Sources

Afanassieff, Marianne. "La genèse de 'L'Église du Saint-Esprit'." In *L'Église du Saint-Esprit*, 13–22. Paris: Cerf, 1975.

Afanassieff, Nicolas. *The Church of the Holy Spirit*. Translated by Vitaly Permiakov. South Bend, IN: Notre Dame University Press, 2007.

——. "The Church Which Presides in Love." In *The Primacy of Peter: Essays in Ecclesiology and the Early Church*, edited by John Meyendorff, 91–143. Crestwood, NY: St Vladimir's Seminary Press, 1992.

——. "The Eucharist: Principal Link Between the Catholics and the Orthodox." In *Tradition Alive: On the Church and the Christian Life in Our Time: Readings from the Eastern Church*, edited by Michael Plekon, 47–49. Lanham, MD: Rowan & Littlefield, 2003.

——. *L'Église du Saint-Esprit*. Translated by Marianne Drobot. Paris: Cerf, 1975.

——. "L'Eucharistie, principal lien entre les Catholiques et les Orthodoxes." *Irénikon* 38, no. 3 (1965): 337–39.

——. "Una Sancta." *Irénikon* 36, no. 4 (1963): 436–75.

——. "Una Sancta." In *Tradition Alive: On the Church and the Christian Life in Our Time: Readings from the Eastern Church*, edited by Michael Plekon, 3–30. Lanham, MD: Rowan & Littlefield, 2003.

Alfeyev, Bishop Hilarion. "The Faith of the Fathers: The Patristic Background of the Orthodox Faith and the Study of the Fathers on the Threshold of the 21st Century." *St Vladimir's Theological Quarterly* 51, no. 4 (2007): 371–93.

Aquinas, Thomas. *Summa Theologiae, Complete English Edition in Five Volumes*. Translated by Fathers of the English Dominican Province. Allen, TX: Christian Classics, a Division of Thomas More Publishing, 1981.

Aran Murphy, Francesca. "De Lubac, Ratzinger and von Balthasar: A Communal Adventure in Ecclesiology." In *Ecumenism Today: The Universal Church in the*

*21st Century*, edited by Francesca Aran Murphy and Christopher Asprey, 45–80. Burlington, VT: Ashgate, 2008.

Badcock, Gary D. *Light of Truth & Fire of Love: A Theology of the Holy Spirit*. Grand Rapids: William B. Eerdmans Publishing Company, 1997.

Baillargeon, Gäetan. *Perspectives orthodoxes sur l'Église-Communion: l'oeuvre de Jean Zizioulas*. Montréal: Éditions Paulines, 1989.

Balthasar, Hans Urs von. *Cosmic Liturgy: The Universe According to Maximus the Confessor*. Translated by Brian Daley, *Communio Books*. Ft. Collins, CO: Ignatius Press, 2003.

Barth, Karl. *Church Dogmatics: The Doctrine of the Word of God*. Translated by G.W. Bromiley. Second ed. Vol. 1. Edinburgh: T&T Clark, 1999.

Basil the Great, Saint. *The Divine Liturgy*. Translated by Members of the Faculty of Hellenic College/Holy Cross Greek Orthodox School of Theology. Brookline, MA: Holy Cross Orthodox Press, 1998.

Behr, John. "The Trinitarian Being of the Church." *St Vladimir's Theological Quarterly* 48, no. 1 (2003): 67–88.

Blane, Andrew. "A Sketch of the Life of Georges Florovsky." In *Georges Florovsky: Russian Intellectual and Orthodox Churchman*, edited by Andrew Blane, 11–217. Crestwood, NY: St Vladimir's Seminary Press, 1993.

Bordeianu, Radu. "Icons." In *Dictionary of Christian Spirituality*, edited by Glen G. Scorgie (Grand Rapids, MI: Zondervan, 2011): 518–19.

———. "Maximus and Ecology: The Relevance of Maximus the Confessor's Theology of Creation for the Present Ecological Crisis." *The Downside Review* 127, no. 447 (2009): 103–26.

———. "Nicholas Afanasiev, *The Church of the Holy Spirit*. Translated by Vitaly Permiakov, edited with an Introduction by Michael Plekon, foreword by Rowan Williams (South Bend, IN: Notre Dame University Press, 2007). Pp. xx + 327 [Review Essay]. " *St Vladimir's Theological Quarterly* 54, no. 2 (2010): 245–54.

Borelli, John, and John H. Erickson, eds. *The Quest for Unity: Orthodox and Catholics in Dialogue*. Crestwood, NY: St Vladimir's Seminary Press, 1996.

Bouwen, Frans. "Ecumenical Councils." In *Dictionary of the Ecumenical Movement*, edited by Nicholas Lossky, Jose M. Bonino, John Pobee, Tom Stransky, Geoffrey Wainwright and Pauline Webb, 336–39. Grand Rapids, MI: Eerdmans, 1991.

Bouyer, Louis. *The Church of God: Body of Christ and Temple of the Spirit*. Translated by Charles U. Quinn. Chicago: Franciscan Herald Press, 1982.

Bria, Ion. *The Liturgy after the Liturgy: Mission and Witness from an Orthodox Perspective*. Geneva: WCC Publications, 1996.

Bucur, Bogdan G. "The Mountain of the Lord: Sinai, Zion, and Eden in Byzantine Hymnographic Exegesis." In *Symbola Caelestis: Le symbolisme liturgique et paraliturgique dans le monde chrétien*, edited by B. Lourié and A. Orlov, 129–72. Piscataway, NY: Gorgias, 2009.

Burrows, William R., ed. *Redemption and Dialogue: Reading* Redemptoris Missio *and* Dialogue and Proclamation. Maryknoll, NY: Orbis Books, 1993.

Cabasilas, Nicholas. *The Life in Christ*. Translated by Carmino J. deCatanzaro. Crestwood, NY: St Vladimir's Seminary Press, 1974.

Calvin, John. *Institutes of the Christian Religion*. Translated by Ford Lewis Battles. Edited by John T. McNeill. Vol. 1. Louisville, KY: Westminster John Knox Press, 2006.

Chryssavgis, John. "The World of the Icon and Creation: An Orthodox Perspective on

Ecology and Pneumatology." In *Christianity and Ecology*, edited by Rosemary Radford Ruether and Dieter Hessel, 83–96. Cambridge, MA: Harvard University Press, 2000.

Congar, Yves. *I Believe in the Holy Spirit: He is Lord and Giver of Life*. Translated by David Smith. 3 vols. New York: Seabury Press, 1983.

———. *Jalons pour une théologie du laïcat*. Paris: Cerf, 1953.

———. *Lay People in the Church: A Study for a Theology of Laity*. London: Bloomsbury Pub. Co, 1957.

———. "My Path-Findings in the Theology of Laity and Ministries." *The Jurist* 32, no. 2 (1972): 169–88.

———. *The Word and the Spirit*. Translated by David Smith. San Francisco: Harper & Row, 1986.

Conradie, Ernst, Charity Majiza, Jim Cochrane, Welile T. Sigabi, Victor Molobi, and David Field. "Seeking Eco-Justice in the South African Context." In *Earth Habitat: Eco-Injustice and the Church's Response*, edited by Dieter T. Hessel and Larry L. Rasmussen, 135–57. Minneapolis, MN: Augsburg Fortress, 2001.

Consultation, North American Orthodox-Catholic Theological. "The Filioque: A Church-Dividing Issue? An Agreed Statement of the North American Orthodox-Catholic Theological Consultation. Saint Paul's College, Washington, DC. October 25, 2003." www.usccb.org/seia/dialogues.htm (2003).

Cooper, Adam G. *The Body in St Maximus the Confessor: Holy Flesh, Wholly Deified, The Oxford Early Christian Studies*. Oxford, NY: Oxford University Press, 2005.

CTSA, Research Team. "A Global Evaluation of BEM." In *Catholic Perspectives on BAPTISM, EUCHARIST AND MINISTRY: A Study Commissioned by the Catholic Theological Society of America*, edited by Michael A. Fahey, 9–26. New York: University Press of America, 1986.

Dalmais, Irénée-Henri. "Place de la Mystagogie de saint Maxime le Confesseur dans la Théologie Liturgique Byzantine." In *Studia Patristica V*, 277–83. Berlin: Akademie-Verlag, 1962.

de Chardin, Pierre Teilhard. "La Messe sur le Monde." In *Hymne de l'Univers*, 19–57. Paris: Seuil, 1961.

de Halleux, André. "Personnalisme ou essentialisme trinitaire chez les pères Cappadociens?" In *Patrologie et oecuménisme: Recueil d'études*, edited by André de Halleux, 215–68. Leuven: Leuven University Press, 1990.

de Régnon, Théodore. *Études de théologie positive sur la Sainte Trinité*. 3 vols. Paris: Retaux, 1892–1898.

Demacopoulos, George E., and Aristotle Papanikolaou. "Augustine and the Orthodox: 'The West' in the East." In *Orthodox Readings of Augustine*, edited by George E. Demacopoulos and Aristotle Papanikolaou, 11–40. Crestwood, NY: St Vladimir's Seminary Press, 2008.

Dionysius the Areopagite, Pseudo. *Pseudo-Dionysius: The Complete Works*. Translated by Colm Luibheid and Paul Rorem, *The Classics of Western Spirituality*. New York: Paulist Press, 1987.

———. *Sfântul Dionisie Areopagitul: Opere complete si Scoliile Sfântului Maxim Marturisitorul* [*Saint Dionysius the Areopagite: Complete Works and the Scholias of Saint Maximus the Confessor*]. Translated by Dumitru Staniloae. Bucuresti: Paideia, 1996.

Dostoyevsky, Fyodor M. *The Brothers Karamazov: A Novel in Four Parts and an Epilogue*. Translated by David McDuff. Second ed. London: Penguin Books, 2003.

Doyle, Dennis M. *Communion Ecclesiology: Vision and Versions*. Maryknoll, NY: Orbis Books, 2000.

Dulles, Avery. *A Church to Believe In: Discipleship and the Dynamics of Freedom*. New York: Crossroad, 1983.

Dunn, James D. G. "Spirit Speech: Reflections on Romans 8:12–27." In *Romans and the People of God: Essays in Honor of Gordon D. Fee on the Occasion of His 65th Birthday*, edited by Sven K. Soderlund and N.T. Wright. Grand Rapids, MI: Eerdmans, 1999.

Dupuis, Jacques, S. J. *Toward a Christian Theology of Religious Pluralism*. Maryknoll, NY: Orbis Books, 1997.

Dupuy, Bernard. "Nikos Nissiotis (1925–1986), théologien de l'Esprit-Saint et de la gloire." *Istina* 32, no. 3 (1987): 225–37.

Edwards, Denis. *Breath of Life: A Theology of the Creator Spirit*. Maryknoll, NY: Orbis, 2004.

Evdokimov, Paul. *L'Orthodoxie*. Paris: Desclée de Brouwer, 1979.

——. *Présence de l'Esprit-Saint dans la tradition orthodoxe*. Paris: Cerf, 1977.

——. *The Sacrament of Love: The Nuptial Mystery in the Light of the Orthodox Tradition*. Translated by Anthony P. Gythiel and Victoria Steadman. Crestwood, NY: St Vladimir's Seminary Press, 1985.

Famerée, Joseph. *L'Ecclésiologie d'Yves Congar avant Vatican II: Histoire et Église: Analyse et Reprise Critique*. Leuven: Leuven University Press, 1992.

Felmy, Karl C. *Dogmatica experientei ecclesiale: Innoirea teologiei ortodoxe contemporane* [*The Dogmatics of Ecclesial Experience: The Renewal of Contemporary Orthodox Theology*]. Sibiu: Deisis, 1999.

Fitzmyer, Joseph A. *Romans: A New Translation with Introduction and Commentary, Anchor Bible Series*. New York: Doubleday, 1993.

Flogaus, Reinhard. "Inspiration – Exploitation – Distortion: The Use of St Augustine in the Hesychast Controversy." In *Orthodox Readings of Augustine*, edited by George E. Demacopoulos and Aristotle Papanikolaou, 63–80. Crestwood, NY: St Vladimir's Seminary Press, 2008.

Florovsky, Georges. "The Boundaries of the Church." In *Ecumenism I: A Doctrinal Approach, Collected Works of Georges Florovsky, Emeritus Professor of Eastern Church History, Harvard University; vol. 13*, 36–45. Belmont, MA: Nordland Publishing Company, 1989.

——. "The Catholicity of the Church." In *Bible, Church, Tradition, Collected Works 1*, 37–55. Belmont, MA: Nordland Publishing, 1972.

——. "The Church: Her Nature and Task." In *Bible, Church, Tradition, Collected Works 1*, 57–72. Belmont, MA: Nordland Pub. Co., 1972.

——. "The Historical Problem of a Definition of the Church." In *Ecumenism II: A Historical Approach, Collected Works 14*. Belmont, MA: Nordland Pub. Co., 1989.

——. "Le corps du Christ vivant." In *La sainte église universelle: Confrontation oecuménique*. Neuchâtel: Delachaux et Niestlé, 1948.

——. "Patristic Theology and the Ethos of the Orthodox Church." In *Aspects of Church History, Collected Works 4*, 11–30. Belmont, MA: Nordland, 1975.

——. "The Problematic of Christian Reunification: The Dangerous Path of Dogmatic Minimalism." In *Ecumenism I: A Doctrinal Approach*, 14–18. Belmont, MA: Nordland Publishing Company, 1989.

——. "The Quest for Christian Unity and the Orthodox Church." In *Ecumenism I: A Doctrinal Approach*, 136–44. Belmont, MA: Nordland Publishing Company, 1989.

——. "St. Cyprian and St. Augustine on Schism." In *Ecumenism II: A Historical Approach*, 48–51. Belmont, MA: Nordland Publishing Company, 1989.

——. "St. Gregory Palamas and the Tradition of the Fathers." In *Bible, Church, Tradition, Collected Works 1*, 105–20. Belmont, MA: Nordland Publishing, 1972.

——. "The Tragedy of Christian Divisions." In *Ecumenism I: A Doctrinal Approach*, 28–33. Belmont, MA: Nordland Publishing Company, 1989.

——. *Ways of Russian Theology: Part One*. Translated by Robert L. Nichols. Edited by Richard S. Haugh. Vol. 5, *Collected Works of Georges Florovsky, Emeritus Professor of Eastern Church History, Harvard University*. Belmont, MA: Nordland Pub. Co., 1979.

——. *Ways of Russian Theology: Part Two*. Translated by Robert L. Nichols. Edited by Richard S. Haugh. Vol. 6, *Collected Works of Georges Florovsky, Emeritus Professor of Eastern Church History, Harvard University*. Belmont, MA: Nordland Pub. Co., 1987.

——. "Western Influences in Russian Theology." In *Aspects of Church History, Collected Works 4*, 157–82. Belmont, MA: Nordland, 1975.

Ford, John. "Ministries in the Church." In *The Gift of the Church: A Textbook on Ecclesiology in Honor of Patrick Granfield, O.S.B.*, edited by Peter C. Phan, 293–314. Collegeville, MN: Liturgical Press, 2000.

Forte, Bruno. *The Church: Icon of the Trinity. A Brief Study*. Translated by Robert Paolucci. Boston: St. Paul Books & Media, 1991.

Garrigues, Juan Miguel. *Maxime le Confesseur: La charité, avenir divin de l'homme, Théologie Historique 38*. Paris: Beauchesne, 1976.

Golitzin, Alexander. *Et Introibo Ad Altare Dei: The Mystagogy of Dionysius Areopagita, with Special Reference to Its Predecessors in the Eastern Christian Tradition*. Thessaloniki: Patriarhikon Idryma Paterikon Meleton, 1994.

——. "Hierarchy Versus Anarchy? Dionysius Areopagita, Symeon the New Theologian, Nicetas Stethatos, and Their Common Roots in Ascetical Tradition." *St Vladimir's Theological Quarterly* 38, no. 2 (1994): 131–79.

Gregory of Nyssa, Saint. *The Life of Moses*. Translated by Abraham J. Malherbe and Everett Ferguson, *The Classics of Western Spirituality*. New York: Paulist Press, 1978.

Groppe, Elizabeth T. "The Contribution of Yves Congar's Theology of the Holy Spirit." *Theological Studies* 62, no. 3 (2001): 451–78.

——. *Yves Congar's Theology of the Holy Spirit*. Oxford, NY: Oxford University Press, 2004.

Habgood, John. "A Sacramental Approach to Environmental Issues." In *Liberating Life: Contemporary Approaches in Ecological Theology*, edited by Charles Birch, William Eakin and Jay B. McDaniel, 46–53. Maryknoll, NY: Orbis Books, 1990.

Harakas, Stanley. "The Integrity of Creation: Ethical Issues." In *Justice, Peace and the Integrity of Creation: Insights from Orthodoxy*, edited by Gennadios Limouris, 70–82. Geneva: WCC Publications, 1990.

Hays, Richard B. *Echoes of Scripture in the Letters of Paul*. New Haven: Yale University Press, 1989.

Himes, Michael J. *Ongoing Incarnation: Johann Adam Möhler and the Beginnings of Modern Ecclesiology*. New York: Crossroad, 1997.

Hinze, Bradford. "Ecclesial Repentance and the Demands of Dialogue." *Theological Studies* 61, no. 2, June (2000): 207–38.

Irwin, Kevin W. *Models of the Eucharist*. Mahwah, NJ: Paulist Press, 2005.

——. "The Sacramentality of Creation and the Role of Creation in Liturgy and Sacraments."

In *And God Saw that It Was Good: Catholic Theology and the Environment*, edited by Drew Christiansen and Walter Grazer, 105–47. Washington: USCC, 1996.

Jakim, Boris, and Robert Bird. *On Spiritual Unity: A Slavophile Reader*, Library of Russian Philosophy. Great Barrington, MA: Lindisfarne Books, 1988.

John Chrysostom, Saint. *The Divine Liturgy*. Translated by Members of the Faculty of Hellenic College/Holy Cross Greek Orthodox School of Theology. Third ed. Brookline, MA: Holy Cross Orthodox Press, 1985.

——. "Third Sermon on Ephesians 1:15–20." In *Nicene and Post-Nicene Fathers, Series 1*, edited by Philip Schaff. Grand Rapids, MI: Eerdmans, 1988.

Kasper, Walter. *The God of Jesus Christ*. Translated by Matthew J. O"Connell. New York: Crossroad, 1987.

——. *Jesus the Christ*. Translated by V. Green. New York: Paulist Press, 1976.

——. "On the Church: A Friendly Reply to Cardinal Ratzinger." *America* 184, no. 14 (2001): 8–14.

——. *Theology and Church*. Translated by Margaret Kohl. New York: Crossroad, 1989.

Kinnamon, Michael. *The Vision of the Ecumenical Movement and How It Has Been Impoverished by Its Friends*. St. Louis: Chalice Press, 2003.

Kinnamon, Michael, and Brian E. Cope. *The Ecumenical Movement: An Anthology of Key Texts and Voices*. Grand Rapids, MI: Eerdmans, 1997.

Küng, Hans. *The Church*. Garden City, NY: Image Books, 1976.

LaCugna, Catherine Mowry. *God for Us: The Trinity and Christian Life*. San Francisco: Harper Collins, 1992.

Lanne, Emmanuel. "Quelques questions posées à l'Église orthodoxe concernant la 'communicatio in sacris' dans l'eucharistie." *Irénikon* 72, no. 3–4 (1999): 435–52.

Leijssen, Lambert J. *With the Silent Glimmer of God's Spirit: A Postmodern Look at the Sacraments*. Translated by Marie Baird. New York/Mahwah, NJ: Paulist Press, 2006.

Lima. *Baptism, Eucharist and Ministry*. Geneva: WCC, 1982.

*The Liturgikon*. Translated by Leonidas Contos. Northridge, CA: Narthex Press, 1996.

Lossky, Vladimir. "Concerning the Third Mark of the Church: Catholicity." *One Church* [*Edinaia Tserkov*] 19 (1965): 181–87.

——. "Ecclesiology: Some Dangers and Temptations." *Sobornost*, no. 4 (1982): 22–29.

——. *The Mystical Theology of the Eastern Church*. Translated by Fellowship of St. Alban and St. Sergius. Crestwood, NY: St Vladimir's Seminary Press, 2002.

Louth, Andrew. "[Book Review of] Aristotle Papanikolaou, *Being with God: Trinity, Apophaticism, and Divine-Human Communion*." *St Vladimir's Theological Quarterly* 51, no. 4 (2007): 445–49.

——. "What is Theology? What is Orthodox Theology?" *St Vladimir's Theological Quarterly* 51, no. 4 (2007): 435–44.

Madathummuriyil, Sebastian. *Sacrament as Gift: A Pneumatological and Phenomenological Approach*. Leuven: Peeters, 2011.

Maldari, Donald C. "A Reconsideration of the Ministries of the Sacrament of Holy Orders." *Horizons* 34, no. 2 (2007): 238–64.

Maloney, George A. *A History of Orthodox Theology since 1453*. Belmont, MA: Norland Pub. Co., 1976.

Matera, Frank J. "Theologies of the Church in the New Testament." In *The Gift of the Church: A Textbook on Ecclesiology in Honor of Patrick Granfield, O.S.B.*, edited by Peter C. Phan, 3–22. Collegeville, MN: Liturgical Press, 2000.

Maximus the Confessor, Saint. *Ambigua: Tîlcuiri ale unor locuri cu multe si adinci intelesuri* din Sfintii Dionisie Areopagitul si Grigorie Teologul [Ambigua: Interpretations of Some Texts with Many and Deep Meanings from Saints Dionysius the Areopagite and Gregory the Theologian]. Translated by Dumitru Staniloae, Parinti si scriitori bisericesti 80. Bucuresti: EIBMBOR, 1983.

——. "Chapters on Knowledge" In Maximus Confessor: Selected Writings, translated by George C. Berthold, 127–80. New York: Paulist Press, 1985.

——. The Church, the Liturgy and the Soul of Man: The Mystagogia of St. Maximus the Confessor. Translated by Dom Julian Stead OSB. Still River, MA: St. Bede's Publications, 1982.

——. "The Church's Mystagogy in Which Are Explained the Symbolism of Certain Rites Performed in the Divine Synaxis." In Maximus Confessor: Selected Writings, translated by George C. Berthold, 183–225. New York: Paulist Press, 1985.

——. "Mistagoghia: Cosmosul si sufletul, chipuri ale Bisericii [The Mystagogy: The Cosmos and the Soul, Images of the Church]." Translated by Dumitru Staniloae. Revista Teologica 34, no. 4–5; 6–8 (1944): 166–81; 339–56.

——. Raspunsuri catre Talasie [Answers to Thalasius]. Translated by Dumitru Staniloae. Second ed. Vol. 3 of the Romanian Philokalia. Bucharest: Harisma, 1994.

——. Sfantul Maxim Marturisitorul: Mystagogia: Cosmosul si Sufletul, Chipuri ale Bisericii [Saint Maximus the Confessor: The Mystagogy: The Cosmos and the Soul, Images of the Church]. Translated by Dumitru Staniloae. Bucuresti: EIBMBOR, 2000.

——. Viata Fecioarei Maria [The Life of Virgin Mary]. Translated by Ioan Ica Jr. Sibiu: Deisis, 1999.

McLeod, Donald. "The Basis of Christian Unity." In Ecumenism Today: The Universal Church in the 21st Century, edited by Francesca Aran Murphy and Christopher Asprey, 107–19. Burlington, VT: Ashgate, 2008.

McPartlan, Paul. The Eucharist Makes the Church: Henri de Lubac and John Zizioulas in Dialogue. Edinburgh: T&T Clark, 1993.

——. Sacrament of Salvation: An Introduction to Eucharistic Ecclesiology. Edinburgh: T&T Clark, 1995.

Meyendorff, John. Byzantine Theology: Historical Trends and Doctrinal Themes. New York: Fordham University Press, 1983.

Meyendorff, John, and Michael A. Fahey. Trinitarian Theology East and West: St. Thomas Aquinas—St. Gregory Palamas. Brookline, MA: Holy Cross Orthodox Press, 1977.

Meyendorff, John, and Nicholas Lossky. The Orthodox Church: Its Past and Its Role in the World Today. Crestwood, NY: St Vladimir's Seminary Press, 1996.

Moltmann, Jürgen. God in Creation: A New Theology of Creation and the Spirit of God. Translated by Margaret Kohl. Minneapolis, MN: Fortress Press, 1993.

——. The Trinity and the Kingdom: The Doctrine of God. Translated by Margaret Kohl. San Francisco: Harper & Row, 1981.

Monge, Rico Gabriel. "Submission to One Head: Basil of Caesarea on Order and Authority in the Church." St Vladimir's Theological Quarterly 52, no. 2 (2010): 219–43.

Nichols, Aidan. Theology in the Russian Diaspora: Church, Fathers, Eucharist in Nikolai Afanas'ev. Cambridge: Cambridge University Press, 1989.

Nilson, Jon. "The Laity." In The Gift of the Church: A Textbook on Ecclesiology in Honor of Patrick Granfield, O.S.B., edited by Peter C. Phan, 395–414. Collegeville, MN: Liturgical Press, 2000.

Nissiotis, Nikos. "The Charismatic Church and the Theology of the Laity." Laity, no. 9 (1960): 31–35.

——. "La pneumatologie ecclésiologique au service de l'unité de l'Église." *Istina* 12 (1967): 323–40.

——. "Pneumatological Christology as a Presupposition of Ecclesiology." *Oecumenica* (1967): 235–52.

*Orthros: The Resurrectional Hymns for Sunday.* Translated by Spencer T. Kezios. Northridge, CA: Narthex Press, 1996.

Rahner, Karl. *The Dynamic Element in the Church, Quaestiones disputatae 12.* New York: Herder and Herder, 1964.

Raiser, Konrad. *Ecumenism in Transition: A Paradigm Shift in the Ecumenical Movement?* Translated by Tony Coates. Geneva: WCC, 1991.

Ratzinger, Joseph. "The Local Church and the Universal Church: A Response to Walter Kasper." *America* 185, no. 16 (2001): 7–11.

——. *The Spirit of the Liturgy.* Translated by John Saward. San Francisco: Ignatius Press, 2000.

Riou, Alain. *Le Monde et l'Église selon Maxime le Confesseur, Théologie Historique 22.* Paris: Beauchesne, 1973.

Rush, Ormond. *The Reception of Doctrine: An Appropriation of Hans Robert Jauss' Reception Aesthetics and Literary Hermeneutics.* Rome: Pontificia Università Gregoriana, 1997.

Schaefer, Mary M. ""In Persona Christi': Cult of the Priest's Person or Active Presence of Christ?" In *In God's Hands: Essays on the Church and Ecumenism in Honour of Michael A. Fahey, S. J.*, edited by Jaroslav Z. Skira and Michael S. Attridge, 177–201. Leuven: Leuven University Press, 2006.

Schmemann, Alexander. *The Eucharist: Sacrament of the Kingdom.* Crestwood, NY: St Vladimir's Seminary Press, 1988.

——. *For the Life of the World: Sacraments and Orthodoxy.* Second ed. Crestwood, NY: St Vladimir's Seminary Press, 1973.

——. *Great Lent: Journey to Pascha.* Crestwood, NY: St Vladimir's Seminary Press, 1974.

——. *Of Water and the Spirit: A Liturgical Study of Baptism.* Crestwood, NY: St Vladimir's Seminary Press, 1974.

Skira, Jerry Zenon. "Christ, the Spirit and the Church in Modern Orthodox Theology: A Comparison of Georges Florovsky, Vladimir Lossky, Nikos Nissiotis and John Zizioulas." Doctoral dissertation, University of St. Michael's College in Toronto, 1998.

——. "The Synthesis Between Christology and Pneumatology in Modern Orthodox Theology." *Orientalia Christiana Periodica* 68, no. 2 (2002): 435–65.

Theokritoff, Elizabeth. *Living in God's Creation: Orthodox Perspectives on Ecology.* Crestwood, NY: St Vladimir's Seminary Press, 2009.

Thumberg, Lars. *Man and the Cosmos: The Vision of St. Maximus the Confessor.* New York: St Vladimir's Seminary Press, 1985.

Turcescu, Lucian. "'Person' versus 'Individual', and Other Modern Misreadings of Gregory of Nyssa." *Modern Theology* 18, no. 4 (2002): 527–39.

Vatican, Council II. *Vatican Council II: The Conciliar and Postconciliar Documents.* Edited by Austin Flannery O.P. New Revised ed. Vol. 1. Northport, NY: Costello Publishing Company, 1998.

Vogel, Jeffrey A. "How the Spirit Hides: Rival Conceptions in Recent Orthodox Theology." *St Vladimir's Theological Quarterly* 53, no. 1 (2009): 99–122.

Wainwright, Geoffrey. "Review of *Ecumenism in Transition* by Konrad Raiser." *Mid-Stream* 31, no. 2 (1992): 169–73.

Ware, Kallistos. "Church and Eucharist, Communion and Intercommunion." *Sobornost* 7, no. 7 (1978): 550–67.

——. *The Holy Spirit in the Liturgy of St John Chrysostom, Holy Spirit Lecture and Colloquium 3*. Pittsburgh, PA: Duquesne University Press, 2007.

——. *The Orthodox Church*. New ed. London, New York: Penguin Books, 1997.

——. "The Value of the Material Creation." *Sobornost*, no. 3 (1971): 154–65.

White, Lynn. "The Historical Roots of Our Ecologic Crisis." *Science* 155, no. March 10 (1967): 1203–07.

Williams, Anna N. *The Divine Sense: The Intellect in Patristic Theology*. New York: Cambridge University Press, 2007.

Williams, George H. "The Neo-Patristic Synthesis of Georges Florovsky." In *Georges Florovsky: Russian Intellectual and Orthodox Churchman*, edited by Andrew Blane, 287–329. Crestwood, NY: St Vladimir's Seminary Press, 1993.

Zizioulas, John D. *Being as Communion: Studies in Personhood and the Church*, *Contemporary Greek Theologians; no. 4*. Crestwood, NY: St Vladimir's Seminary Press, 1985.

——. *Communion and Otherness: Further Studies in Personhood and the Church*. Edited by Paul McPartlan. New York: T&T Clark/Continuum, 2006.

——. "The Development of Conciliar Structures to the Time of the First Ecumenical Council." In *Councils and the Ecumenical Movement*, edited by Faith and Order Secretariat, 34–51. Geneva: WCC, 1968.

——. "Ecological Asceticism: A Cultural Revolution." *Sourozh* 67, no. February (1997): 22–25.

——. *Eucharist, Bishop, Church: The Unity of the Church in the Divine Eucharist and the Bishop During the First Three Centuries*. Translated by Elizabeth Theokritoff. Brookline, MA: Holy Cross Orthodox Press, 2001.

——. "Implications ecclésiologiques de deux types de pneumatologie." In *Communio Sanctorum: Mélanges offerts à Jean-Jacques von Allmen*, edited by Boris Bobrinskoy and Yves Congar, 141–54. Geneva: Labor et Fides, 1982.

——. "The Institution of Episcopal Conferences: An Orthodox Reflection." *The Jurist* 48 (1988): 376–83.

——. "Ordination-A Sacrament? An Orthodox Reply." In *The Plurality of Ministries*, edited by Hans Küng and Walter Kasper, 33–40. New York: Herder and Herder, 1974.

——. "The Orthodox Church and the Third Millennium." *Sourozh* 81 (August 2000): 20–31.

——. "The Pneumatological Dimension of the Church." *Communio* 1 (1974): 142–58.

——. "Preserving God's Creation: Three Lectures on Theology and Ecology." *King's Theological Review* 12 (1989): 1–5.

——. "Primacy in the Church: An Orthodox Approach." In *Petrine Ministry and the Unity of the Church: "Toward a Patient and Fraternal Dialogue": A Symposium Celebrating the 100th Anniversary of the Foundation of the Society of the Atonement, Rome, December 4–6, 1997*, edited by James F. Puglisi, 115–25. Collegeville, MN: Liturgical Press, 1999.

——. "The Theological Problem of 'Reception'." *One in Christ* 21, no. 3 (1985): 187–93.

# INDEX

Note: The bold entries show that the pages are directly related to the keyword and they deal with the theme consistently